Super Investing

5 Proven Methods for Beating the Market and Retiring Rich

BILL BODRI

Top Shape Publishing, LLC
1135 Terminal Way #209
Reno, Nevada 89502

ISBN-10: 1480258032   ISBN-13: 978-1480258037

DEDICATION

This book is dedicated to those self-reliant people who want to make investment decisions on their own independent of Wall Street hucksterism. They want to use the very best investment methods available that have been proven over very long periods of time. They want to grow their wealth without being snookered into Wall Street's "buy and hold" maxim that, though fraught with risks, promises steady fees to managers who cannot even beat the markets.

George Soros once said you might be able to make a billion dollars from a $25 book if it contains the right ideas you are looking for, and while my hopes for you are not so ambitious, I sincerely wish that this book helps you with your own personal investment goals, whatever they may be. It reveals the exact investment rules others have used, and which you can also personally employ, to grow wealthy through the road of investing.

This book is also dedicated to your children, the next generation to come after you. My hope is that this collection of investing rules and lessons is so valuable that you decide to teach them to your children in turn to help them grow and preserve their own wealth in life. Many of these lessons warn them against events and situations that might someday imperil their future. They also need to learn that they must get started at investing early in life and need methods more solid than typical technical analysis indicators, or the "buy options" or "chase the winning stock" dream sold to the public that typically wastes one's time and causes people to lose money.

Lastly, this book is especially dedicated to those who have already accumulated some degree of wealth and are now presented with the responsibility of investing those funds in order that they might be used to support philanthropic charitable causes that serve society and help to better the world. While I hope this knowledge helps everyone accumulate the degree of wealth they desire, it is especially dedicated to such individuals who desire to contribute to others with such lofty goals.

CONTENTS

ACKNOWLEDGMENTS

I would like to thank everyone who contributed to helping make this book a reality, especially my editors Barry Miller, Jeremy Antbacke, and Gerard deCondappa who helped correct and improve my many drafts. I owe a special debt of gratitude to John Newtson, who first introduced me to Benjamin Graham's simplified investing technique that he used at the end of his life, and who provided an alternative explanation of what Warren Buffett was really doing through his many investment strategies. John got me started on the idea of a wealth accumulation for the benefit of families, and the hopes to help create a new future where "great families" arise in each nation and use their resources to contribute to the public good as in days of old. Without that ideal, I doubt I would have done this book.

Knowing the difficulties of fostering "good government" that always continually works for the benefit of the public (rather than those who control it by buying influence), John and I encourage families to take on the role of supporting good works in society instead of expecting the government to solve the problems. The social welfare funds simply won't be there for governments to do as much as they previously did in the past. The injection of beneficial impulses into society will have to come down to individuals with the requisite money, means of influence, power and will to act. We have already seen signs of this fledging idea being adopted by the already mega-wealthy such as George Soros or Bill Gates, Warren Buffett and many other signers of GivingPledge.org.

We hope that an era of contributive "great families" will arise, both large and small, who can morally grow generational wealth and then use it for the benefit of positive cultural impulses in society. We don't expect that governments will have as much power to solve major social problems in the future, but we know that Bodhisattva-minded individuals will step forward to play helpful roles where governments can or will do nothing. It has always been that way throughout history. However, those who do so must have the means to do so, which means they must in part accumulate a degree of wealth through business and investing. Whether your monies are large or small, I hope this book helps everyone, but particularly those individuals who have an ultimate goal of benefitting society through whatever monies they thereby accumulate.

i

1
INVESTING CAN BE ONE OF YOUR ROADS TO RICHES

This is a simple book on how to grow your wealth through several proven, powerful investing methods. Specifically, it contains the simplest but best performing investing methods that I have found in over thirty years of investment research. Most people want to become rich, and while there are many roads to wealth, most people don't have the means to become wealthy other than through the road of savings and investments. If that's you, this book contains five very simple, historically proven investing techniques that have often grown stock portfolios at consistent rates of 20% or more per year over *many decades*, and are easy to put into practice on your own. Despite their fantastic track records, you may not have ever previously encountered these techniques because they go against Wall Street's often advertised idea that you should simply buy and hold stocks in order to become wealthy, or let Wall Street do the work of managing your money for you. In today's volatile world where the Wall Street players are often not to be trusted, the idea of being a passive investor is not safe any longer, and so these are more active investment strategies to help you protect and grow your wealth.

Like Wayne Green, founder of several of the best selling magazines of all time, I have always advised people that the very best way to become wealthy and control your own destiny is to start your own business. Again, if you want to become wealthy, the best way is to start your own business. Unfortunately, most people cannot or don't want to do this. Even so, the plain truth is that an inordinate number of people have become well off as a result of starting a business that was in tune with what they wanted to contribute to the world, and which materialized some form of what they believed to be their life purpose. Famed investment fund manager Ken Fisher wrote a book, *The Ten Roads to Riches: The Ways the Wealthy Got There*, where he listed the ten most common ways by which people most often got rich in life, and at the top of his list also appeared this idea of starting your own business:

1. Start a successful business of your own (ex. Bill Gates, Donald Trump, Mark Zuckerberg)
2. Become the CEO or extremely high paid executive of an existing firm that will reward you extremely well (ex. Jack Welch)
3. Hitch yourself to the coattails of a superstar visionary who is going places and ride along his wave of success (ex. work for a startup that succeeds)
4. Become a celebrity yourself and turn fame into wealth (ex. George Foreman, Paris Hilton)
5. Marry into money
6. Use the law to take money from other people (ex. Erin Brockovich)
7. Capitalize on or leverage other people's money to make your money (ex. be a portfolio manager or banker collecting fees on the money they manage)
8. Invent an endless future revenue stream such as the perennial royalties from a book, movie, invention, song, etc.
9. Make money from real estate using the power of leverage
10. Save hard, avoid debt and invest well

The large majority of people cannot make use of any of these proven avenues to riches except for the last. Therefore the many roads for accumulating wealth are out of bounds for most people except for the one avenue of investing. This book is therefore devoted solely to that road of investing, especially for the target of accumulating a retirement nest egg that can become a large family legacy.

Perhaps you need more money *now* so that you can live better, or so that you can more easily pay for expenses such as your children's college education. Maybe you want to accumulate more for retirement because your savings aren't sufficient and you know you shouldn't depend on government programs and promises for your retirement years. Perhaps you want to have enough money that you can be financially independent and thus free to say "no" to wrongs when you see them. Perhaps you subscribe to the noble ideal of doing great deeds in the world and therefore want to establish a great charitable legacy that requires funding.

Whether you are trying to increase your current income, become financially independent, set the stage for a comfortable retirement, or establish the initial core of what I call "generational wealth" that is large enough to help the world *and* fund the dreams of several generations, what should you do? What investing strategies should you employ and what steps should you take? If you are just an ordinary individual with an ordinary job, is it really possible that you can accumulate such wealth? Is it possible that someone can use some plan over the course of twenty, thirty, forty or even fifty years of compounding and position themselves to be in the leagues of millionaires, or even the mega-wealthy?

It is indeed possible, but it also requires some money to start with as well as periodic additions to that initial capital. While saving money is difficult, nearly anyone can find a way to accumulate the necessary starting capital required for investing. The first thing you must do, however, is sit down to take a pause and think deeply. You must carefully set some targets and objectives, and then consistently devote yourself to a wealth building course of action to fulfill them. You must stop carelessly spending your savings or throwing it away through speculation. You must put it to work in proven investment techniques that *safely* compound money at extraordinary rates of return. Of course, it is important to also consistently add more funds to that growing sum wherever and whenever possible.

While you probably cannot take advantage of any of the other ten roads to wealth from Ken Fisher's list, you should discuss this list with your children for several very important reasons. It is rare that elders take the time to talk to the younger generations about the various means by which people typically become wealthy. Can you recall a time when anyone ever talked to you about this and gave you teachings and advice? Because we don't teach them otherwise, today's youth usually take money for granted after they get a job and don't think about long term planning. They pile on personal debt, live beyond their means, and primarily learn how to spend money rather than save it or invest it. No one teaches them general rules for investing, and so they must learn it on their own, which typically entails losing lots of money in the process. When it comes time for their retirement, the outcome is that many people are broke because they have saved little and invested nothing at all. This book is meant to help counter that tendency.

There are many personal finance topics, such as covered in the book *Rich Dad, Poor Dad,* that we should share with our youth today. The task of

---

how to manage one's money and grow one's wealth are some of the critical life topics which deserve intelligent discussions. You can use Ken Fisher's list to open a discussion on these topics, or even give this book as a gift to help the younger generation get started with investing. As regards the topic of investing and wealth compounding, it contains the very information I needed to know in my youth when I didn't actually know what I needed or wanted. Having this information back then would have changed my life in a profound way, and so I hope you can teach some of these systems to the next generation if you see these methods can help them. If you introduce these concepts to someone at an early enough age and they then start along on the road of wealth compounding using these techniques, I am convinced that their financial situation will absolutely dwarf that of their peers over time. Those with the greatest advantage are those who start earliest with these approaches.

Because the topic of wealth also ties into the topic of life in general, I have also tried to include various human interest lessons within this book that bring up important issues about one's ultimate life purpose, perspective and fulfillment. I have met countless millionaires and several billionaires in my life time, sharing meals and deep discussions on a variety of topics, and from all these encounters am a firm believer that accumulating wealth that lasts is not divorced from personal character, merit and one's values.

There certainly is a *character aspect* to success with investing because you need self-control and discipline to cut losses short and stay with your basic methodology, patience to bear uncomfortable drawdowns, calmness to transcend the emotions of fear and greed, unbiased intellect to look at how things really stand, and so on. I also believe that there is often a *moralistic foundation* to wealth accumulation that also not only helps you succeed, but which often explains why some people can accumulate great generational wealth while others simply lose all that they have accumulated in the end. Henry Kravis, billionaire co-founder of Kohlberg Kravis Roberts & Company, said, "If you don't have integrity, you have nothing. You can't buy it. You can have all the money in the world, but if you are not a moral and ethical person, you really have nothing."

Along these lines when it comes to wealth accumulation, what people think are virtues in life are often not virtues at all. I have met a handful of people who lived so frugally that their family members, in surprise, only discovered that they had actually been millionaires after they died! You might consider this outcome as representing some type of success, but no one ever suspected this result because those individuals had lived painfully by denying even the tiniest purchases that might had added little joys to life. Frugality is typically a virtue, but if it extends too far—to the extent of miserliness or stinginess—this virtue has become a fault. An entire family can suffer by pursuing an imagined virtue that is its own opposite. The value of money is not in how much you have but in what it actually does for you and your family when you use it. It ultimately has to be used to have value. We must remember the tale of Ebenezer Scrooge who got absolutely no value from his coffers growing larger. He only became happy when he started using his wealth to bring joy to others and relieve them of pain and suffering.

You must think about how you will use any money you earn through investing, especially if it grows to become an appreciable sum. Ultimately it has to be spent to give meaning to all the work you do to accumulate it. The value of money only appears when it is used, so you must think about your ultimate goals and purposes for wealth and for life in general. I am talking about goals other than just good living. Many people have no reason for wanting to build up a financial fortune other than to see a personal bank account grow ever larger, which makes the entire effort a rather meaningless pursuit once they pass away. They neglect family, friends, health and moral values for business but no one gives a funeral oration upon their death saying "they were a great worker." As Colonel Sanders of Kentucky Fried Chicken fame once quipped, "What's the point of being the richest man in the graveyard—you can't do any business from there!"

When writing this book, I was therefore constantly hoping it would eventually come into the hands of those who want to do something greater and more meaningful with whatever they subsequently accumulate in life, and because I believe these methods can definitely help someone accumulate large sums of money when given enough time, I was hoping some individuals would give some thought as to how they might use their monies to have a more positive impact on society other than just donating it to a college or charity organization. We are entering an era where the greatest good for people and society will probably be done by wealthy philanthropic individuals while they are alive, rather than by governments (who are finally tightening their budgets because they have spent too much over the decades), so I think these issues are rather important.

In *The Richest Man in Town*, the billionaire Jonathan Nelson mentioned that at the beginning of his career he met a CEO who had accumulated an amount of money so vast that he could never spend it or give it away in the his remaining lifetime. However, this CEO told Nelson that whenever he was sick he would cross the state line and stay in a hotel across the border. "I can only spend 180 days a year in my home state for tax reasons. I don't want to waste a single working day when I feel good." Reflecting upon this comment, Nelson realized something was amiss in this type of behavior, but could not quite put his finger on it. Nevertheless, he knew that this was no way to live. This wealthy man was a huge success by virtually every commonly held measure, had money he could not even count, and yet was leaving his own home when he felt ill to cross state lines just to save a few tax dollars.

Similarly, one of my own millionaire friends once told me that he could not buy a magazine or cup of coffee on a street corner because in doing so it actually pained his heart knowing that he was wasting money. On the other hand, he said that he could easily buy an ugly $150,000 tapestry and hang it on his wall despite its ugliness because he knew it was an investment. When I heard this, I realized this wasn't a virtue but was actually a mental problem, and told him so. His "virtue" had become its opposite. It is counterproductive to life to set upon the course of accumulating riches if you become shackled like this or like Hetty Green, the Witch of Wall Street, who valued her bank statement more than her own health or the health of her children. A millionairess, when her son broke his leg she tried to have him admitted to a free clinic for the poor rather than pay for a good doctor, and she refused to have an operation for her own hernia because it cost $150. Her frugality had helped her become rich, but it had developed into a miserliness that negatively warped normal human relationships. If your personality becomes negatively warped by financial prosperity such that you lose sight of human values, what have you gained?

This is definitely a book on a variety of fundamentally sound, proven investing methods that, given enough time and the right circumstances, can indeed accumulate gargantuan wealth for some disciplined people. However, you must also ponder all these issues concerning what you should do with any money attained through these techniques if you are that successful. Life is in the doing, not in the locking away; money only has value when it circulates.

As Gerald Loeb (a founding partner of E.F. Hutton) was fond of saying in order to prod good people, "Why do you go to all the trouble of making this money? What's it there for? To look at?" These are good questions to ask because you must remember that you cannot take money with you into heaven. As George Mallory (the famous mountaineer who climbed Mount Everest) said, "And joy is, after all, the end of life. We do not live to eat and make money. We eat and make money to be able to live. That is what life means and what life is for."

Andrew Carnegie, who was once the richest man in the world, said, "The man who dies rich dies disgraced." He was simply saying that if you accumulate wealth in life without using it to good purpose, then in his eyes you have been a failure in life. Your money has been accumulated to no purpose. Without touching the lives of people in a positive way, you have accomplished nothing at all in terms of higher purpose. You must therefore think deeply on why you are accumulating money and how you might use it other than just willing it to heirs who might squander it through destructive tendencies.

In any case, this is a book on superior investing methods for increasing your wealth and that's where the emphasis will lie. While investing is the most reliable of the ten most common roads to riches, and while I believe you have before you some of the top tier investing techniques that will continue to work over your lifetime, no one can guarantee that any of these methods represent a fool proof plan for getting richer. Even when investments are successful, unexpected things can happen. This is one of the overlooked rules of investing in that fate is often unpredictable.

Life is fragile, stock markets are fragile, banking systems are fragile, and countries are fragile. An accident or plague can kill hundreds in an instant, a dictator can confiscate everything you have accumulated in life (I have known more than a dozen families from different countries to whom this has happened), and a war can destroy all the wealth your family has built up over many generations. In a world of constant transformations, the twists of fate can utterly destroy the best of assets and investment schemes. Fame and fortune cannot be depended upon to last. This is why I say that in times of adversity it is only your family, friends, and accumulated merit that can possibly save you. Thus once again, you must think of the value of great human relationships instead of just wealth, and think about how money can be used to help others both prosper and be happy in life.

Another issue you must deeply consider is that while American stocks have gone up over the long run, and while there is the good and reasonable expectation they will continue to do so into the near future, there is absolutely no guarantee that their growth rates will continue to place them at the helm of the world economy especially when we look at the potential of the East. Everyone always assumes that America will reign supreme for many future decades, but as people are discovering through the problems of the member states within the European Union, there is no real guarantee for any country that its stocks, bonds, or currency will maintain their values if destructive forces eat away at a country's economic foundations.

Even though the U.S. dollar is presently the world's reserve currency, in the past that title was held by other nations until they eventually lost their supremacy status in turn. One after another this always happens for as the Chinese say, "Empires wax and wane, states coalesce and cleave asunder." No one remains the leader forever. History shows that the role of the leader always turns to someone else over time. Most fiat currencies have never lasted for more than forty years either, and excessive debt levels like we are presently seeing in the world have usually played a predominant role in almost every depression, crash, deflation and hyperinflation in history. In short, *unanticipated* macro scale economic changes are sure to hit whatever country you live in, and can certainly happen to the world's present hegemon. We must remember that few predicted that the Berlin Wall would come down, China would start adopting capitalistic ways, the U.S. would offshore its manufacturing base, and emerging markets would become the new engines of world growth. All these things and more have happened in less than twenty years time. If you could not predict such *giant* trend changes, then with what surety can you forecast that your nation will always have a healthy future? You must remember this warning of risk when considering various long term investing strategies.

Now there are many approaches (a multitude of ways) by which people have made fortunes in the financial markets through the route of investing. However, it's a known fact that the effectiveness of many popular investing techniques often fluctuates over time. This is why I have always sought long run investment techniques that capture something fundamental as their basis and which have worked over many decades. And even when you find such investment methodologies, once again there is still no guarantee those techniques will continue to crank out positive returns into the future. Even if a basic investing methodology continues to remain sound, the exact parameters it uses for decision making might also have to be adjusted over time. For instance, today we might be using a P/E (price to earnings) ratio of 10 as our criteria for selecting stocks, but we might be using a P/E of 14 just a few years later because lower P/Es cannot be found.

Since there is no holy grail or single solution to investing, since the investing methods that work must show a certain degree of flexibility, and since people have different personalities that attract them to different investment styles, I have tried to select a variety of techniques that appeal to different personalities and which—in twenty or thirty years time—can be easily adapted for a new investing environment and still continue working. Many of these methods can be adapted to work for various foreign (non-U.S.) markets, too. The investing techniques I'm introducing are the ones that have shown stable high rates of return over many decades, are based on fundamental underpinnings, are easy to duplicate, and are likely to continue working in some form or another into the future.

Since no single investing technique is guaranteed to work forever, in the best of worlds you would combine several techniques together to use in growing an investment portfolio. Some markets or asset classes do very well for long periods of time, and then do quite poorly for an equally long period of time. A perfect example is gold whose price in the early 1970's grew from $41 to $800 by the end of that decade, and then fell for nearly 20 years. Since nothing goes up forever, it therefore makes sense that you should use a diversified investment approach to managing your money that rotates you into different asset classes and markets over time, and which borrows the "fund of funds" idea to combine several diversified investment management techniques together. Sometimes it's your asset allocation and sometimes it is your disciplined methodology that allows you to avoid catastrophic risk (and preserve your wealth) during the periodic market meltdowns known to destroy wealth. By using different investment methodologies that focus on different markets and asset classes, you can help reduce some of these risks.

The need for diversification of investment methods and asset classes reminds me of a personal story one of my college classmates once told me. He came from Nicaragua, and he told me about his grandfather who had worked hard to build up an immense fortune that was completely lost in the stock market crash of 1929. His son, my classmate's father, decided that he would not repeat his father's mistake of having all his eggs in just one basket, so he decided to diversify the family's holdings so that they weren't just in the stock market. Over time he painstakingly built up diversified investments in many sectors of the Nicaraguan economy, and his family became one of the richest in the nation. It owned chemical factories, commercial real estate, plantations, import-export companies, an American car dealership, and of course stock market investments. Even though he had undertaken this successful strategy of diversification, his father had neglected one important thing—country risk. The family lost all its wealth once again when the Sandinistas came to power and confiscated many of their holdings! Short moral: in today's world, there is need for international diversification.

If your country is ruined by war, such as has recently happened in Iraq and Libya, the value of your domestic savings and investments may also turn with the fate of the nation. Japan is uniquely facing the danger of the Fukushima nuclear plant continuing to radiate the country and its fishing grounds along with demographic and other depressive economic conditions. The typical Greek is facing the possibility that his net worth will be destroyed through a currency devaluation. Spain is facing a sovereign debt default. Who knows when these countries will return to a level of stable prosperity?

While Germany wisely prevented the outsourcing of its manufacturing sector over the last two decades, America has foolishly offshored most of its manufacturing base in search of lower costs (and thus its middle class job opportunities). Thus the country is now lacking a robust internal capital base and suffering the inevitable degenerating consequences of globalization, namely trade imbalances, unemployment and high national debt. Perhaps it will even see the end of the dollar used as a reserve currency. Basically, its prosperity has plunged because of deficits that are more than financial. The one economics book I always advise people to read to understand these matters is the unrecognized classic, *How Rich Countries Got Rich and Why Poor Countries Stay Poor*, by Erik Reinert, which examines the past six hundred years of economic history across many nations. It clearly shows that every country which loses its industrial manufacturing base always eventually becomes poor through that loss.

Furthermore, you cannot replace that loss through an economy based on finance or speculation, or by printing money "out of thin air." If manufacturing goes, the wealth goes as well.

You must produce and then sell something to see strong wealth grow within a nation, and you must store that wealth in the middle class if you want to see true national prosperity. This is why, as Jeremy Grantham has pointed out (and as paradoxical as it sounds), the history books clearly show that economic growth and stock markets have done better when Democrats were in power rather than Republicans. One of the reasons is that Democrats tend to look after workers, which as Henry Ford discovered ages ago turns out to be good for demand, and thus the markets. On the other hand, whenever you push the middle class into poverty by removing their jobs and saddling them with debt, or whenever you push an entire economy into speculation, it always leads to financial turmoil and economic decline. This is what the U.S. recently tried to do with its housing market by producing a mortgage bubble. We are sure to see a similar problem with student loans that are difficult to discharge even through personal bankruptcy. The prosperity of a consumption-based economy dependent on the economic well being of its consumers cannot last long if that base is imperiled, and that production base has been destroyed. If a consumption-based economy depends primarily on consumer debt as its fuel, that prosperity just cannot last over the long run because consumer debt levels can eventually go to extremes, and then we see a collapse.

As the economist Joseph Schumpeter noted, many types of financial wars and economic struggles are going on all the time. To grow your wealth and keep it you have to be attuned to these forces of "creative destruction" so that you can preserve your funds and move them into the greenest pastures when necessary. Determining where the new green pastures lie and moving into them is one of the roads to riches, and I laugh when people point out how Michael Corleone, in the Godfather epic, demonstrated this principle by moving his family into the attractive casino gambling business. The point is, if we want to grow wealthy through long term investing, we need adaptive investing techniques that can help us find new pastures to move into, or which help us survive when negative weather affects the one pasture we own until its grass can become green once again.

International diversification and asset class diversification, while only stressed in one of these five techniques, become ultra important when the prosperity of our host nation comes into question, and long term decline is a real possibility if governments institute wrong policies. The idea of growing your wealth through some static buy and hold strategy in the midst of deteriorating forces is ludicrous, so you must always remember to be flexible and open minded to active investment management techniques. I feel so strongly about this that I wanted to name this book, "Forget Buy and Hold" because going forward, I believe it is a mistake for investors to firmly anchor themselves to the typical 60-40% buy and hold domestic stock and bond strategy usually touted by Wall Street.

On the other hand, if you can identify a large unstoppable trend that represents incredible demand such as commodity price inflation, the growing shortage of some necessary substance, or an increasing preference for real goods over paper assets, … you might accumulate a small fortune by riding that trend using a "buy and hold" strategy throughout that multi-year trending period. Unfortunately, in this book we cannot go into this most fascinating form of investing that involves a combination of demographics, economic patterns, macro supply and demand trends, long wave cycles and the fate of nations for long term buy and hold investing. We must restrict ourselves to more active investment techniques you can easily execute on your own, one or more of which will appeal to your personality and investment style, that involve more frequent buy and sell decisions.

These techniques have been selected because they offer both safety *and* wealth accumulation throughout all types of economic environments, including the difficult ones. However, you should understand that the truly mega-wealthy *always aspire towards a genuine understanding of macro trends and cycles in world affairs* so that they can position their massive assets for dependable growth over long term horizons. Mega-wealth accumulation often involves buying and holding certain types of assets over extremely long periods of time, especially with a contrarian mindset, but even then we cannot say that you should do this forever. The prudence of risk control and diversification must play a role in the accumulation of wealth and these principles are often at odds with the strategy of buy and hold.

Even so, the wealthy are sure to study mega-trends for their investment potential. Knowing the long term trends, smart individuals with the required resources often position themselves so that they can slowly but gradually gain monopolistic control over very large markets and forces just as the Rothschilds aimed to do. The poor public rarely studies matters deeply like the mega-wealthy, and is therefore easily influenced by clueless talking heads on television who have no sense of history or long term market forces, but commonly mislead them into wrong investment decisions again and again. The mega-wealthy I have known, on the other hand, try to think independently rather than just accept what they hear on the news or read in the papers. They diligently study fundamental forces to understand the long term supply and demand situations for markets. That detailed study and subsequent understanding always helps guide their long term investment decision making. Many become rich through that type of understanding, but as stated, it deserves an entirely different type of book to explain it.

For instance, in America we're now facing the retirement of 80 million baby boomers who are seeking to downsize their homes. They are leaving an average home size of 2,500 sq. ft. for 1,000 sq. ft. condos, but will eventually turn to even smaller dwellings in assisted living facilities as they get older. They will need to sell their present homes to the 65 million Generation Xers who earn less than their parents and grandparents, who have trouble getting mortgages, who have large college loans that are already a large cash flow burden, and whose employment security is at an all time low. Knowing such facts and that foreclosures are currently high due to other circumstances, we can easily forecast that the supply and demand situation is not good for American home prices into the near future. In the 2010 census, we found that America had 19 million vacant homes, and that inventory is not going to clear quickly.

Despite what you may hear on the news, such are the facts, and from these facts and the knowledge of demographic trends, employment trends and how markets work, we can foretell that property is a terrible investment at this time because it lacks a large potential for gain. Property prices will also certainly fall if we encounter another recession (which inevitably happens every few years), if property taxes go up, if home purchase tax credits or interest deductions disappear, or future mortgage loans all become adjustable rate mortgages (forcing homebuyers to assume the interest rate risk). A variety of possible but likely scenarios only make the future prospects of real estate worse than the present, and so many are stand aside because they feel that current decline in property prices is likely to continue. Whether the conclusion is true or false, this is an example of how the mega-wealthy train themselves to analyze and evaluate various investment situations.

The good news for the young, however, is that 85 million Echo Boomers will start buying homes from the 65 million Generation Xers in about 10-12 years time, which will start the clock again and initiate another property boom at the bottom of a 25-year bear market. At that time real estate prices will probably be a lot cheaper than they are now and buying property, rather than renting, will look like one of the worst investments possible on planet Earth. Unforeseen circumstances may change that forecast dramatically, which one will have to review at that time, but if all goes as stated, that future period may indeed represent a contrarian's giant opportunity for getting rich through real estate once again. By understanding the long term demographics and the supply and demand situations they will generate, a wise investor can anticipate that he has about a decade to save up money before he can buy homes in the best neighborhoods at low prices. This is the type of understanding that comes from a macro analysis of demographic spending patterns and long term market forces, a style of analysis popularized by Harry Dent (*The Great Boom Ahead, The Great Crash Ahead*) and others.

Unfortunately, we will not go into this type of fundamental analysis because this book restricts itself to simple formula-type investing techniques with more frequent buy and sell decisions. Real estate investing, which has been a common road to riches for many, is therefore not a topic covered. Real estate, art, businesses, and commodities are all ways to diversify your investments and grow your wealth, but we will be restricting ourselves to systematic investment techniques that tell you when to buy and sell stocks and other liquid financial assets in the world markets.

Companies rise and fall, industries rise and fall, asset classes rise and fall, countries rise and fall, everyone is born and then eventually passes away. No one can guarantee that any particular investing method will increase your wealth by the end of your own unique investment horizon. There are always real risks that are out of reach of our knowledge and you should understand that from the start. In particular, there is the risk of ignorantly committing to ineffective investment methodologies that cannot work through an unforeseen crisis and preserve your wealth.

Nonetheless, after many years of research in the investment arena, spending time in New York and Asia, I've assembled a set of extremely impressive techniques for stock market investing that have brought continuous 15-20% year returns over decades of good and bad times and *throughout all sorts of negative economic environments and adverse situations.* What are some of the most impressive investing techniques that you can actually duplicate on your own so that you become a super investor? You are about to find out.

2
WHAT RATE OF RETURN SHOULD YOU EXPECT?

When I was living in Asia in the nineties, I happened to pick up a book by Robert Heller called *The Age of the Common Millionaire*. This was written well before many of the latest fad books that have looked into the habits of millionaires or how they made their fortunes. Heller had analyzed many famous family fortunes as well as the growth rates in the net worth of many dynastic families. What surprised me was that he found that most of the mega-wealth fortunes, once made, increased over time at an average rate of only about 7% per year. Yes, only 7% per year! That's certainly a low number, and it should help us establish a benchmark for certain expectations.

Reading Heller's book was the first time I ever sat down and actually considered what the mega-wealthy were earning over a 50-year, 100-year, or even 150-year period of time. Later I found Jeremy Siegel's *Stocks for the Long Run* which said that the real return (inflation adjusted) on stocks over 250 years was 6.9%; it was 7% between 1802 and 1870, 6.6% between 1871 and 1925, and 6.9% since 1926. Once again we have a rate of return around 7%, so the figures tally between what the wealthy actually earned and what the academics say they may have earned.

Bonds have done even worse than stocks over the long term with annual returns at about half of these numbers. Real estate or property investment did not perform anywhere near as well as stocks either. The reason stocks have done better is that they must compensate you for the fact they have several times the volatility of bonds. In order to hold risky assets that fluctuate so much, you have to be compensated with a higher rate of return.

People often think that real estate investment is the key to riches, but even real estate has not produced extraordinarily large returns over the long run. Property cycles do exist, and real estate as an investment vehicle travels in and out of fashion over time due to the ease of credit and various market supply and demand factors. Robert Shiller, author of *Irrational Exuberance*, looked all the way back to 1890 and found that real estate produced truly outstanding returns *only twice* in this long history. The first time was after World War II when returning troops were starting their families, and the second period was from 1998 to 2005, which for many reasons turned out to be an artificially manufactured real estate bubble. We experienced that housing bubble due to a perfect storm of permissive lending practices together with other plumping conditions, and are not likely to see high returns in real estate for awhile until the excess housing inventory clears and demand picks up once again.

Housing's *long run rate of return* has actually averaged around 3% a year, which is just barely above the inflation rate and half the rate of appreciation of stocks. In the thundering inflation period of the 1970s it rose 8.1% per year, which was its greatest rise in history, and 5.9% per annum in the 1980s. With the long run CAGR for real estate running at about 3% per year, an illiquid house is certainly not a better investment than the stock market or bonds. In recent years, millions of people were conned by bankers, real estate agents, the press and public euphoria into believing that their home would be the biggest positive investment that they would ever make in their lives, but housing should never have been presented as an investment at all! A home is actually a consumer item that can possibly preserve some of your capital if you purchase the right property in the right location at the right price. As for being a "for-sure" investment, who can guarantee that it will always go up in price? We have just seen that illusion collapse brilliantly. While many people have made their fortunes from real estate investments, many people have also suffered incredible losses. Most of the public now has unrealistic expectations as to how much their property might appreciate in the years ahead. Real estate appreciates much less than stocks over the long run, which only rise at about 7% annually.

From all these numbers, you can see why Warren Buffett, in his 2007 letter to his investors, criticized mainstream retirement strategists for telling their clients that the stock market has reliably delivered returns of 10% or better to investors and therefore that is what they should expect going into the future. One source, Cornerstone Investment Services, reported that the annual rate of return for the S&P500 since 1871 has been about 5.63% to 5.85% annually, which of course is less than our 7% target once again. Even when you look at S&P 500 earnings, measured from peak-to-peak they have also grown no faster than 6% annually over time. Thus, if stock prices are related to the earnings growth rate then we still have the same low 7% CAGR range once again, if at that. We keep revolving around 6-8% returns that one might earn on stock investments *over the long run.*

To help this sink in, you should know that conservative pension funds in their calculations also assume they will only be able to make an average 7-8% yearly return over time, and the Social Security Administration's Office of the Actuary (OACT) has generally used a 7.0% real return for stocks throughout its 75-year projection period. Hence unless you are exceptional, 7-8% is what you should expect for the *long term growth rate* of your assets using a simplistic buy and hold strategy. I just call this "7%" for short. This is the conservative number you should use for various investment calculations, and sometimes even this number is too high as we shall see. The basic idea is that the odds of getting a rate of return like 15% or 20% is much harder than you think. A CAGR of 20% over many decades is extraordinary, but most people don't know this.

While of course you should certainly strive to earn more than 7-8% per year, and while the stock market will often return 20-30% in a single year, to be a successful investor you must know these numbers and use them to set some realistic expectations. Assuming that all things are in your favor, every extra year you add to your period of growth should add, on average, an extra 7-8% to your total wealth if you can secure this return.

No one can deny that there have been single years and extended periods of time when stocks have shown extraordinarily high returns much greater than this, and we might even see continuous yearly returns of 20-30% again at some time in the near future. There are times when some "hot" markets, such as the emerging markets or commodity price run-ups, will even return 50%, 75% or more in a single year or multiple years in a row. But the future is unpredictable, and you cannot bank on rosy hopes or cheerful expectations when trying to grow your wealth. If you do, you are doomed to disappointment.

Thus, one of the principles of wealth investing is not to try to predict the market. Do not depend on forecasts. No one can predict the market, so instead you want to *try to capture as large a portion of whatever returns the market can possibly give you.* To do this, you want to devote yourself to reasonable, logical, robust, and proven long term strategies that, when consistently applied in a disciplined fashion, take the volatility and unpredictability of the market into account and aim to grow your funds over the long term better than 7% per year.

You also don't want to place your trust in methods that have been backtested to fit prior history to perfection because of the simple fact that curve-fitted investment models usually don't work into the future. Their historical success, derived through curve-fitting, is actually just a fiction of your mind. You want to depend upon fundamentally sound investing methods that have been generally good (much better than average) throughout all sorts of environments because those are the ones most likely to continue working into the future. You are looking for methods that have sound logic, are simple to apply, and have an excellent proven track record. You don't want to use complicated methods divorced from reality and which have been optimized to the hilt. Methods that veer far from Occam's razor in construction or which depend on complicated math will usually fall flat when it comes to future performance.

When the mega-wealthy became rich, that wealth was quite often due to cashing out the value of a business that they had built up slowly over time. People like Henry Ford or Andrew Carnegie worked their entire lives to build firms that they eventually sold, and thereby realized tremendous financial gains. Some people, like Mark Zuckerberg of Facebook fame, luckily realize that tremendous wealth sooner rather than later in life, but in any case, business owners tend to earn a lot of cash, or convert their businesses into cash, and then typically turn that cash over to investing. The growth from investing, when successful, then turns those funds into something substantially larger over time that I call mega-wealth or generational wealth when it can last several generations.

Thereafter, over the long term those mega-fortunes usually do not grow at exponential growth rates anymore. While very high growth rates might have characterized their original businesses as they prospered, the hard fact is that their money afterwards typically grows at a very slow rate of around 7-8% per year over the long run. This CAGR is what you should actually expect for your portfolio gains unless you use some superior investing techniques such as those featured within this book.

Part of the job of accumulating large generational wealth entails keeping it intact rather than seeing it lost through taxes, excessive spending, or incompetence. It seems to be one of the lessons of history that the third generation of a business patriarch usually loses the wealth it inherits because it did nothing to create it. Because the third generation knows little about building a business, it usually only becomes expert at spending easy money rather than making it. Perhaps this is not a bad thing because it forces money to go back to whence it came. It then ends up circulating in the economy once again rather than remain concentrated in the hands of the unproductive.

History also shows a tendency for wealth and power to become concentrated in the hands of a few and then be lost again, so this tendency might be considered as a sort of natural law of human culture, too. All trends tend to return to the mean after sufficient time, so that money accumulated is then lost unless some force maintains the upwards ascent. Various cultures suggest that this force that enriches individuals and families is called "merit." Merit does not last but must be continually replenished by good works otherwise the merit as a source of wealth runs out. Did you know that of the original members of the "Forbes 400" list of wealthy Americans from 1982, only 24 members of that original list still held a place on it in 2012? People think wealth is all due to intelligence and good investment or business decisions, but I firmly believe that merit plays a role. This is one of the many reasons why I believe that a family aspiring to reach the levels of the Medicis, Rockefellers, Rothschilds or other mega-wealthy must continually perform many acts of merit in order that its wealth may continue to flourish over centuries.

Having lived in Asia during the 80-90's roaring bull market years of Taiwan, Thailand, Hong Kong, Singapore, China, Korea and other country tigers, another principle I have observed is that when stock market returns have been extremely high for several years, people often start quitting their jobs because they expect to make an easier (and more exciting) living off the market. They begin to think they are excellent stock pickers because all their investments have gone up, but they are usually just confusing a bull market with brains. During mega-bull markets, monkeys can toss darts at financial newspapers to pick stocks and do well, but few realize that the presence of a bull market is what explains their success.

Self-deception regarding the level of our true abilities comes easy during such bullish periods. About 80% of a stock's volatility is due to the overall direction of the market, so most stocks end up following the overall trend of a rising market and *this* is what creates profits for most individuals.

This is usually the actual reason behind their investing success, whereas they typically come to believe that it is due to their skills. If an individual can still achieve great returns during a bear market, which is inevitable, that's when we might we say that they are truly good investors. That's the test: can they do well during a bear market?

When people start telling you that they are giving up their jobs to make an easier living trading stocks, you can take it as a clear sign that the market is overheated, nearing a top, and it's time to stand aside. You should take it as a fundamental rule that markets don't go up forever, and the world doesn't work in such a way that most people can earn easy returns by speculating for a living. When you hear people planning to do this, it means it is time to get out of the market.

It takes a lot of work to consistently earn double digit returns as a stock trader or investor. Thus it is an old Wall Street adage that if a shoeshine boy (meaning a taxi driver, waiter, hair dresser, etc.) starts giving you investment tips, it's the type of typical behavior that marks the ending phase of a financial market bubble. Your alarm bells should go off when things like this start to happen. Furthermore, when a certain type of investment—whether it be gold, stocks or real estate—starts being advertised on television as a way to make money, or TV shows on that type of investing start to proliferate, then once again you should know that the end of that trend is nearing. House flipping, day trading, numismatic coins, internet websites … you'll know when you see it advertised on television that the trend is no longer something to bet upon.

By the way, this shoeshine boy adage comes from the life story of Joseph Kennedy, patriarch of the dynastic Kennedy clan. In the winter of 1928, Joe Kennedy's shoeshine boy starting giving him stock tips, and so Kennedy knew it was time to get out of the market, which he promptly did to avoid the painful crash of 1929. He provided us with the famous quote often repeated, "You know it's time to sell when shoeshine boys give you stock tips. This bull market is over."

Bernard Baruch, the legendary Wall Street trader, also wrote about the behavior of the common man at the height of the 1929 bubble: "Taxi drivers told you what to buy. The shoeshine boy could give you a summary of the day's financial news as he worked with rag and polish. An old beggar who regularly patrolled the street in front of my office now gave me tips and, I suppose, spent the money I and others gave him in the market. My cook had a brokerage account and followed the ticker closely. Her paper profits were quickly blown away in the gale of 1929."

More recently, there is a story of the retired investor Jack Dreyfus, founder of the Dreyfus Funds, who visited fund manager Stanley Druckenmiller in 1987. Dreyfus said, "As you know, I haven't looked at the market for twenty years. However, I've been very concerned about the conversations I've been hearing lately when I play bridge. Everyone seems to be bragging about all the money he's making in the market. It reminds me of everything I read about the 1929 market." After doing some requested analysis about excessive positions in futures contracts, Druckenmiller came to the same conclusion that the market was speculatively overheated and it was time to sell. However, he reached his conclusion on the Friday just before the famous "Black Monday" when stock markets around the world crashed. I remember that day well. Due to his study, Druckenmiller was able to sell everything with confidence on that Monday and go short. He later found that Dreyfus had hedged his holdings two months earlier at the very top of the market because he understood the implications behind the card game discussions. Dreyfus believed in a contrarian approach to investing, and used to say, "Sell when there is an overabundance of optimism. When everyone is bubbling optimism and running around trying to get everyone else to buy, they are fully invested. At this point, all they can do is talk. They can't push the market up anymore. It takes buying power to do that." You can take this as an apt explanation for how the markets truly work.

A bull market is like a rising tide that tends to lift all ships, and thus it tends to be very forgiving about poor stock selection. Many people succumb to the unrealistic dream that their brokerage account will ever increase during a bull market, and this happens en masse to the public just near a top. Just as there is no such thing as a perpetual motion machine, there is no such thing as a bull market that will last forever because once the last buyer is drawn in, there is no one left to power the advance further.

In many ways the contrarian's view of the market is absolutely correct, which is that people are the most bullish right before a correction and most bearish at a market bottom. You can and should track sentiment indicators to monitor these swings in mood. People are the most bullish at the peak moment when there are no more buyers to propel an advance one dollar more. Conversely, they are the most bearish when there are no more sellers to send a market price lower. These are principles you should learn if you want to safely sit through ten, twenty, thirty or more years of market volatility and still grow your funds through investing. You must learn how to calmly keep your head and stick to your proven investment strategies while the public noise tries to entice you into some hot market whose trend is soon to end.

Now that all these various issues are behind us, before we delve into the super investment techniques that have shown great performance over the long run, we must first tackle one other important topic. We must also understand how the compounding of interest helps accumulate riches over the long run. For instance, in terms of fundamentals it certainly would be nice to expect 15% or 20% investment returns every year, but who can consistently get that sort of performance? Very few people! Nonetheless, some investors can continually earn such returns because they have a disciplined way to grab a bite out of the fact that the average S&P500 stock fluctuates 35-40% from its high price to its low price in any given year. You can use that market volatility as a source of profits if you have a method that tells you when to both buy *and* sell such stocks rather than simply remain a passive investor. In other words, *the inherent volatility of stocks gives plenty of opportunities for upside profits if you can find some reliable way to buy them cheap and automatically sell them at higher prices*, and can do so on a regular basis. There are indeed such investing methods, and this is why stocks will be the focus of our investment techniques.

As earlier stated, without the possibility of using long term cycles analysis, demographics or macro trend type approaches to investing, shorter term stock investment techniques will therefore form the focus of our means for wealth accumulation. And if you are going to invest in the stock market, you should also know what rate of return you should expect as a buy and hold investor based on current and projected economic conditions. You should not risk your financial security without knowing this number, and you should also know that it has been derived through rigorous analysis involving extensive historical testing.

To start off, in 2009 John Bogle—founder of the Vanguard Group and creator of the world's first index mutual fund—wrote *The Little Book of Common Sense Investing: The Only Way to Guarantee Your Fair Share of Stock Market Returns*. Within this book, he gave a large number of reasons why the future market returns over this next decade (2010-2020) would be around just 7-8% per annum. After all the "intermediary" costs of the mutual fund industry, Bogle warned that investors would actually get much less than this figure, so we already have an expectation for this decade that is smack on top of our own long term estimate of a 7-8% return per annum.

Now there are several ways to forecast the expected returns for stocks over the coming decade. Although 5-year and 7-year forecasting methods are also available, people normally use a 10-year forward horizon. This is because ten is a round number that's long enough to be considered "long term" and yet short enough that most people can still imagine that time period into the future. John Hussman's method of calculating future 10-year horizon returns, which I consider the most sound, uses *Forward Operating Earnings* to arrive at the projection, and it is a number you should periodically check by googling "Hussman" and "Forward Operating Earnings" on the web now and then. There is a lot of work that goes into calculating this number, and the historically tested Forward Operating Earnings method produces as accurate a forecast of future stock market returns as you will get. This should be your realistic estimate of possible returns that should help you avoid unrealistic expectations.

According to this technique as I write this in 2012, forward operating earnings are currently forecasting future 10-year returns of less than 5% per year! This tallies with Bogle's warning that your expectations should be dropping, and together these sources say that you should expect much less than 7% per annum. This is already after the returns from 2000-2010 that have been called the "lost decade" because they were so dismal, nearly flat. Even Warren Buffett said the following in a November 1999 *Fortune* magazine interview: "Let me summarize what I've been saying about the stock market: I think it's very hard to come up with a persuasive case that equities will over the next 17 years perform anything like they've performed in the past 17. If I had to pick the most probable return, from appreciation and dividends combined, that investors in aggregate—repeat, aggregate— would earn in a world of constant interest rates, 2% inflation, and those ever hurtful frictional costs, it would be 6%!"

The important point is that you now know that this benchmark number is always available from a variety of sources and that it provides a yardstick for expectations of yearly returns over a 10-year future. Whenever you see that this expected rate of return is very low, the idea of remaining a fully invested buy and hold investor should be severely questioned when other options promising greater returns are available.

Furthermore, now that you have this number, there are several ways to use it. Naturally it becomes one of the yardsticks by which you can evaluate particular investments or investing techniques that you might want to use over that 10-year horizon. When you become serious about stocks and choose the investing to grow your wealth, this expectation becomes important as do several other principles about wealth compounding over the long run.

I cannot begin to even count the number of excellent books, such as *The Zurich Axioms* by Max Gunther, which provide extensive lists of excellent do's and don'ts that can help guide investment decision making. Because there are so many readily available sources for the principles of investing, there is no reason to try to come up with an extensive list for this book. However, while this may seem like old school to seasoned investors, there are some things we should also go over before our introducing our investing techniques, and this is where the comparison to a 7% CAGR comes into play.

A person of today normally works approximately 45 years (age 21 to 66) before retiring. Thus, depending upon when you get started on the road of investing, you might have ten, twenty, thirty, or even forty years or more available for growing your wealth through a long term investing strategy. If you apply compounding principles over a sufficiently long time horizon, they will have a big impact on your investment success.

DON'T LOSE MONEY AND CUT YOUR LOSSES QUICKLY

The first rule of compounding your investment returns is *not to lose money*. If you don't make money in one year, then you have only lost the chance to earn a return but haven't lost any capital. You have only squandered an opportunity cost. However, if you lose your capital then you have to earn even more, percentagewise, to get back your principal. It is more difficult to get to break-even once again. It is therefore much harder to recover from a loss than it is to make money.

For instance, if you lose 10%, you have to earn 11% to be even again. If you lose 25% then you have to make back 33% to get to breakeven, and if you lose 33% you have to make back 50%. The big one is when you lose 50% of your money, which can often happen with certain volatile investment markets. Even the stock market can drop 50% in a bear market. If you suffer such a loss, what percentage gain would you then have to earn to make back your lost principal? The same 50%? Wrong! If you lose 50% on your investment, you must make *100% on some investment* just to break even again. You must double your money, and how often does that happen? If you could easily do that you'd be rich already. If things are even more terrible and you lose 75% of the money you put in an investment, you're even worse off because now you must realize a 300% gain just to get back to even again—the equivalent of compounding at 10% for 15 years. Basically, once you lose money it's harder to make it back.

As Warren Buffett said, "Rule #1 is never lose money. Rule #2 is to never forget Rule #1." Billionaire Warren Buffett always first focuses on what he can lose in an investment, and only afterwards does he think about return. His very first question about any investment is whether it is subject to any type of catastrophic risk where he can experience a large loss of his capital. Most investors do the exact opposite and think about the upside potential of an investment first, and only secondarily consider the risks if at all. Once Buffett concludes he can lose money in an investment, he immediately says "no" and stops thinking about it entirely. He won't even consider it if he thinks there's a chance he can lose substantial money. Thus, he tries to eliminate the potential of a loss from the very start. How different this is from how most people operate.

Hence, preserving your capital throughout any type of investment system that you follow is the primary rule of investment risk management. If you lose your capital, you have to make back a larger percentage than you lost just to return to even. Therefore to prevent losses, people use all sorts of money management techniques such as diversification, stop orders, asset allocation and so forth to prevent the loss of capital.

People always think a stock or other investment will make money when they get into it, otherwise they would not buy it in the first place. Unfortunately, most people don't take the risks of an investment into account when they first make that purchase, so they don't adequately prepare for the potential of a loss. Because they succumb to hope when they first purchase an investment, they allow small losses to turn into big losses, and then they suffer from the catastrophic losses that Buffett so feared. Or, when things go well people commonly succumb to greed and allow big gains to turn into small gains, or even losses, because they don't lock in their profits after the trend changes. This is why the most successful investment systems have well defined rules for selling positions. Few systems ever try to hold a stock to its peak, but usually try to harvest some profits during a run-up or sell the investment entirely. When to sell is usually the most difficult decision of any investing system.

The big key to amassing wealth, as we shall see, is not getting wed to any particular investments forever but to periodically sell them, due to well defined rules, and then put that money to work in new investment opportunities that have a fresh chance of gaining once again. Whether you buy and sell houses or stocks, you must eventually liquidate (sell) the asset after it has gone up in price, and then try to repeat the process all over again. If the asset looks like it will drop in price for the longer term future, you should try to get out with a small loss to protect the erosion of your capital, and put that money into better opportunities in the meantime. You basically try to invest in such a way that you avoid losses and just compound whatever positive returns the market can give you, even if they are smaller than you would like.

Taxes are also considered another type of loss since you have to pay money to the government from whatever you earn through investment gains, so if you can compound your return in some tax free manner, this is also one of the methods the wealthy use to become richer over time. The wealthy often do this through trusts and offshore investment vehicles, as the secretive case of Mitt Romney demonstrated, but now you can avoid taxes with IRAs and 401(K)'s.

COMPOUNDING IS YOUR FINANCIAL PLAN, SO START INVESTING EARLY

Compounding is the key to any big growth in your financial position over time, and is what Albert Einstein called "the eighth wonder of the world" that keeps wealth growing exponentially. It is your magical best friend, and the cornerstone of any financial plan to grow your wealth. While the first rule of investing is to avoid losses, the second would have to be to compound your returns for as long as possible with as high a return as possible, and to do so you should start compounding *as early as possible*. That is why it is very important we transmit much of this information and style of thinking to the younger generation to help them get started at investing while avoiding the errors we have commonly made ourselves.

Many people have tried to make the case that a person in their twenties should start saving so that, with a decent rate of compounding earned by smart investing, they can become millionaires well before retirement age. Few, however, ever seem to want to take on the challenge. I believe one of the reasons is because no one ever presents this outcome in such a way that startles people enough that they become motivated. Hence, I'll try to do this using several striking examples.

Let's start by examining a real life situation that actually applies to many people. Let's say you have accumulated $10K in credit card debt that is charging you an effective interest rate of 19% per year. That's a pretty fair picture of reality although many credit cards charge even more. If we assume a minimum credit card payment of $200 per month, it will take you over 8 years to pay off the balance you owe. Furthermore, you'll end up paying the credit card company $19,800 to get rid of that debt, which is almost *double* what you borrowed. This illustrates the problem of debt. Most people get into trouble because of debt, but start feeling richer and getting richer when they finally get out of debt. Companies, as you well know, often go bankrupt because of too much debt.

Since we can assume that you can support a monthly credit card debt of $200 (because you have gotten into this situation in the first place and continue successfully making such payments), let's see what would happen if that money were instead put toward investments that earned a decent rate of return. It involves some sacrifice, but let's see what would happen were you to redirect this monthly $200 towards retirement savings. You are not going to get rich quickly, so we already know that you will have to compound that money over a long time period of time and keep putting in funds along the way to get the maximum return possible by retirement. You'll see in the next chapter that there are even tools available to help determine which time of month is statistically best for contributing more money for this compounding objective.

Just for illustration purposes, let's say you were able to earn a tax free return of 13% per year on this money. In that case, you would become a millionaire in 31 years. So the target is possible. To make the figures more conservative, let's assume that you don't get started investing at age 21 but at age 25, and continue to work for just 40 years (25 to 65). If you were able to divert that $200 monthly credit card payment to compounding this entire period, you would eventually accumulate $3.24 million for retirement! If your money only compounded at 7% per year, you would accumulate $525K by the end of that period, a 10% annual return would net you $1.26 million, a 13% rate of return would accumulate to the $3.24 million we mentioned, 15% compounding would grow to $6.2 million and a 20% average rate of return would net you $33.48 million. The amount ultimately earned would depend on the compounding rate, how much money you reinvested, and how early you got started on such a plan. That $200 per month is roughly $2400 per year, and yet given enough time and the right compounding rate you could see that it could easily make you into a millionaire.

Once again, the key to becoming rich in this way is getting a high compounding rate, making periodic contributions, and avoiding losses. A single loss can hurt that long run rate of return quite terribly, which is why Buffett hated losses. For example, let's assume that you earn 20% returns for three consecutive years in a row, but suppose that you lose 20% in the fourth year. For the first three years your compound average rate of return (CAGR) is 20%. However, due to the loss in the fourth year, the overall CAGR (compound annual rate of return) for the entire 4 year period now drops to just 8.4%. The single loss has cut your rate of return in half! Had you simply made nothing the fourth year, perhaps because you stayed out of the stock market, your compound rate of return would still have remained quite decent at 14.7%.

As you can see, your total return drops tremendously when you suffer losses, so the first and primary rule of investment risk management is to avoid losses and preserve your capital. This is why traders and investors tell you to cut losses quickly and let profits run, but they also have rules for when you should exit profitable positions. They also commonly tell you to allocate your money between different assets, investment vehicles and investing methodologies so that this overall diversification helps you cut down on drawdowns and losses. The idea of diversification is that you can decrease drawdowns and build portfolios with higher returns for the same or less risk. In fact, you can put together a group of risky assets and as long as they don't all move in a correlated fashion, the combined portfolio can be less risky than its parts with lower drawdowns and losses.

Unfortunately, most people never consider the risks for their investments because they always think that they are going to make money when they enter a trade. But even the best investing techniques produce losses, so you need some way to measure your risks and adjust your position sizes according to those risks. You can do this through timing models, fundamental models or evaluations of the market climate. You can use timing indicators, trend indicators, or value indicators to evaluate investment risks. The job of an investment strategist or manager is to find the best methods that help you secure an absolute positive return while minimizing your risks.

Now let's hammer home the point about starting upon an investing plan as early as possible in life. Once you have some methodology to secure a superior rate of return for your investments, the length of time you compound will have enormous leverage over the ultimate size of the wealth that you eventually accumulate. These two factors determine your wealth: your long-term rate of return and the length of time over which you can compound those returns. If you stash away $2,000 a year beginning at the age of 25 in a fund averaging 7% per year, you would retire at 65 with $427K. If your investment methodology returned 10%, 13%, 15% or 20% per year, you'd retire with $974K, $2.3 million, $4.1 million or $17.6 million respectively. The growth or compounding rate changes your final outcome substantially.

Let's be conservative and consider how the example of a smart investor who decides to save $2,000 annually that he puts in a tax-deferred account (such as an IRA or 401(K)) and earns an average 10% annual rate of return on his money. If he does this for 10 consecutive years (so that he only puts in a grand total $20,000) and then adds nothing else for the next 20 years, his portfolio value at the end of that period will be $214,438. He only put in $20,000, but it will grow nearly tenfold in size!

On the other hand, let's consider what happens to an investor who starts late in the game, rather than our early friend, and who therefore does nothing during the first 10 years of this same investment horizon. Then let's assume that all of a sudden he wakes up, finds out he's behind the curve, and then tries to make up for lost time by investing $2,000 annually for each of the next 20 years. While our early bird investor will see $214,438 in his bank account at the end of the 30 years, our tardy investor will invest more money but only see $114,550. In coming late to the party, yet committing *twice* as much as the first investor (for a total of $40,000), he can only accumulate about *half* the wealth of the first investor who was wise enough to start investing early. Invested *twice* as much and got *half* the possible wealth! The moral is to start saving and investing NOW!

Another example can also make this clear. Let's start again with two individuals aged 22, Roberto and Donald, who are going to deposit $2,000 into IRA investment accounts and who will both compound their funds at an even better rate of 12% per year. As before, these two individuals will do things a little differently from each other.

Age	Roberto	Donald
22	$2,240	0
23	$4,509	0
24	$7,050	0
25	$9,896	0
26	$13,083	0
27	$16,653	0
28	$18,652	$2,240
29	$20,890	$4,509
30	$23,397	$7,050
35	$41,233	$25,130
40	$72,667	$56,993
45	$128,064	$113,147
50	$225,692	$212,110
55	$397,746	$386,516
60	$700,964	$693,878

65	$1,235,338	$1,235,556

Roberto starts early and invests $2,000 for six consecutive years *and then never does anything again*. He puts in only $12,000. Donald spends everything he makes during those six early years, and only "wakes up" to realize he should start investing at age 28. From that point on, he invests $2,000 every year until retirement, which comes to $74,000 that he invests. When they both retire at age 65, let's see how much money they have each accumulated.

Actually they made the same amount of money at the end, but smart Roberto put in far less capital and benefitted far more because he started investing earlier. He had less pain and greater gain just from starting earlier. As you can see, the earlier you start saving the better off you will be because you don't have to add as much money to your account as does someone who starts saving and investing later. To grow your money it comes down to:

* Saving and then investing as much of your income as possible

* Extending the years of saving and investing by starting out as early as possible

* Increasing the rate of return at which your money grows (which also means sheltering it in a tax deferred vehicle)

Market Logic, of Ft. Lauderdale, once published a similar study to this tale of Roberto and Donald using a 10% growth rate. One investor opened an IRA at age 19 and put in $2K for seven consecutive years, and then stopped. The second investor made no contributions until age 26, which is the year that the first investor stopped putting in money, and then put in $2K per year until retirement at age 65. What was the result? The first investor, who only put in seven contributions for a total of $14K, did better than the second investor who put in 40 contributions for a total of $80K. Those seven early years of compounding were worth more than the 33 extra payments and their compounding results of the second investor! The first investor saw a 66-fold increase over what he invested while the second investor saw a 11-fold increase in his $80K investment.

The moral is, *start investing your money as early as possible* to give yourself a long enough time period, with plenty of leeway, to grow your money as large as possible. Your retirement is in your hands so you must something about it *now!* Try never to lose any of your principal (at least try not to lose any big money through potentially disastrous investments), but compound your funds diligently through a combination of safe, powerful investment techniques and add to your investment funds regularly over time. The higher your compound annual growth rate, the more dramatic will be the effect that an early start will have on the final size of your bank account.

These few examples are something you should show teenagers or college grads to encourage them to start putting away $2,000 per year whenever possible and start investing it. Whether they get 7%, 10%, 15% or even more on their money doesn't matter. The important point is that they must start early! I didn't do this when I was young because no one ever showed me the comparisons or drummed it into my head that I have to save for myself, but this is what you have to do. Having travelled the world and seen all sorts of poor countries, it is paramount that we teach our younger generation that this is what they must do, rather than depend on family members, Social Security or the government when they retire, in order to prevent their older years from being a time of poverty.

How can anyone spare that money for investment? As *The Richest Man in Babylon* and various other advisors have suggested, you must encourage over-spenders to eschew debt and live below their means—rather than become consumption addicts—so they can save at least 10% of their income each year and invest it. It takes sacrifice, but that sacrifice means that they will not be destitute in old age (when the government is unlikely to take care of you). We must all work to change the culture of a consumption-based economy fueled by personal debt, and encourage everyone to start planning for their own retirement early rather than dreaming that they will be able to depend on government assistance when they become older. Other than family members, who might not earn enough money themselves, you simply cannot rely on anyone else to provide a safety net for you as you get older. This new type of thinking must begin to take hold everywhere, especially as governments start to cut social programs for the next twenty years or more.

The nation has to change the way it educates the public, and we must be taught to start thinking long term from the very moment we enter the workforce and start making money. Many people will shake their heads with acknowledgement upon reading this because they know full well that things would have turned out entirely different in their own lives had they had this good advice and started saving and investing much earlier. Hence, I've tried to give enough examples to make the comparison sink in, as well as provide realistic expectations for what you can expect to earn over the long run. The methods we'll see earn far more than 7-8% per year, but when you are doing your planning you should always see what happens when you assume you'll only make 7-8% per annum until retirement.

MANAGE YOUR ASSETS USING MULTIPLE INVESTMENT STRATEGIES

There is a very old saying that every investment has its day. This isn't really true, but it gives us a chance to discuss the fact that markets, sectors, and asset classes fall in and out of favor over time. For instance, certificates of deposit actually beat stocks in returns from 1994 to 2009 and bonds outperformed stocks from 1968 to 2009. Sometimes an asset class shines, and then sometimes that luster fades away; nothing performs well forever.

For several years an asset class, like precious metals, may be booming, and then it can enter a "go nowhere" sideways market, or start upon a precipitous decline that lasts for years. As we saw with Japan, stocks or even real estate may enter a massive bull market that sucks in the entire world's money but which then enters a multi-decade bear market. Real estate can go up for years and then become the worst investment for a generation. Emerging market stocks become all the rage, and then fail to deliver any returns at all when the world enters a period of slow growth or recession.

In short, the hot market sectors always change over time. Bear markets become bull markets and bull markets become bear markets. The fate of industries and stocks is that they can and will rise and fall. Therefore—and this is the key—you need to become flexible in your investment approach if you want to compound your wealth over the long run. Being flexible and adaptive with various rotation strategies, rather than just buying an asset and then forgetting about it, is the necessary way to grow an investment account.

Even different types of investment styles can go in and out of favor over time. A favorable investment technique can outperform all others for awhile, and then enter an underperformance phase as the economy enters an entirely different type of economic environment. At any moment in time, some type of stock fund is therefore outperforming others that are devoted to an entirely different investment style. Without some forward projection analysis to depend upon, it's a common story that by the time that this type of investment finally attracts your attention because of its recent stellar returns, it's just about ready to turn the corner. As a contrarian might explain, it only finally attracts attention from the crowd when that investment has nearly run its course.

It is a strange quirk that investors often enter a sector or strategy near the time it's due to underperform, and leave it right before it outperforms, so if we are going to devote ourselves to long term investing and don't do any form of analysis, we'll need some methods that can help us avoid this trap. We'll need methods that do generally well over the long term through thick and thin, through good and bad market periods. We cannot always be betting on the horse that won the last race. So to grow your wealth more safely, and help prevent a loss of your principal, one of the most important things an investor can do is to allocate their funds to various proven investment techniques that have worked over the long term, and are likely to continue working into the future because they are based on fundamental principles. You want to be using investing strategies that have some logic behind them and are *based on fundamental factors which give you a conviction that price alone won't give you.* In the best of worlds, you are seeking investing methods that can perform 3% or better per year than a buy and hold strategy. You also want to be sure that this 3% alpha (extra return margin that is in excess of the risk borne by the investment) is real because you have track records proving that method's success.

While some people want to use just a single system to grow their wealth, often a much wiser decision is to use a combination of investing methods so you are not over-dependent upon just one method that might temporarily fall out of favor. No matter how well it may have done in the past, there is no guarantee that an investing system or technique will be able to continue performing well into the future. The diversification into different investing methods helps prevent the loss of capital if things do indeed turn sour.

You can understand the power of diversification from a simple comparison of two individuals and their investment styles once again. Let's say that Tom takes the route of certainty, because he doesn't want any market risk, and invests $10,000 in a 7% bond set to mature in 20 years. He is therefore going to receive 7% per year and get all his principal back after twenty years have gone by. In twenty years time, his investment will have grown to $38,697.

John, on the other hand, also invests $10,000 for 20 years but decides to practice some diversification of investment techniques. He splits that $10,000 into five separate $2,000 amounts that will each be managed using a different investment methodology. Let's further assume that each of those five investment slices performs differently over time, most of them poorly. For instance, let's pretend that he decided to trade the first $2,000 slice on his own, and ended up losing everything. Pretend that the second slice earned absolutely nothing at all, not even bank interest, but he didn't lose it. Let's assume that the third slice earned just 4%, which is a little better than real estate but less than the long term return earned from the bonds. So far he's not doing so well, so let's say that the fourth slice of $2,000 was put into the stock market and earned the long run expectation of 7% per year, and his fifth slice earned an impressive 15% because he used some tested method—like those within this book—that continued to do well into the future.

Twenty years later we can compare the two results. While Tom's money has grown to $38,697, John's asset allocation strategy has seen it grow to $46,853 … and he did a lousy job managing most of his investments! This exceptional result shows both the power and possibilities of asset allocation and diversification.

Rebalancing a portfolio on a periodic basis is also another commonly used strategy to help boost returns when you are in several asset classes or using several different investment techniques. We won't go deeply into this topic, but periodically rebalancing your portfolio also usually produces better returns and lower portfolio volatility.

All in all, now you know what to expect in terms of typical investment returns, and so you therefore should understand what is outperformance. The difference between 7% and 9% a year might not sound like much, but after 20 years of yearly compounding that small 2% difference leads to enormously different outcomes. You also reviewed some lessons about the power of compounding that you probably already knew, but there's always some benefit to revisiting the basics. You can never overstress the fact that in order to grow your wealth you should start investing early, cut losses short, add regularly to your investment funds over time, ignore short term market fluctuations while staying focused on a proven investing technique, diversify your approach with different asset classes and investment techniques, and ignore the enticing temptations of the crowd that might pull you away from your proven investment methodologies. Another big rule, as we shall see, is to BUY VALUE. "Value maintains its value and offers a good chance of price appreciation." Because you should buy value, you must learn how to wait for it and not be impatient. You must learn to practice patience and wait for times when the value situation for any type of investment becomes outstanding. Don't feel pressured to do anything but be willing to wait months or years for your next investment. Don't try to force the market to make you a living, but act like you don't need the market. Don't try to chase the market (such as high flyer stocks) but wait for great value situations to come to you because you know the long term statistics.

We could have greatly expanded upon this list as to the benefits of being prudent, studying cycles and market history, evaluating risks, and *not feeling pressured to make money in the markets,* but these issues are covered elsewhere and it's time to get into the details about the actual superior stock market investing methods you can use for the goal of growing your wealth and retiring rich. It's time to get to the actual methods used by super investors.

3
SEASONAL MARKET TIMING

The first super investing method involves seasonal investing, and is the simplest of the five investment techniques we will be covering. Amazingly simple, it still beats the market and is very easy to put into practice on your own. It also beats most actively managed mutual funds, including Wall Street's professionally managed growth stock portfolios. For example, we'll soon see how it could take a $10,000 investment in NASDAQ stocks to $818,196 during the time that a buy and hold investor would only make $280,936, and how it could grow that same $10,000 in Dow stocks to $2,074,294 versus $600,206 made using a passive buy and hold strategy. Actually, the returns from this strategy are even understated because we are not including any interest earned when it takes you out of the market.

As Vanguard Funds founder John Bogle and others have noted, managed mutual funds usually lag market performance by about 2.5-3.5% every year. They typically fail to beat the market averages they set out to beat because of their expenses. About 96% of funds fail to beat index funds, and of the 4% that beat their benchmark index, the after tax results average only about .6% of additional gain! Their management fees (1.5% expense ratio) represent a very large portion taken out of an investor's total potential return, and the costs of portfolio turnover (1%) and sales charges (.5%) decrease returns as well. In short, mutual funds as a whole simply cannot earn the returns of the market index because they have their own expenses, and if you try to find the few mutual funds that might consistently beat their relevant indices, it's a futile search. Since investors who try to pick individual stocks themselves tend to do even worse than the actively managed mutual funds, I will therefore introduce an investment methodology that is an alternative to buying mutual funds, stock picking, or investing in an index fund using a simple "buy and hold" strategy.

This investment methodology is simple, easy to use, and *has superior returns to buy and hold with far less risks and drawdowns*, so it makes sense that our collection of best investment rules to grow your wealth should start off with something amazingly simple. After over thirty years of investment research, this is in fact the best purely technical trading method that I've ever discovered at its level of simplicity, and so this is the best method to start us on our search for superior investing methods that can help us grow a nest egg of retirement riches. Some will like this technique while others will not because they prefer something more rigorous that promises yet higher returns. Nevertheless, we must start at the bottom of the ladder of simple investing systems. Of the five super investing methods we will introduce, you must pick one or more that match your personality because those are the only ones you are likely to work with, and many people will like this simple technique. If a method is too complicated or doesn't match your personality, you probably won't put it into practice at all, so that matching is important. Many people will particularly like this technique because they only have to worry about the market just two times per year if they use it.

With this seasonal investing technique, you are going to be invested in the stock market roughly just six months of every year, so there is only one buy and one sell decision per year. You'll be investing your funds only during what has historically been the *best six months of every year*, and which has avoided many of the devastating market crash periods and volatile situations that we often annually see in the summer and fall. Thus, this strategy is called the *best six months of the year seasonal timing strategy*.

You would think that picking this historically worst time of year to stay out of the market is basically just curve fitting, but something is going on here since many other countries totally unrelated to the U.S., and which have entirely different economic systems and tax codes, also show this annual tendency for a summer-centric six month period of lousy stock market returns. This universality of results hints that perhaps something fundamental is being captured by this simple timing method, and we always want to be using an investment technique based on fundamentals.

Along the lines of this powerful technique, I am also going to introduce a related seasonal charting technique that will probably become one of the best stock market analysis methods you will ever encounter, and you will wonder why no one previously invented it. I originally developed it as a way to help guide investment decisions without all the hoopla of complicated indicators and expensive computer services. I was seeking a common sense alternative to charts full of confusing indicators where my head was more important than technical analysis. I hope it rapidly becomes one of the first tools you turn to when you hear a stock discussed in the news, or when you want to evaluate some potential investments and see their immediate future potential. You will even find this seasonal technique especially useful when you want to buy or sell stock options with the maximum chances for success. This makes it extremely valuable for possibly adding a few percentage points of return to a stock portfolio every month, and that in itself is a valuable methodology for both short term trading and longer term investing.

Many brokers and financial advisers tell you to buy options, but since more than 95% of options buyers lose money, this special charting technique will help you reverse those odds by determining when to sell options in a risk adverse manner so that you are one of the consistent winners. It will help you find those particular seasonal time periods when it makes sense to sell covered options for extra portfolio returns, and it will help reveal the rare times when buying options seems worth the risk. The methodology is based on seasonal timing analysis applied to individual stocks, which is related to our best six months of the year investment strategy, and is fully described in *The Commonsense of Seasonal Trading*.

But first, let's get back to the topic of the seasonality of stock market indices in total rather than discuss the seasonality of individual stocks and how you might use that information to boost your individual stock investment returns.

INDEX SEASONALS

No one really knows for sure why there is a consistent seasonal pattern to stock market prices, but there is. What we do know is that researchers (Bouman and Jacobsen) have found that a repeated negative seasonal pattern in stock returns, from May to November of each year, occurs in an incredible 37 out of 38 countries, even going as far back as the 17th century for British share prices! If there wasn't something fundamental captured by this timing technique, then why would all these countries show the same common results, and why would they extend back as far as the 17th century? The stock market returns in all these countries are systematically negative (or lower than what you can earn on short-term interest rates) during the period from May to October every year, which is the basis behind the famous adage to sell stocks at the beginning of May ("sell in May") and then buy stocks back again at the end of October. Whether this tendency can be explained or not, the pattern does indeed exist even though many scratch their heads saying it shouldn't be there.

A repeatable type of seasonal result doesn't just hold for the general market. As we will soon see, many individual stocks tend to annually repeat the same general trading patterns again and again. That consistent trading pattern should also not be there, many argue, but it certainly reappears with regularity. Therefore let's see how we can take advantage of this reality rather than fight it because if a consistent pattern appears in so many markets going as far back as the 17th century, the question becomes whether you can make money by using it. Can you make more money by somehow piggybacking off this typical pattern rather than just buying and holding 100% of the time? The answer is "yes" if you use market timing methods which hitch themselves to that basic seasonal expectation, and assume this pattern should repeat itself.

Many investment advisors tell you never to try to forecast the market or try to time the market. Instead, they suggest that you should simply buy an index fund and then stay invested for the long run while ignoring all sorts of market corrections, including severe drawdowns and periods of volatility. If that's the case, you won't achieve the returns of this "seasonal best six months of the year" strategy that puts the buy and hold strategy to shame.

Buy and hold often asks you to sit through some mighty painful drawdowns. It assumes that the market will always recover after a severe drawdown and rebound to prior highs, which is generally a good assumption if the country and its GNP keep marching forward. When you are insisting on a passive "bullish for all seasons" strategy, you are inherently making this assumption that a country's economy will continue to move upwards even though this is not always the case. The modern instances of the invasions of Libya and Iraq show that countries can be devastated by war, or, their economies can be derailed for a significant amount of time as has happened to Japan in its "lost decade" (1991-2000) that has now become a *second lost decade* (2001-2010) as well. A bear market has knocked 75% off the value of its stock market, and then kept stock prices suppressed for twenty years!

You want your assets parked elsewhere during such long periods of stagnation, during wars and other catastrophes, and during special economic times when, as other instances, a country suffers debt defaults or its fiat currency becomes worthless due to hyperinflation. Thankfully this has not recently happened to the United States or Europe. However, the fact that situations can change means that this is definitely a possibility one day, and the potential for change is a lesson that long term investors should take to heart. For instance, hyperinflation has happened enough times in history that you should know that it can occur in any nation if its leaders institute poor economic and monetary policies. Fiscal crises also become common when government expenditures exceed revenues and debt servicing costs climb to extremes.

When leaders choose poor policies, it only becomes a matter of time until the market catches up with the incompetence. There is a famous saying that "God has not granted the boon of perpetuity to any state or nation." As goes the wisdom of a nation's leaders, so goes the fate of a nation and the fate of its stock and bond markets. In looking at past history, it is easy to see that economic collapses occur frequently and are often to some extent predictable because of a nation's poor policies.

In short, remaining a perennial bull in any market does not protect you from several possible unfortunate scenarios. If we look at long term economic cycles going all the way back to the 1300's, we can find tremendously long periods of Western economic growth followed by tremendous periods of stagnation and decline. Over such long periods of time, successive powers have emerged as the leading nations of their time in roughly 150 year cycles, and the great money was to be made by investing in the superpowers of each period. Right now the flow of investment capital is slowly moving to the emerging markets and Asia, just as it once moved from Britain to the United States. Those flows accelerated when short-sided U.S. policies encouraged the offshoring of its manufacturing base, which Germany refused to allow happen (which is why it has remained strong), and this trend will most likely continue during our lifetime, with profound economic ramifications, despite what politicians may say.

A famous Chinese novel, *Romance of the Three Kingdoms*, starts out with the telling phrase, "Empires wax and wane, states cleave asunder and coalesce." With this in mind, we must remember that while the U.S. has been the premier place to invest over the last century, this does not mean it will remain the premier location into the future. As Americans we typically shout patriotic slogans and expect to remain *numero uno* because it's been that way for several generations, but things can and do change. In order to be able to grow to mega-wealth status, you must remember that other countries (such as China, Brazil, India, Turkey, etc.) may represent better investment possibilities than the U.S. in the future and become a safer place for capital to grow as time goes on. You cannot remain solely America-centric if you want to grow your wealth as large as possible and in the safest possible way.

The flexibility to ignore the domestic "buy and hold" mantra and move your funds to more promising markets over time might be the best single piece of advice anyone ever gives you for growing your capital, which is one of the purposes of this book. In short, I don't think it's wise to be a perennial domestic bull which is why this seasonal strategy is especially helpful and a start at changing one's attitudes along these lines. Hedge funds, for instance, rarely think about permanent positions and they typically make the most money through active investing. In long term investing, *realistic pragmatism and flexibility* are both required to protect and grow your capital while many international changes go on. If through analysis or common sense you can anticipate an imminent stock market crash, or if you no longer trust a financial institution with your money, you should definitely preserve your assets by removing them from the market or that institution and putting them elsewhere. My college friend's Nicaraguan grandfather could not do so before the crash of 1929, but Joseph Kennedy was able to do so.

Now the "best six months of the year strategy" has historically tended to keep you out of many market declines, but there's no guarantee it will exempt you from the largest declines of the future. Nevertheless, it is the simplest investment strategy I have ever found for those of a perennially bullish persuasion yet it captures far more return with far less risk. You basically get into the market the best six months of every year, and get out of the market during the six months when the market tends to do its worst.

A frequent argument against this automatic strategy is that an investor who misses even a small number of the best market days during the "off" investment period would underperform the market over time. The counter-argument is that an investor who misses even a small number of the worst periods would significantly outperform a buy and hold strategy over time. Which camp is right? Historically speaking, *skipping the worst months has increased returns over buy and hold many times over.* Sometimes that means giving up some summer-autumn profits, but in terms of the total track record, this simple timing strategy has produced a better rate of return with less drawdowns than staying totally invested all year long. Those results don't even take into account the interest you would have earned during the "out" periods, which would make it shine all the brighter. So here are the rules to this super investing system that uses the seasonality of the stock market …

THE RULES:

The basic strategy has you investing in the stock market between November 1st and April 30 each year, and then getting out of the market and investing in bonds, money markets or other interest rate vehicles between May and November. This is the idea behind the famous saying to "sell in May and go away, but come back to be seen near favorable Halloween," which in turn is based on the original British saying to "sell in May and go away, stay away till Saint Leger's Day." Thus, now we know approximately when we want to be in or out of the market. However, this basic strategy has a dynamic aspect to the timing that alters the exact date you would use each year to enter or exit stocks. The strategy uses the MACD indicator (moving average convergence divergence indicator invented by Gerald Appel), favored by stock market technical analysts and found on nearly all charting software, as a trigger to determine the exact day to enter or exit the market around these two calendar poles. I tend to use the **ThinkorSwim.com** software to monitor the MACD as it has many other indicators, too, but you can use other services as well.

Starting in April and running through May, one waits to leave the market only after the MACD indicator finally gives a cross-over signal to "sell." Starting in October and running through November, one monitors the MACD indicator again on a daily basis and waits to re-enter the market when the indicator finally gives a "buy" cross-over signal. This little bit of

SUPER INVESTING

dynamic behavior improves the returns of the simple six month strategy many times over! It gets you in earlier and keeps you in longer during market uptrends, and gets you out earlier and keeps you out longer when the market is in a downtrend. By making the basic calendar rule dynamic, you increase your returns and decrease drawdowns, too.

The Stock Traders Almanac, by Yale Hirsch, reports that this simple strategy, which it developed based on the initial work of seasonal analyst Sy Harding, has produced extremely reliable investment returns with reduced risk since 1950! That's a positive track record over six decades long, and having such a long term track record is one of our requirements before recommending a super investing method. Before you decide if you want to start using it, let's look at the actual performance of this method.

Starting with an investment of $10,000 (starting in 1950 for the Dow and S&P and 1971 for the NASDAQ), the following table derived from the **StockTradersAlmanac.com** website shows how this initial $10K would have grown for the Dow Jones Industrials, S&P and NASDAQ to the end of 2011. It also shows the compound average rate of return, or CAGR, that you would have achieved using a buy and hold strategy or the best six month seasonal period switching technique. The best six months of the year trading strategy clearly shows a far better return per year and represents far less risk and much less drawdown. Its CAGR beats buy and hold by 1-3% per annum, and that difference adds up to a lot over time.

The Compound Annual Rates of Return for Two Investing Methods

	Buy and Hold Returns		Seasonal Switching	
Dow Jones	$600,206	6.8%	$2,074,294	9.0%
S&P500	$740,484	7.2%	$1,398,585	8.3%
NASDAQ	$280,936	8.5%	$ 818,196	11.3%

These growth numbers do not even include interest earned during the six month summer period when funds are sitting idle, which would boost the compound growth rates even higher! Given that the average yearly T-bill and T-bond rates were roughly 4-5% and 6-7% over these long time frames, and assuming that we would get half of that return when we parked the idle summer funds in T-bills or bonds, we can conservatively add yet another 2-3% of yearly outperformance to the rates of return earned by the simple MACD seasonal switching system.

S&P sector analyst Sam Stovall has even suggested in *The Seven Rules of Wall Street* that investors might consider switching into either the S&P Consumer Staples (XLP) or Health Care sectors (XLV) from May to October as a rotational strategy instead of T-bonds or bills. This is yet another alternative although I have not seen computations showing how much additional return this adds to the system. People usually don't like simple investing systems because they then think they must not work due to the simplicity, but this one outperforms in spades.

If you are going to follow only one simple market timing rule rather than buy and hold, this is the one I would use. Starting October 1, you are looking for signs of a market uptrend using a standard 12-26-9 MACD indicator, and you get into the market when it gives a "long" or "buy" cross-over signal. Beginning April 1, you are looking to exit your position as soon as the market starts declining, once again the trade being triggered by a "short" or "sell" MACD cross-over signal. You can trade the system using index funds to avoid management fees, and the trading rules are just that simple. People can even subscribe to the StockTradersAlmanac.com newsletter if they want to receive real time trading signals twice a year when they don't want to compute them on their own.

There are plenty of free charting programs on the web which chart the MACD indicator, so there is absolutely nothing to buy if you want to implement this system yourself. When you're not in the market, you simply park your money in a money market fund and earn interest. For a *simple strategy* that produces far better returns than a simple buy and hold strategy and which eliminates lots of risk and severe drawdown periods, I've never found anything better. There are lots of investing strategies that are better than buy and hold, but they are not usually this simple or have such a long track record of outperformance. As stated, we're starting at the bottom of the ladder of both complexity and possible returns based on how much time you can afford to put into managing your money, and how much complexity you can handle in trying to become wealthier through investing.

While no one can say for sure why the six month summer period is so poor for trading, many logical reasons have been suggested. The clear fact is that it works in more than just the American market so something universal is going on. Thus it satisfies the criteria for a methodology that holds up over a long period of time and which captures something fundamental for its underpinnings.

It would be interesting if research were done overlaying some fundamental timing model, market climate or valuation model on these two "risk on" and "risk off" investing periods to determine if even a small amount of conditioning information could improve results. There is always the possibility that the summer-autumn returns were reasonable when the market was undervalued or interest rates were falling, or that the November to April returns were exceptional in similar circumstances. If one could determine the right conditional factors that might have identified over or underperformance conditions for this simple strategy, you could improve further upon this basic timing mechanism.

INDIVIDUAL SEASONAL STOCK PATTERNS

Most seasoned investors know about the calendar seasonality of the stock market indices, but going one step further, many market legends have used some form of seasonal analysis to trade individual stocks, too. Those who watch market seasonality include famed trader Larry Williams, and I once read that the stock trader Dan Zanger, who started in 1998 with just $10,775 that he promptly turned into $18 million in less than two years, also advised watching seasonal patterns. Zanger developed his own version of a famous investing technique called CANSLIM that takes into account a variety of different factors for stock selection. His track record of making 29,000% in one year's time has made him the world record holder for personal portfolio performance for a one-year and 18-month period. In short, many famous stock traders reference seasonal stock charts for their trading, and commodity traders use them, too.

The basic idea of stock seasonality is that individual stocks, like the larger stock market indices, have a general seasonal trading pattern that frequently repeats itself on a yearly basis. If you know that individual seasonal pattern and can tell when a stock is currently following it, you might then use it—with its historically derived projections of upcoming highs, lows, and breakout periods—to make safer money than from just subjecting yourself to the "random walk" of the market.

No one trading rule or methodology works all the time, and this caveat holds for stock seasonal trading, too. If a stock isn't following its normal seasonal trading pattern then you wouldn't want to trade it using any type of seasonal investing methodology. You should trade it using some other technique or skip it entirely and go on to find another stock that is following its seasonal pattern when you want to use seasonality investing. This is just common sense; never try to fit a square peg into a round hole. If an individual stock or market index doesn't fulfill the criteria required for trading it via a certain methodology, then you shouldn't trade it using that technique. Therefore, if a stock's current trading pattern isn't already following its typical seasonal pattern with a 70% correlation, I wouldn't use seasonality to trade it at all.

The basics of seasonal stock trading are as simple as that; if a stock is already following its typical seasonal pattern then you can use that pattern to guide your trades. You are then betting that the typical trading pattern of the seasonal will continue. There are many different forms of seasonal trading, but this is the simplest: you trade a stock according to its expected seasonal price pattern *when it is already following that pattern.* If it is already following that pattern, then you can get in or out of the market using a MACD indicator or other system trigger (such as a trend line break) that you set against the seasonal expectation just like we did with the best six months of the year strategy.

If you want to use seasonals to trade a stock and it's not already following its seasonal pattern that year, you would "pass" on any trades until it got back in sync and started to follow its normal pattern once again. On the other hand, you might make a bet that it *would begin to start following its pattern near an expected top or bottom* and put a MACD or other trigger around that expected time period, but that's a totally different type of trading. You are basically saying, "It's not following its normal seasonal pattern right now, but might once again do so right about this typical flex point (high or low) period. *I am going to bet on a return to the normal seasonal through this trade.*" You are still using seasonal expectations, but with a different type of trading method. One style of trading bets that the seasonal pattern right now will continue, and another type bets that the market which is not following its normal seasonal pattern will soon start doing so.

By just thumbing through a chart book of stocks together with their normal seasonal trading patterns, you will readily find many cases where stocks have been closely tracing out their normal seasonal pattern, including even very tiny up and down wiggles in the expected price pattern. When known patterns are already being followed, it's just human nature to expect that the rest of the anticipated price pattern will come to pass. Indeed, some stocks will truly follow their typical seasonal patterns for months at a time before they deviate from the expected pattern, and those are the ones you're hoping to find for *seasonal trading* or *seasonal investing*. When we say "seasonal trading" we are referring to quickly getting in and out of the market based on systems which trigger trades at the time of expected seasonal turning points, namely expected seasonal changes in trend. If we say "seasonal investing" then the implied trading pace is much slower. Here we are referring to longer term buyers interested in seasonal lows where they can safely add onto their positions, sellers interested in seasonal highs where they can liquidate positions at the best prices, and stock owners who want to know when they can more safely write (sell) calls to collect the premiums on long positions they are holding.

The general rule behind these various types of seasonal trading is to identify when prices have been recently following the normal seasonal price pattern with high exactness, and then assume that they will continue following the pattern into the near future (due to momentum, fundamentals or because of market correlations). There are never any guarantees that a stock will continue to follow its normal pattern into the near future, but there's no guarantee any other stock investment or trading method will work into the future either. That's why you always trade everything in a risk adjusted fashion, taking your risks into account before assuming a position. All you can ever say is that stocks now following their historical trading pattern might continue doing so until they no longer do so; something works until it no longer works. There's no guarantee that any stock will continue to follow any pattern even one more day into the future, but with seasonal trading you try to make money off the expected pattern nonetheless.

Trading and investing are a game of odds, edges, probabilities and risks, so to make money you have to get used to this type of uncertainty in the markets. My own extensive experience in seasonal trading has lead me to hunt for stocks that are already following their typical seasonal patterns, and then use some confirmation system (such as a MACD) to tell you when to buy and sell according to that seasonal expectation because the trend has truly turned in the expected direction. Alternatively, I often screen for value stocks and then buy them at seasonal junctures right before expected bullish patterns. When you build seasonal patterns correctly, it gives you a tremendous trader's edge that is a significant advantage. You can start with stocks already following their seasonal pattern, or you can start with candidates you want to buy and then look for the most appropriate seasonal entry points. In either case, you are still using seasonal patterns.

Even if you don't want to trade using seasonal patterns, there's still another reason to want to know the normal seasonal tendency for any stock. Let's say you have some model that can tell you that you are currently in a bull or bear market. If you're in a bull market, it makes sense to be invested in stocks that should also experience what is normally their bullish seasonal period rather than stocks in the midst of their normally bearish seasonal period. Those stocks *whose seasonals align with your trend* are the ones that are likely to continue going along with your expectations, so which ones would you rather be in? If the trend is bullish, just scan for all the stocks already following a large bullish seasonal, and then you have a subset you can choose to trade or invest in. If you can confirm your expectations with fundamentals, you are thus combining both fundamental and technical analysis in a logical manner.

Stacking your portfolio in this manner can definitely help you outperform a bull market by avoiding laggards and losers. If you expect the market to tank and you want to go short, what better choices are there than to *short the stocks that have bearish seasonal tendencies right then* anyway? By performing seasonal analysis on individual stocks, you can stack your portfolio with companies whose bullish or bearish seasonals already line up with your larger expectations. If you expect a bull market then you can buy stocks going through their bullish seasonal period right now as an example. Or, you can use seasonals to create "market neutral" portfolios where you buy stocks with bullish seasonals and short stocks with bearish seasonals at the same time.

There is yet another way to use stock seasonal patterns that fundamental value investors should want to know about. In terms of fundamental analysis, when a stock is following its normal seasonal trading pattern this also suggests that things are going on as normally expected for the company. The company's annual sales and earnings cycles, which become reflected in its stock price because of the efficiencies of the market, are probably doing nothing out of the ordinary because prices are following the usual seasonal trading pattern. The expectation is that there's nothing especially wrong or "out of whack" when everything seems to be following the normally expected seasonal tendencies.

On the other hand, if share prices suddenly *stop* following the typical seasonal pattern, then that deviance alerts you to the fact that something— for good or bad—is out of the ordinary! A fundamental analyst wants to immediately know this because they need to investigate what's happening. Without the seasonal pattern as a reference basis for comparison, they have little else they can use as a yardstick to tell them that something is truly out of the ordinary. You need some way to compare what the shares normally *should be doing*, and seasonals supply that dispassionate yardstick of expected normality. When you derive the annual seasonal trading pattern for a stock, which can dramatically differ from the basic seasonal pattern of the overall market, you create that relevant yardstick of normal expectations which you need. The big question is then how to best construct the seasonal pattern for the most accurate forecasts possible.

Here's where I suggest you approach seasonal trading differently than the way most people use it, which tends to lose money. First, you should construct an *adaptive* seasonal pattern that is more accurate than just the static seasonal pattern constructed from all your price data. An adaptive or similarity seasonal forecast more accurately reflects how the market has been trading by only using previous years that traded just like this one. Second, you should construct *conditional* seasonal charts that show how a stock has historically performed during past bull or bear markets, prior recessions and expansion phases of the business cycle, or other sets of opposite market conditions. They are seasonal charts drawn up for a particular fundamental environment, and thus these conditional seasonal trading patterns show the underlying sensitivity to certain market factors. I call these "factor" seasonal charts because they show how a stock has historically been influenced by different market moving *factors*, namely entirely different market "climates" or economic conditions. They reveal how stocks have been historically affected or influenced by different environments, and their patterns of trading in those different environments.

Once you start making these adaptive and factor seasonal charts for individual stocks, you will know how your stock has traded in time periods similar to this current one, including previous environments matching the environment you are now experiencing … or expecting. Various factors can bias trading patterns this way or that, and that's why these are called "factor" seasonals in honor of the *factor analysis* technique taught in business schools to explain stock market returns. By creating individual seasonal charts for different types of environments, you are showing how a stock's trading has historically been affected by different factors.

The idea behind "factor analysis" is that a stock's performance is affected by (sensitive to or influenced by) different types of factors such as interest rates, inflation, or other economic conditions. No one really knows which economic factors are the most important influence on the market in the future since Mr. Market weights the effects of factors differently over time, but if you can identify the typical factors that are affecting market returns *now* and can predict them into the future, you can then use that understanding to predict future stock movements, especially if you can determine which factor has the predominant influence *right now*. How do we apply this concept to individual stocks? In this case, you historically derive the typical trading behavior (pattern) of a stock under different past economic, political, or financial environment factors and see if those charts offer predictive abilities in any way. They certainly do!

You can create factor seasonal patterns for all sorts of different types of trading environments. You can create factor seasonal charts showing how a stock typically trades in bullish or bearish monetary environments, during rising or falling interest rate conditions, when there is a rising or falling dollar, during increasing or decreasing inflation rates, and even when Republicans or Democrats are in political office. You can create factor seasonal charts for any type of environment you can think of as long as you have a clear history of the previous dates isolating the different climates.

All these seasonal chart patterns created for various types of conditions ("factors") can help a technical or fundamental analyst set their trading expectations for when a stock seems to be following that pattern, and when the environment you are presently experiencing is characterized by that factor as well. Is the stock following the seasonal pattern it normally makes during a recession, and are we in a recession? If so, you then have an expectation of how the stock will trade due to that factor seasonal pattern. Is the stock following its "inflation rate factor seasonal chart," and are we in that type of economic environment? If so, you now have an expectation of the general price path it might follow from that chart. Is the stock following the seasonal pattern it typically makes when a Republican is President, and is a Republican President in office? These are just examples of the types of factor seasonal charts you can derive.

What is probably the most useful predictive pattern for trading decisions is the *adaptive seasonal forecast*. If you decide to create a seasonal pattern using ten years of past price data, normally you would just average up the normalized patterns of each of those ten individual years to create an average ten-year seasonal pattern, which is a static pattern that doesn't change. However you can also create a more "adaptive" seasonal pattern that uses just half of those years (five of them), and which tends to project a more accurate price pattern forecast into the near future than just the purely static seasonal. Which years should you include in your computations? The ones that have most closely matched how the market has recently been trading. The "most similar seasonals" are the ones whose price patterns have the highest correlation with the current market prices.

Figure 1: A perfect adaptive seasonal forecast for BP Oil good for 1-3 months into the future. You must always redraw adaptive charts on a monthly basis.

If you are using twenty years of data to create a static seasonal chart, an adaptive seasonal projection might only use ten data years from within that group of twenty to create its best adaptive forecast. Which ten years? You rank each of the twenty years in terms of how closely the trading pattern for each year looks like this year's pattern (you see which years have the closest correlation to the current trading pattern), and then use those prior years which best resemble the market to create your chart. In other words, you use those years whose trading patterns best match or mirror the pattern of how the current market has been recently trading.

This adaptive or similarity seasonal chart usually produces a much more accurate forecast than a static seasonal chart, and often picks future trading tops and bottoms to within days. This makes it an extremely useful tool to the value or dividend investor who wants just a slightly lower price before he buys a stock but doesn't know if he should wait a bit longer. This type of chart puts the odds in your favor for determining a better buying period.

As stated, you can produce factor seasonal charts (also called "environmental" or "climate" seasonal charts) that show the historical trading performance of a stock under different types of fundamental environments such as bull or bear markets, increasing or decreasing interest rate scenarios, and even different exchange rate conditions (an increasing or declining dollar). You will find that some types of factor seasonals are extremely predictive for certain types of stocks, such as interest rate factor seasonals being good for predicting banking stock movements. Together with the adaptive seasonal forecast, having a stock's typical trading pattern for different economic environments can really help you make much better investment decisions because you can see how that stock typically trades in the environments that might affect its economics, and thus profits and stock prices. Sometimes it follows those patterns exactly! This type of analysis should help you with your goal of making more money in the markets. Once you master it, it will help you with many other investment methodologies including the best six months of the year strategy itself.

Over the years I have found that the two most useful factor seasonals are a stock's typical trading pattern during **recessions versus business expansion** periods, and its typical seasonal pattern during **bull or bear markets**. Those different environments can dramatically change the shape of the typical seasonal pattern you would normally expect, which is another reason why people who try to trade just a static seasonal chart often lose money with unsophisticated analysis.

If you produce these two factor seasonal charts and the most recent adaptive seasonal chart for a stock, they can become the basis of many highly profitable trading systems. Static seasonal charts show the normal tendency for stocks to make tops or bottoms at particular times of the year, but adaptive similarity seasonals take into account the most recent trading information to produce better expectations. Even so, they are usually only good for 1-3 months into the future, though sometimes longer, and you should never expect an adaptive pattern to hold for the entire year.

All these seasonal charts show you the periods when a stock usually goes up or down during the year, so you can use those charts to determine many things such as when you should ignore individuals "pushing" a stock on the television news right near its seasonal top. Often you can discover through the seasonal charts when people are trying to manipulate the markets in various ways, such as when they want to push up stock prices so that they can unload their shares through distribution.

Figure 2: The Bull-Bear Market Factor Seasonal chart for Walmart showing

the stock trading as if it is in a bull market environment (2012).

Either a stock has recently been following one of its factor seasonal patterns or it hasn't, and either it will continue to follow those computed patterns into the immediate future or it won't. As stated, there are no promises, just as there are no promises with *any other stock selection or trading system!* You can use these charts, but you cannot depend on them.

As stated, an adaptive seasonal forecast is usually good for only about 1-3 months into the future. It's stable but not stable enough, so you should produce new adaptive seasonal charts every month to adjust to recent market behavior. Some patterns, once computed, will even remain stable (and accurate) for 5-6 months into the future when the company's economics are running just as expected. However, you should produce new adaptive charts every month or so to keep updated on any new pattern that might be developing. I firmly believe this type of information will help you make more money with your investments, and much better decisions than flying blindly or by working off news headlines, but you will just have to see for yourself whether or not this is true.

Until the adaptive and factor seasonal methodology becomes so popular that absolutely everyone uses it, at which time its ability to help you outperform astute traders might decline a bit (because the extra edge it offers is arbitraged out of the market), chances are that if a stock has been closely following its normal pattern then it will continue to do so into the *near* future. It's just a question of how closely it will continue to follow its pattern and for how long. Actually, the real question is not "how much" or "for how long" but rather, how can you use that forecast in a risk adjusted way that has a reasonable chance of making you money? How can you put the trading odds in your favor using these special seasonal charts?

I originally invented this methodology many years ago to help those managing money find better entry and exit points for their positions, and it is actually the most valuable and dependable trading method I have ever found for stocks and commodities. I am revealing it here to help you as much as possible with your future investment and trading decisions because it's much better than listening to people on television for stock tips. Usually you decide to get into a stock position for some reason other than seasonals, but you can use seasonals to greatly assist your timing for buying and selling. In my experience, proven seasonals (meaning that the market is already following the pattern) tend to be far more reliable than cycle projections, Elliott Wave counting, Gann angles, trend following projections, and so forth for most types of trading and investing. *You can even start with a certain investing method and then apply seasonals on top of that method to greatly assist you in your decision making.*

For instance, if a stock is following the typical pattern it usually makes during the expansion phase of the business cycle, and if you are in such a typically bullish period, your "business cycle expansion phase factor seasonal" can give you a very good expectation of the future price pattern for that stock and when it should move up or down or make a high or low. For a long position trader, such a factor seasonal chart can help you decide when you might raise your stops, lighten up your positions, write covered calls, or buy puts for portfolio protection. You can use the projected seasonal pattern to help maximize your gains with whatever investment strategy you are using.

Figure 3: The Expansion-Recession Factor Seasonal chart for AT&T showing its normal seasonal price behavior for two entirely different types of economic environments.

If a stock is following its normal bear market pattern and you're in a recognized bear market, you can use that information to help you short sell the stock, sell covered calls, or buy puts at better time periods. You can use the Bear Market Factor Seasonal information to even know when a stock *tends to rally during a declining bear market!* A correctly constructed factor seasonal chart will give you a forecast of all the upcoming wiggles you might expect, *including some upwards bullish periods during a normal bear market*, and it's simply up to you to decide what to do with that information.

This is the basis of my form of seasonal trading for stocks and market indices, and you are looking for the situations when you can make money from this sort of analysis. After you see it work, you will have to agree that many stocks and market indices *do indeed follow* a consistent, repeating seasonal trading pattern just as does the overall market itself. If you have a disciplined way to find those trading patterns and put a trading rule on top of those seasonal expectations, you can use this to make excellent money! Long term investors, such as dividend players and fundamental analysts, can use this in addition to shorter term traders as well. But while forward adaptive and factor seasonal projections can be extremely accurate, you should never bet the house believing that these seasonal patterns will come true exactly as predicted.

Just because a stock has been following its seasonal pattern doesn't mean the forecast will continue to hold, so you should never throw all caution to the wind and make trades without the typical prudence you would normally use for other types of stock trading. As Warren Buffett and other famous traders and investors have explained, you must worry about your risks of loss first! No matter what your trading or investment methodology, you therefore should always use appropriate risk management techniques such as stops and limited leveraging. Nevertheless, long term investors, short term traders, options players, fund managers, hedge fund traders, and even day traders pay big money to have information like this to help determine trades where they might have an edge. I'm going to give you the software that allows you to do this for FREE!

So that's it for our discussion of market seasonality and adaptive/factor seasonal trading. We have our first investment strategy—trading the six best seasonal months of the year using a MACD to get better entry and exit points—which is a market timing rule superior to buy and hold that requires just two trading decisions per year. You invest in the market during what has historically been the best six months of the year and the rest of the time you stay in cash. However, you time your entry into and exit from the market using a MACD indicator around May and October so that the system greatly outperforms a simplistic calendar day strategy of entering and exiting on the same date every year. Now that you know about adaptive seasonals, that type of seasonal chart, applied to the stock market index, can help you increase your gains as well.

The consistency of superior returns for the best six months of the year strategy, while assuming far less market risk and producing much smaller drawdowns, has held up for over sixty years! It's a simple system, and since some people only like simple trading systems, we are starting out with the most basic system possible that produces far better returns than Wall Street's often recommended buy and hold strategy. It also has far less risk. Even a teenager can follow this strategy, and teenagers should certainly be taught the market's propensity for lousy or losing returns during the summer and autumn months of the year from May to October.

You also have a new analysis methodology, the **adaptive seasonal pattern** and **factor seasonal charting method**, that can be used on individual stocks as well as market indices to make forward pattern forecasts and price projections. You can use this unique seasonal projection technique in many ways for trading and investing, and I believe you will be using it far into the future. Options traders absolutely love this method once they learn how to use it after some experience.

As long as you know the general seasonal price pattern of a stock, you can use the adaptive seasonal trend forecast along with a MACD cross-over signal (or some faster cross-over system) to generate better buy and sell signals that take advantage of expected seasonal trends. Therefore you now have an excellent way to know when to reasonably expect typical market highs and lows. Value investors, fundamental analysts, dividend investors, and options traders will all find that taking seasonals into account usually leads to far better (much more profitable) decision making.

The best six months of the year strategy and factor/adaptive seasonal strategy for individual stocks (or market indices) are better than the simplistic buy and hold strategy drummed into the heads of most investors. You will find that seasonals applied to individual stocks will also help you improve your returns significantly over the typically blind buy and hold strategy. Hence, you now have not just one but two new systems you can use to increase your wealth that are better than the passive buy and hold strategy, and you'll find that the second strategy of adaptive and factor seasonals will help you improve returns for almost every other type of investment methodology you use.

Lastly, to help you get started with these new techniques I wish to *give you for free* the "Seasonal Pro" software I personally use that produces the factor seasonal and adaptive (similarity) seasonal charts discussed in this chapter. You can even use this free software to put into practice the best six month of the year seasonal switching strategy. It cost me tens of thousands of dollars to develop the Seasonal Pro software and would cost you several hundred dollars were you to buy it, but I'm giving it to you as a gift to help you with your future investing. There is no obligation whatsoever, but just my best wishes for your future investment and trading success. Naturally it is not guaranteed to make you money (or in any other way), and of course you are totally responsible for your own profits and losses from using it. My hope is that it helps you achieve your investment goals of becoming a better trader and investor and that it (and the associated seasonal trading philosophy within this book) helps to catapult you several steps closer to being able to accumulate generational wealth and create a Legacy IRA. You can download it for free at:

http://www.markettimingresearch.com/seasonalsoftware/

4
ANALYTICALLY TIMING
FUNDAMENTAL INFORMATION

When I worked on Wall Street, my job was to invent various investment strategies and money management rules that were used to manage billions in funds. I would research the fundamental or momentum factors which moved various markets and then turn those findings into systematic investing rules. These rules would then be turned into computerized trading systems that would automatically buy and sell commodities, foreign currencies, stocks, bonds, and precious metals whenever the time was appropriate.

To develop an investing rule, you always had to think of fundamental principles and how markets reacted under different environments or in different situations. Once you had some observation of how markets fundamentally worked and an idea on how you might make money from that fundamental tendency, you then had to historically test your ideas against many different years of prior price history to see if it was true. You were not just looking for a systematic way to make money off that tendency, but a system that consistently made more money than by putting it in the bank, than buying and holding an index fund, and which did so with far less risk than the typical buy and hold investor.

Our investment funds would trade just about any liquid asset possible. The process would be to historically test all sorts of buy and sell models on very long price series to see if they produced positive returns, and then use the very best models to trade the funds we had under management. While we investigated all sorts of complicated models, the most successful ones usually ended up being very simple trend following rules that would tell us when to go long, go short, or just get entirely out of a particular market such as Treasury bonds or the Japanese Yen. We'd call getting out of the market "going flat" or "going neutral" because it meant we wouldn't have any position in that market, neither long nor short. Today this is called a "risk off" position.

At that time, which is still the case today, no purely technical trend following method did well enough to serve as a stock market timing system that held up over long periods of time. Instead, as the investment research stars Marty Zweig and Ned Davis Research had showed, *the best stock market timing models came from putting analytical analysis methods on top of fundamental information*. I always called these models **"analytically timing"** or **"technically timing fundamental information"** and believe they represent the best approach to make sense of all the government statistics and fundamental information that comes to you about the market. When you mathematically analyze such data, only then can you turn it into a reasonable buy or sell decision, and if you want to invest in the stock market you should use technically timed fundamental information.

One of the most successful types of these models involved monitoring interest rate differentials to come up with stock market buy and sell decisions. If credit was easy (so interest rates were low) you'd expect stocks to go up, and if credit was getting tighter you'd expect the market to go down. Many studies have shown that investing in stocks when the Fed was tightening credit produced far lower returns than when the Fed was easing credit, although this hasn't been true during all periods. There are always caveats to this general observation, so what you have to do is take that general fundamental tendency and turn it into some tested systematic trading system that can accept the losses when the relationship decouples. Hence, various timing models might analytically compare the rates between T-bills and the discount rate, changes in the T-note rate, the spread between the T-bond and prime rate, yield curve differentials, or some more fundamental metric (like the difference between the S&P earnings yields and the T-Bond yield) to come up with a trading system that would be profitable for the stock market over very long periods of time.

Ned Davis Research, which is a literal powerhouse providing exceptional investment research for institutional investors, and many others have published all sorts of successful investment rules based on timing interest rates differentials, and these monetary models have worked over very long periods of time. Once while in Hong Kong I was talking to a Japanese equities fund manager with whom I was working, and behind him on his wall was a 100-year historical chart of the Japanese stock market showing this sort of relationship. At the bottom of the chart were two lines indicating the levels of the Japanese short term interest rates against the country's discount rate, and you could clearly see that when the short term yields were more or less than what banks were being charged, the market was either going up or down appropriately. This manager had been sitting in front of this chart for years and had never once noticed this fundamental relationship that had also ruled the basic direction of the U.S. stock market.

Back in New York, like many other investment houses we eventually created our own profitable market timing model for the U.S. stock market based on interest rate differentials. It was far more profitable and reliable than anything we had ever discovered through trend following research. At that time, a large Wall Street house was one of our marketing partners and had just sold a commodity fund we managed that had a substantial stock market component within it. Before the famous crash of '87, our stock market timing model, based on these interest rate differentials, had turned negative on stocks. Therefore we were holding a very large short position on the S&P futures market even though the stock market kept climbing higher.

Every day our institutional marketing partner would check the performance of our funds, and management saw that we continued to maintain a short position in stocks (because of our model) while the market continued going higher. One day our partner could stand it no longer and called up saying, "We're not going to claim that we have any expertise at all in the various commodity markets you trade in this fund, but one thing we do think we know is stocks. You're short the stock market and it keeps going higher. Don't you think you should reduce that position?"

Bowing to the constant pressure, at their request we finally reduced our exposure just days before the big stock market crash of 1987 sent shockwaves throughout Wall Street, pummeling stock prices in a day that old timers will long remember. Afterwards, when all the smoke had cleared, had we maintained our position according to our fundamental model we would have made an extra 20% return on our portfolio that year. We didn't secure that return because we listened to emotional "experts" rather than simply follow our time-tested fundamental model. The story illustrates the benefits of trading according to tested models, and the dangers of emotional trading as well.

Since that time, the question of which type of interest rate model still works best in timing the market has become problematical. In fact, I have my doubts that the long term fundamental relationships between interest rates and the market still strongly hold *at this particular point in time* because of excessive government interferences in the market. I believe we've entered an "end game" period of unprecedented circumstances when the government has so manipulated rates that the basic causality that used to strongly exist between stocks and interest rates has degraded, and it is hard to come to correct conclusions of value and price discovery using interest rates solely as your guide. If you don't have an honest interest rate, then no one can make accurate investment decisions and industry cannot make correct capital allocation decisions either, and this is biasing the market. However, when the government stops manipulating the market, these models will start shining in all their glory once again because a fundamental relationship is truly there, but until the end game is over I am wary about fully trusting them.

For instance, once Japan pushed itself into a 0% interest rate environment (ZIRP) years ago in hopes of stimulating its economy, it has been stuck in that situation for twenty years and has not been able to get out. All the quantitative easing in the world hasn't been able to fix the constipation. The Japanese have run up huge deficits and now have one of the highest debt-to-GDP ratios in the world, and the future demographics of the nation don't look rosy anymore. If Japanese interest rates simply went from 1% to 2%, it would use up all the country's tax revenues to finance the debt as once happened in Hapsburg Spain. The low interest rates, artificially maintained by the government, have never stimulated its economy, and to raise them after having lowered them to the bottom risks both economic and financial catastrophe. This is an example of a government following errant policies for a long period of time, in turn producing unintended consequences from which there is no escape. You can't use the low interest rates to make proper investment decisions, and only know that if rates rise the debt bubble will pop and your investments may be imperiled.

The only reason Japan has survived this situation for so long is that the Japanese have used their vast savings of the last 50 years to fund their government debt. However, the dynamics are such that the country is aging and the savings rate will soon go negative, and if we put this together with its trade deficits, the future *long term* outlook for Japan is extremely negative.

Japan's currency will most certainly suffer devaluation over time. Money printing is guaranteed. History teaches us countries which run large deficits with increasing debt levels cannot create wealth over the long term, and so a financial disaster is openly in the making. Monetary policy cannot be used to solve structural issues. Money printing cannot create wealth.

All governments, no matter how modern or "smart," make mistakes and then end up kicking the can of consequences down the road, rather than fix the accumulating problems, for only so long until they finally have to pay the piper, and that day of reckoning will eventually occur to the Japanese. The U.S. is heading for its own end game of debt restructuring as well, along with a collapse of the dollar's status as a reserve currency due to improper moves by the politicians, bankers and the Fed. As the plot lines of the ancient Greek tragedies continually point out, wrong conclusions, misconceptions and lack of understanding produce unintended but fateful consequences. The performance of Japan offers many lessons for the U.S. because it shows the ineffective results of a zero interest rate policy meant to stimulate, and illustrates what can happen when smart people don't bite the bullet and do the right thing earlier rather than later.

However long it takes, after the market manipulation and interference ends things will eventually return to a new level of normality again where the true fundamental relationships between stocks and interest rates are restored, even after a debt collapse or issuance of a new currency. When that happens, this type of timing model will no doubt come into vogue again, and so is something you should keep in the back of your mind to guide long term investment decisions during the long periods of non-extremes. As an example, just a very simple stock market timing model of comparing T-bill yields to their rates six months ago finds that when the rates increase, stocks only gain at about a 5% annualized return. However, when interest rates are falling and the rates are lower than six months ago, the annualized stock market rate of return is about 20%! This is a timing model along the likes of the following:

If T-bill Yields < T-bill Yields 6 moths ago then you are Bullish;
If T-bill Yields > T-bill Yields 6 moths ago then you are Bearish;

This type of simple interest rate model—which involves comparing the current T-bill rate (or T-note yield) with the rate six months ago, and to invest accordingly—is a very crude rule that we're using only to illustrate the basics of how you can do market timing using fundamental information. Even though it's crude, it can certainly help classify a time period as good or bad for stocks and thus help you become a better investor.

Few things can be taken as certain in the world of investing, which is a world of uncertainty, so the best you can hope for is that the environment is favorable when you decide to invest in the stock market. Nonetheless, there is strong empirical evidence showing that a drop in the T-bill rate seems to predict an environment of generally higher stock market returns. But as noted, the value of short term rates as a predictor of stock market movements has decreased recently as the Fed has interfered more and more with the markets, and the relationship has uncoupled to some extent.

A relationship holds until it no longer holds, which is why you must never depend entirely on just one system, method, equation or relationship to guide your investing future. There are always periods of time when even the strongest fundamental relationships decouple and stop working for awhile until market forces reach equilibrium again. But fundamental relationships do tend to eventually reassert themselves and cause price extremes to revert to the mean, going back to normal, and this is what investors bank on in the investment field. Nevertheless, investors must be cautious when fundamental tendencies decouple, which is why the famed investor Barton Biggs once said, "There are no relationships or equations that always work." Having evaluated such models for many years, I readily concur. There is especially the possibility of a catastrophic outcome for those who depend on fancier and fancier algorithms for trading or investing because there always comes a day when markets start deviating from those models. Whenever I have developed investment rules in the past, my philosophy has always been that simplest is best, and simple algebra is preferable to complicated math because it almost always leads to more robust models.

One of the times when some particular fundamental relationships stopped working sent the multi-billion dollar Long-Term Capital Management hedge fund into bankruptcy after a Russian financial crisis. Its monies were managed by all sorts of complicated mathematical models developed by two Nobel prize winners and their team, and the normal relationships they depended upon one day just stopped working. Basically, they bet on models which stipulated how things should normally work, but which did not work during "fat tail" extreme events which, while rare, happen every now and then. An unusual set of circumstances caused these models to decouple from mirroring market actualities. Thus, you cannot depend on mathematical correlation relationships always working in the markets, but if the relationships you depend upon are truly fundamental, after being out of sync for awhile they tend to reassert themselves after any interferences subside. The question is whether you can survive during the periods when they temporarily go out of sync because "temporarily" can translate into a big price swing and large losses.

Basically, at some time in the future the basic relationship between interest rates and the stock market (that has held up long term over many prior decades) will no doubt become stronger again once the interfering hand of the Federal Reserve and central banks are removed from the scene. At that time this book will still be around to remind the reader of what may once again work after the interference disappears, but until then, the markets are not functioning correctly because of artificial manipulations. You can certainly say this for the LIBOR rate and for prices in the gold market and foreign exchange. Nevertheless, if you are not presently living in the United States then you can do some research on the relationship between stocks and the short term interest rates (or the yield curve) of your own country to develop a similar simple buy or sell model for investing.

One of the big lessons I learned from many investing experiences over the decades is that using analytical methods to technically time fundamental information is the only objective way to interpret and then make use of that fundamental information. This is why I like using interest rate or monetary models for the stock market. Nothing works better, and they are far superior to relying on your guts or emotions when you are managing billions of dollars. Of course it is said, as reported by his son, that billionaire investor George Soros gets out of his losing positions when his back starts to ache with pain, but you cannot depend on subjective indicators like this to help guide your own personal trading. You must guide yourself by investment models rather than by emotions or aches and pains. You cannot just look at a chart of fundamental information either, such as P/E ratios or market sentiment or the yield curve or GNP growth rate, and come to a conclusion without some type of mathematical processing of that information to uncover an objective way of using it. You need to analytically backtest various assumptions on how to use financial information and see whether it offers any predictive abilities for bullish and bearish market periods. This is the approach I firmly recommend.

To make sense of any particular statistic or piece of fundamental information, you must go back throughout history and find out what it has actually meant in terms of market returns when the number has been high or low, increasing or decreasing, or when it has crossed some fundamental barrier, and other things like that. You can only make rational investment decisions using fundamental information when you derive objective standards or propensities from studying past history, such as discovering that gold goes up during negative real interest rate environments. With some work, those lessons and the standards you derive can then become the basis of profitable trading and investment rules. It is only through analysis and the development of trading rules that the numbers in the news can become investment guides.

Even when you are devoted to a particular style of stock market investing—such as momentum investing, growth, contrarian or value investing—the best approach to using fundamental information is to use the past history of those numbers to derive a behavioral relationship with market returns. Then you can produce tested rules that will help your investing decisions. Without any research as to what the level of any fundamental statistic actually means, you are always at the mercy of clueless television news commentators who just spout nonsense about the meaning of this or that. For instance, interest rates might suddenly go up by a half percentage point, but what should that mean in terms of your stock position? What does that usually do to the market in the current type of environment you are in? Without any historically derived trading model which uses interest rates, you cannot know the relevancy of any changes in such fundamentals, including whether a small change is significant or not.

Without any type of model derived from historical testing, you have absolutely no way to objectively interpret any such events and whether they have any probable effect on stocks and the market. You cannot just jump to the conclusion that something in particular will happen because of an event, but must go back through history to prove (or disprove) the possible effect you imagine. If you don't do this, most of the time you will just be making investment decisions under false assumptions. You will imagine the ghost of a market relationship where there is nothing there at all.

In short, you should always monitor fundamental information using analytical techniques (technical models) when you want to use that information to trade the markets. When you apply mathematical analysis to fundamental data to help determine clear buy or sell environments, it becomes far more valuable. When you "technically time fundamental information," which is *fusing the two market approaches of fundamental analysis and technical analysis together into a single combination*, you can create some wonderful models that tell when to buy and sell the market. You can determine levels where risks are high or low, and when you should get in or out of the market for superior returns.

Even purely technical traders should use technical trading rules that are adaptive to different fundamental environments. As an example, a common rule that Marty Zweig once popularized in his book, *Winning on Wall Street*, was to buy or sell the Value Line index if rose or dropped by 4% in either direction. This is an extremely simple technical trading rule based purely on price movements. However, a better rule that changes according to fundamental conditions would adaptively vary that 4% trigger according to the market environment, as illustrated in a fictitious trading algorithm such as the following ...

> If fundamental conditions are Bullish according to some model
> > Then buy when the market rises by just 3.1%
> > Or sell when the market falls by 5.2%

> If fundamental conditions are Bearish according to some model
> > Then buy when the market rises by 4.3%
> > Or sell when the market falls by just 2.5%

Don't use these numbers because they were randomly invented. They simply illustrate how you might react faster in becoming long or short when you take into account the underlying fundamental environment of the market. In my opinion, the best trading and investment models are not perfectly symmetrical, which is what economists typically assume, but treat long and short trades, namely buys and sells, quite differently. People trade differently in different types of economic or fundamental environments, and so the models for those environments should not be mirror images of one another. This same principle actually holds for the effectiveness of monetary and fiscal policies as well. For instance, monetary policy is usually very effective during boom times but not so much during downturns. Fiscal policy works well in downturns but is not as effective during economic upswings. Usually the simple econometric models people build do not account for these differences. The simple ones typically make the mistake of assuming that government intervention policies are equally effective throughout all types of environments.

When you are developing stock market investment rules, it's extremely important to make sure that they try to capture some underlying genuine fundamental mechanism that explains parts of the market's direction or volatility, and are not purely the result of curve fitting past historical data. You must avoid creating models that over-fit the past because curve-fitted models are never good for future predictions at all. While I have an MBA and advanced engineering degrees whose philosophies stress "optimization" and "maximization," my rule for creating investing systems is to always be looking for something that is "generally good" or "above average" in capturing a type of behavior, rather than "perfect" or even "optimal," and which holds over the long run. It is far better to use a rule that is generally good (capturing above average but not maximum possible returns) in all sorts of environments than pursue something "optimized" or "optimal" that perfectly fits the past but doesn't ever work in real time. In any case, the big lesson for stock market investors is to try to avoid using a purely trend following or technical approach to the market but always try to combine technical analysis with fundamental analysis and look for rules that work over the long run. You can indeed combine the two approaches with technically timed fundamental information.

People commonly build investment models which assume that people invest and trade the exact same way in bull and bear markets, or during recessions as opposed to periods of business expansions, but trading behaviors change dramatically for different economic environments. That's why I invented the factor seasonals discussed previously. You need to have different investment models for different types of environments just as credit card and insurance companies create different predictive models for different income brackets and age groups. If you were trying to predict someone's weight using their height, as another instance, you would first separate the individuals into male and female categories and then build two separate weight prediction models for each of these groups. If you lump everything together, however, your model will lose a lot of accuracy.

To invest in the markets, it is best to have separate trading and investing strategies for recessions and bear markets than to use the same models for bull markets and the booming expansion phase of the business cycle. It's common sense to trade differently in different types of environments, but most people usually stick with just one methodology that only works in bull markets and then wonder why it doesn't work as well during bear seasons.

All my life I've searched for really good long term timing models for the stock market, including separate investing rules for bull and bear markets that would be easy to compute so that anyone could use them. You should be asking, "Is there a general rule that I can easily compute on my own so that I can time the market and do better than the simple buy and hold investor?" The MACD-adjusted "best six months of the year strategy" was the first introduction to such a model, but now we will step up the power a bit and move to incorporating fundamental information into our decision making.

Many people have been pioneers along these lines in producing complicated models that soundly beat the market indices over long periods of time, but they usually involve many complicated computations or difficult to find or quite expensive data. Therefore their models are hard to duplicate and you must usually become be a client of a large research house in order to gain access to their predictions. However, one of the most respected researchers of such models has been Nelson Freeburg, who publishes the *Formula Research* newsletter that evaluates their performance. The many back issues of this great newsletter contain computer simulations on countless investing models that have outperformed the markets over long periods of time. One of the simplest rules Freeburg has tested, which investment advisor Mark Pankin also revealed on the internet, has such a long term track record that it works all the way back to the 1920's! Since then it has returned 10.6% per year over all this time *at half the drawdown* of a buy and hold strategy, and it's probably the very easiest of the analytical fundamental models that you can duplicate.

You can indeed use this simple fundamental model (called the "Triple 40 Timing Model") to get you on the right side of the market, determine your degree of risk, leverage or allocation, and you can even use it to bias your other trading strategies. Using this model you become bullish because the market fundamentals are bullish, and when the model turns bearish it is because a simple fundamental relationship that moves the markets becomes bearish. We'll get to its details in a moment, but first must briefly review the concept of the "market climate" which is similar to the principle of factor seasonals.

THE "MARKET CLIMATE" APPROACH

As you know, the two basic approaches for stock market index investing are to either "buy and hold" or "time the market." In terms of analysis approaches, there are also *technical analysts* who only look at internal market price action to make their decisions, and *fundamental analysts* who look at external data such as earnings, valuations and various other fundamental factors (debt load, cash flow, sales growth, etc.) to guide their investment decision making.

Buy and hold investors believe that stock market returns cannot be predicted, but hope to receive long term compound growth annual rate returns in the range of 10-12% if they always stay invested. That's usually their expectation even though the returns you receive can vary widely over time, and the long term average CAGR is probably much lower as we have discussed. Furthermore, the buy and hold strategy embodies an inherent, implicit assumption that the country's GNP keeps marching forward and is not sidetracked by some calamity that would make "buy and hold" look ridiculous.

Famous value investor Warren Buffett put their philosophy best when he said, "I think you can be quite sure that over the next ten years there are going to be a few years when the general market is plus 20% or 25%, a few when it is minus on the same order, and a majority when it is in between. I haven't any notion as to the sequence in which these will occur, nor do I think it is of any great importance for the long-term investor." On the other hand, we have consistently seen (through the modern examples of Japan, Zimbabwe, Spain, Greece, Libya and Iraq) that the actual fate of many modern nations can defy that assumption of constant forward progress, so this implicit assumption of perennial forward progress is important if you insist on keeping your assets in just your home market. There are always "end game" scenarios when your monies should clearly leave the market.

Now market timing advocates are different than fundamental buy and hold investors because they believe that future stock market performance can often be predicted, and so they try to create timing systems and models that forecast bearish or bullish trends which they then use to guide their investing. They are also more open to the idea that they might have to rotate their investments into different asset classes and sectors at different times, and so they are not necessarily wed to just one single market.

Yet another investment approach is the "market climate" method popularized by fund manager John Hussman of the Hussman Funds, who had attained a 35% per year track record managing funds between 1988 and 1994. This method tries to classify the market as a certain type of climate, and that climate is either favorable or unfavorable for stock market investing. The market climate, or environment, is much like our factor seasonals in that it sets the tone for what you can historically expect for your future returns. Thus determining the market climate becomes the basis of picking the most appropriate investment strategy.

In other words, the risk of loss in the stock market is not the same at every moment of time because there are some conditions which have a stronger tendency to produce higher or lower returns. If you know those conditions and can find out where you are in relationship to them, then you have a smarter way to invest than just blindly buying and holding and sitting through all sorts of painful market drawdowns. If you know the typical returns you can expect under different market conditions, knowing the current market climate together with that history can help you achieve superior investment returns. You can avoid environments that typically produce drawdowns, and invest with more leverage during bullish time periods.

It is impossible to avoid every whipsaw or downturn in the stock market. It is impossible to always correctly anticipate what the future will bring. That's why fundamentalists say you should never try to predict the market and just always stay a perennial bull. However, sometimes your risks from staying invested in the market are just way too high if you subscribe to this notion. Sometimes the risks of being in the market will also be rewarded more richly in certain market climates over others. It pays to know whether you are in any of those situations. At any point in time you need some objective way to judge the tradeoff of potential future returns to your present risk of losses from the market.

Let's get a handle on this concept by discussing something simple—P/E ratios. The P/E or "price to earnings" ratio is a popular valuation measure for individual stocks, or the market as a whole, that is used to tell us if they are relatively costly or cheap. It has averaged about 14 for the S&P over the long run. When you look at history, the record clearly shows that high P/E ratios correspond to lower future market returns. In fact, when the P/E ratio has approached 20, stocks have typically returned less than T-bills for as long as a decade or more. When the P/E ratio has hit 20, prior market gains have also often been given back quite painfully.

High P/E periods typically have lower dividend yields, which is important since Standard and Poor's reports that the dividend component of the market was responsible for nearly half of the total return of the last 80 years of the index, and even more if you go back further. Dividends represent a very important component of the total return you can expect to receive from the market as a long term investor. Market periods that start out with a high P/E ratio also often end with a lower P/E, and market returns correlate to that trend in the P/E ratio. Basically, there are all sorts of reasons behind the fact that when you start with a high P/E ratio, you can expect that market returns in subsequent years will be well below average. Why? Because the P/E ratio will eventually fall, and with that decline your returns will decrease as well. But what about low P/Es?

Historically speaking, many of the best years of stock market returns were associated with periods when a low P/E ratio was increasing. Lower or negative returns usually occurred when a high P/E ratio was falling. When P/E ratios were rising, a "rising tide lifts all boats" has been historically true and we were usually in a bull market. When P/Es were dropping, however, positive stock market returns became harder to get and even index investing could land you in a world of hurt.

Historical statistics and logic together basically say that there are times when equities offer a little or a lot of upside potential based on the level of the P/E ratio and its trend. If you know this type of information, your approach to stock market investing should change dramatically based on this parameter. If there are other ways to segment the market into periods of negative or positive returns as well, you should take that information into account when making investing decisions, too.

Many investors use just the market P/E ratio alone to help them determine if the market is over or undervalued, and thus worthy of investment because of a stronger potential for returns. However, with the Hussman "market climate" approach, you to try to characterize the quality of the stock market using two dimensions rather than a single criteria such as the P/E ratio. Each of these two dimensions embodies a variety of separate factors that are all collapsed together into one single measurement. The market climate (and market potential) is then characterized by the two metrics of *market valuation* and *trend strength*.

In a loose way, these two metrics actually correspond to the two dimensions of technical and fundamental analysis we have been discussing. You want a measure of valuation that provides a fundamental measure of potential market gain, but you also want some technical measure of trending strength since you don't want to be buying stocks while prices are still declining. You want to ride an upwards trend as far as possible, including when the market starts heading into overvalued territory because you never know how far it will ultimately go. Putting the two dimensions together allows you to combine technical and fundamental analysis, and then partition the market into situations or "climates" with different potentials.

In the market climate approach, these two dimensions of "market valuation" and "market trend strength," when put into a 2x2 table, yield four distributions which are used to grade the investment climate as either bullish or bearish, favorable or unfavorable. The market only falls into one of these four climates unless you create even more divisions of this basic square, and that investment climate can be used to determine the kind of investment methodology that you should favor when you are pursuing investment returns.

It would be interesting to match this together with seasonal investing or overlay it against other market models that independently identify bullish and bearish conditions, and which by themselves are quite accurate. With enough research, it might even be used to help identify the right sectors or assets classes likely to outperform during different environmental conditions, an idea similar to what S&P analyst Sam Stovall tried to do when he studied which S&P sectors performed best or worst during different parts of the business cycle. If you had a method like this that could accurately classify the investment climate for different world stock markets and asset classes, it would certainly help guide your asset allocations, too, but such models are usually only available inside the secretive research corridors of the super hedge funds that never tell the rest of the world what they are doing.

The exact formulas which Hussman uses to define his various climate measurements are confidential, but every now and then you will find people deriving similar types of models which they openly publish in books or on the internet. The two dimensions of *valuation* and *trend strength* have become the standard cornerstones for many of these models. Various academic studies have proved Hussman right in discovering that stock portfolios constructed using both valuation and momentum metrics usually outperform the overall market. Hussman's 2x2 classification scheme results in four basic investing climates, and each suggests a different type of investing approach:

> Valuation Favorable & Trend Strength Favorable – Buy
>   aggressively for chances at capital appreciation
> Valuation Favorable & Trend Strength Unfavorable – Buy
>   cautiously to increase market exposure moderately on declines
> Valuation Unfavorable & Trend Strength Favorable – Remain
>   constructive; maintain a generally positive market position
> Valuation Unfavorable & Trend Strength Unfavorable – Hedge to
>   preserve and protect your capital (reduce your position)

Hussman's valuation metric reflects the fundamentals of stocks as assets. It incorporates the ratio of stock prices to the expected stream of future income or cash flow earned by securities over time. His trend strength index incorporates within one metric the current market price action, interest rates and other factors that drive prices toward or away from "fair value." It basically indicates whether the market is going up or down, and whether the trend is strong or not. Using a *fusion approach* that combines both fundamentals and technicals—trend, valuation, economic and interest rate factors all combined together—and rooting itself in *historical analysis*, it satisfies my requirement for some form of fundamental and technical analysis used together in a single market model.

These types of classification models never chase short term market fluctuations, which are notoriously difficult to predict. Market climate models don't predict the short term direction of the market at all but are geared for the intermediate to longer term investor. They simply aim at objectively classifying (identifying) the present market climate, environment, or potential—however you wish to call it—and then you base your investment decisions for what to do upon that classification. It's extremely logical.

If the numbers say that the current potential for stock returns is low and you feel you are at a market top or have just entered a bear market that no one yet recognizes, you would reduce your market exposure in order to protect your wealth and preserve your assets. Many famous investors tell you that you have the long term ahead of you, so you should always *choose a sound sleep over a very risky chance for marginal extra profits*, and that's what you would do here. On the other hand, if the public in a bear market is shouting that "the end of the world is near" when your model has turned positive, these are the contrarian times to go against the crowd psychology of negative emotions (and pessimistic magazine covers) to buy great assets at a discount. Baron Rothschild said, "buy when there is blood in the streets," which J. Paul Getty also said is one of the keys to entering the tier of mega-wealth status. Warren Buffett simply said that investment success means avoiding excitement, expenses, and to "be fearful when others are greedy and greedy only when others are fearful." Investment models can help you go against the powerful emotions of fear and pessimism so that you can do this and make great money at it. It is one of the keys to being a great value investor.

The basic idea of the market climate, which is incontrovertibly true, is that some market conditions represent higher return to risk tradeoffs than others. Therefore you can, and should, vary your investment commitment or trading methodology using some form of objective analysis of the investment climate which gives you a yardstick of future expectations. Knowing the current market climate you are in identifies your probable returns for being invested in the market, and thereby helps determine when you should be aggressive with investments or be out of the market and into something else in order to preserve your wealth.

Because they objectively measure current conditions and are based on solid historical analysis, market climate models can be extremely valuable for guiding your investment decisions. When you're in conditions that have historically produced hostile market returns, you should assume a defensive stance for your stock investments. If the conditions you are in have traditionally been favorable for market advances, you should take a more positive, bullish stance with your money. You don't actually try to predict the market with market climate models. You are just trying to identify the current conditions, and since you know the typical returns for all types of environments, you can then use that information to adjust your positions accordingly. Market timing models typically tell you to just buy or sell, but with market climate models you can come up with all sorts of different strategies for different environments, and can know when the long or short weighting should be greater or lesser.

There's always something intelligent to do with your money at any point in time, and this method helps you determine the risk to reward ratio of being in stocks at any moment. This method is quite different from, and yet similar to the "factor seasonals" which show how a stock has normally performed in particular types of fundamental environments, and which once again wed technical and fundamental analysis together. In this case, however, we try to objectively determine the market environment and then afterwards decide what to do. In the case of the fundamental factor seasonals, we go a step further in that we produce a projected future trading pattern for an investment based on its past trading history within that particular environment. Some individuals just want to know what the historical percentage change of a stock or market has been under certain conditions, whereas the factor seasonals give you the actual historical trading pattern for various different climates or environments.

Hussman's market climate approach uses proprietary formulas and incorporates many different factors in its calculation, so it is very difficult to duplicate on your own. Luckily for investors, Hussman often publishes his current market climate reading on the internet, which I suggest you check for now and then. This allows you to objectively know where you are in terms of the big picture, and also reveals the future returns you might expect from the stock market at any point in time based on past history.

The problem with complicated models like this is that you are always dependent on other people to produce the results for you, and what happens when they stop reporting their results? While more complex models can increase your investing returns, with each layer of complexity you add to a model, the fewer the number of individuals who can duplicate it on their own until you are left with no one able to do it at all. So while John Hussman's market climate reading is usually available on the internet, what is more important is deriving the lesson that buy and hold is not always best, market conditions change, you can measure those conditions, and through objective historical analysis you can determine the most favorable or unfavorable times for investing. You cannot forecast what return the market will give you, but you can determine when it is a good time to buy, hold, lighten your position, protect it with puts, short or just stay out altogether.

In the long run as an investor you are interested in safety first so that you don't lose your principal, and then you are interested in maximizing your returns for the degree of risk you are willing to take. No investor can accurately predict what he will make over the next twelve months through investing, so the best you can do is try to situate yourself so that you won't lose a lot of money if the market tanks, and then let the market return whatever it will since you cannot force it. Everyone wants to make more than 20% per year but you cannot guarantee such returns, so you should always be seeking a sufficient return on your principal for the risks that you are willing to take. The market climate approach helps you get a handle on this, as does this next fundamental timing model that everyone can duplicate.

THE "TRIPLE 40" TIMING MODEL

As stated, in searching for models to guide your investing so that you can hyper-compound the growth of your investment funds, you should always be searching for methods that are simple in construction, simple to apply, fundamentally sound (their principles are based on sound logic), and which have an excellent supporting track record. One model people that perfectly fulfills all these desired characteristics is the "Triple 40 Timing Model," introduced by analyst and money manager Mark Boucher, who we will later encounter again. This is a very simple timing rule that combines both the technical and fundamental condition of the stock market just as we have emphasized. It has worked over extremely long periods of time, and in its own way can be considered a two-state market climate model. The basic idea is that you should be in the market when stocks are trending upwards (stocks are above their moving average) and when interest rate trends—which are used to identify the fundamental force behind the market—are favorable. You want to be out of the market when stocks are going down or when the monetary environment, as measured through interest rate trends, becomes unfavorable.

The rules of this timing system are simple, which is why this model is preferred to more advanced timing systems that most people would not be able to compute on their own anyway, or which would not be available to you unless you were willing to spend hundreds or even thousands of dollars in research services. Remember, we want to do better than a buy and hold investor while risking a lower drawdown, and even a one percent difference in returns per year in our favor will accumulate to an incredible wealth difference when given enough time. We want something simple, but it must be based on fundamentals so that it truly ties into how the market actually moves and why.

If you want to make money through investing, I believe in simplicity but don't necessarily agree with legendary Fidelity Fund manager Peter Lynch who once said, "If you spend more than 15 minutes a year worrying about the market, you've wasted 12 minutes." That's advice coming from a fund manager who worked long hours every day on investment analysis who was also marketing a buy and hold mutual fund. To become a super investor you cannot just be a blindly passive buy and hold investor who spends no time paying attention to the markets at all. It's just too dangerous to do that anymore. Even a buy and hold real estate investor has to keep his pulse on the market to know in what direction prices are heading. Hence, advising investors to hold onto their hats and stick their heads in the sand during all market conditions is just nonsense.

Nevertheless, if it does take you more than several minutes per day to compute some timing model, you probably won't continue to do so for lack of discipline, and then you won't succeed with that technique in trying to become a super investor. However, while you can definitely find more complicated models that have produced higher rates of return than this model we're about to introduce, what are the use of those techniques if you can't duplicate them and then use them? You can only become a super investor using methods you can duplicate on your own. That's why in this book we're starting out with the simplest investing methodologies possible and then slowly moving to methods involving far more complexity.

THE RULES:

With the Triple 40 Timing Model, you only have to calculate three 40-week moving averages, and you do this just once per week. From these three averages you then determine if you should be long or short in the market, so bullishness or bearishness is your trading signal or market climate. What are the rules; what do you do? You must calculate a 40-week moving average of the S&P500 index, 90-day T-bill rates, and 10-year T-bond rates (using weekly Friday data). Most free stock charting services on the internet have this information readily available at the push of a button or two, and since the information changes slowly you usually only need to check things out just a few times per month, namely every weekend to see if anything has changed.

The rules are very simple. You buy stocks if the S&P500 index is above its 40-week moving average and *at least one* interest rate is below its moving average (meaning interest rates are declining). You sell if the S&P500 drops below its 40-week average *or* both interest rates are above their moving averages (meaning interest rates are rising). Note that to become bullish you only need one favorable fundamental interest rate trend to match the price trend of the market, while bearishness requires both conditions:

- Buy if the S&P500 is above its 40-week moving average AND at least one interest rate is below its 40-week moving average
- Sell if the S&P500 is below its 40-week average OR both interest rates are above their 40-week moving averages

This is an extremely simple investment timing model with strong fundamental logic. You cannot go long unless stocks are trending higher, and you cannot remain long if stocks are trending lower. You cannot go long unless the interest rate environment appears favorable to some degree, and you certainly cannot remain long if the interest rate environment is unfavorable because all rates are definitely rising. Now the question is, how has this simple system performed?

Nelson Freeburg of *Formula Research* reported that from 1970 to 2002 it returned 13.8% per year compared to 10.9% for the S&P, which is about 3% extra per year, and its drawdown was only about one-third of the market's pain! It's not always right because only around 65% of signals were profitable, so it produces a whipsaw every one to three years. It loses a little bit of performance during bull markets, but the benefit to the model is that it is extremely stable throughout all types of economic environments. As a long term investor who cannot predict what tomorrow brings, this type of stability is what we are seeking.

What's most impressive is this model's longer term performance.

When tested all the way back from the 1920's to 2002, the model still worked in outperforming the market! It is incredibly impressive when any model works this long, which is *over seventy years!* This suggests that it has captured something fundamental about the market through its simple design rather than is just jury rigged (curve fitted) to show the strongest possible historical returns. Of course that is also a possibility, but the model does have a strong fundamental logic to its structure. As regards its long term track record, it has returned 10.6% per year compared to 9.3% for the S&P, and at half the drawdown risk.

Many people eschew such models, which try to mathematically process fundamental information and transform it into a trading system, because they simply don't trust them. They typically base their investment decisions on what people say works rather than guide themselves by the results of extensive testing. They want to trade according to market opinions, gut feelings, and their own emotions that don't reference any history at all. However, as Warren Buffett wrote in his 1962 letter to investors, "You will not be right simply because a large number of people momentarily agree with you. You will not be right simply because important people agree with you. You will be right over the course of many transactions, if your hypotheses are correct, your facts are correct, and your reasoning is correct."

This basic interest rate model satisfies all these criteria. It combines fundamental and technical information. It is based on sound fundamental reasoning, does much better than the market rate of return, and even holds up for more than seventy years! If you want to be using market timing, this is one of the simplest and yet robust timing rules you can find. The buy and sell signals it produces can also be considered the determinants of a bullish or bearish market climate, so if you do not want to use it for outright market timing, you can certainly use it to classify the market for its bullish or bearish potential.

There are all sorts of ways to analytically time fundamental information, but this is the best of the *simplest* timing models I have ever found that combines the technical market trend with fundamentals to determine when the investing environment is bullish or bearish, and it has worked for decades. It has worked through all sorts of conditions, incorporates the powerful fundamental basis of classifying the monetary environment that influences investments via interest rates, and basically "times" that fundamental information to keep you on the right side of the wealth making portion of the stock market. When we use simple and logical rules to combine technicals with fundamentals, as we have here, the models have a tendency to remain robust and dependable. They may not be "optimal," but they are certainly "above average good" which means they work throughout all sorts of market environments producing better than average returns. With this one simple rule alone you can also classify the market potential, use it for market timing index funds, or bias your other trading strategies.

In progressing from a seasonal timing model that is purely technical to a model that incorporates interest rates, we've gone to a more fundamental timing model that does much better than buy and hold once again. If you want to pursue the world experts who build these sorts of models and do this type of research, you should certainly check out the publications of the Ned Davis Research group, Marty Zweig, and Nelson Freeburg's *Formula Research* newsletter.

We have also discovered in this chapter that if you can identify the market's climate through metrics that capture the market's trend strength and valuation levels, that information can help you make more appropriate investing decisions. Our Triple 40 Timing Model actually does this because it combines a trending variable with interest rate trends. Hence, with both the MACD-adjusted best six months of the year strategy and the Triple 40 market timing model, we now have two ways to trade index funds. You might combine the two methods together to create an entirely new system, or can just use each one to trade a portion of your funds. In any case, it is time to move to methods that involve specific asset allocation rules and more complicated stock selection techniques for superior investment performance.

5
WINNING MOMENTUM INVESTING

One of the most insightful books for creating investing systems is a little known classic, *The Hedge Fund Edge*, written by Mark Boucher. Within this book Boucher tells the story of how he met a very low key private European money manager, with failing health, who after many years in the investment business decided to teach Mark his highly secretive method for managing billions in client funds for extremely high returns.

The track record of this secret methodology should grab your attention, as should its basic set of rules since it was said to have worked for well over three decades. Few investing methods work consistently over long periods of time, and when they do it is usually because they have captured some sort of fundamentally sound approach to market investing. You won't have all the tools readily available to exactly duplicate this technique, but the lessons are so valuable that you will be able to immediately apply what you learn elsewhere to great advantage.

This highly secretive European manager reported extremely impressive returns with very low risk. His long term compound annual growth rate (CAGR) for managing funds was greater than 19% per year since the mid-1950's, and that's without ever having had a drawdown greater than 20% on the money he managed. Furthermore, in over thirty years of managing money he had only seen one negative calendar year on his investments (-5% in 1974)!

These are incredible results. Mutual funds would literally break down the doors with offers to hire anyone who could duplicate such returns. If you started with $100,000 and compounded your performance at 19% per year over thirty years, you'd be left with over $18 million before taxes. Clearly this is a method for creating generational wealth, and the return doesn't even factor in the possibility of adding funds along the way for greater wealth accumulation.

This is the type of performance that can build a financial dynasty if it is kept up over time while avoiding taxes, and the methodology he used to capture these returns was both extremely simple and extremely logical. When you remember that the large financial fortunes could only grow their own funds at a long run rate of return of around 7-8% over the generations, this is the type of method we want to use to grow our wealth over many years if we desire an active form of diversified investing.

So how does it work?

The method concentrates on monitoring all the stock markets in the world and buying those that are currently advancing better than all others (as determined by a relative ranking), but only getting into those investments if there seems to be a fundamental basis supporting those advancing moves. You buy the world's best performing stock markets by rotating into a country's market when it starts outperforming everything else, and you get out of these investments when they fall out of the top tier of outperformers. Additionally, the basic rules of diversification and money management are also applied to protect the total portfolio from excessive risks and drawdowns.

In a sense, these rules are similar to those commonly used by commodity and foreign currency fund managers. These investment businesses typically use a trend following approach to manage billions in positions, and those methods make buy and sell decisions based on market price movements alone. These trend following models never stipulate that a price trend has to have a strong fundamental basis behind it and yet for many markets, just making trades based purely on the trending pattern of price movements can produce substantial profits. The trick is that you must trade enough markets together and then you can capture some big movements from within this pack.

The weakness of a pure trend following approach to investing is that when you trade on just price movements by themselves, without insisting that you verify there are fundamental reasons behind those moves, it opens you up to tremendous price gyrations and sharp reversals. Prices will often suddenly go against you, and then you must get out of your positions because your trend following systems will trigger a signal to exit the market ("go neutral" to a "risk off" condition) or reverse positions (go from long to short or short to long). Without a fundamental basis behind your investing, but just buying or selling based on the shape of price movements alone, you never really know if you are investing in a true long term trend. You are always subject to rapid whipsaw losses whenever you reverse your position, and you never know if it would be better to hold a position through extreme market volatility instead.

When I was in the business of creating computer rules to manage such funds, the way we avoided significant portfolio drawdowns (and catastrophic losses) was by diversifying ourselves into many different assets and by using many trading models. We would hold many positions in many different markets, most of which were uncorrelated to each other, and furthered our diversification by using multiple models to trade each single market. We also always used adaptive money management principles that continually adjusted the risks of our positions, and every rule for entering a market had a well defined rule for when we should leave that position. In other words, *there was always a clearly defined exit strategy for each and every market position.* These computerized rules not only helped us manage our risks but entirely eliminated emotions from the process of investing.

In commodities fund management, you are always trying to capture the short term, intermediate term and long term trends of the various markets you are in, and you want to layer the profits from various positions together. Sometimes you can capture gigantic upward or downward trends that last years, and sometimes a trend you thought had just started disappears almost immediately as soon as you enter the trade. Quite often with this type of trading you could accrue a sizeable chunk of unrealized profits from a steady trend that took months to unfold, but those "virtual" profits could disappear overnight due to a single adverse price swing. All you needed was a large price movement in the opposite direction suddenly appearing out of nowhere. The gold and silver markets, for instance, were famous for extreme one day moves that suddenly took away profits earned over many months, which is the same case today because those markets are very heavily manipulated.

As long as you had good asset allocation rules that prevented you from putting all your trading bets in one basket, and practiced prudent money management skills that had you adaptively managing risks, then when a big winner came along (or when multiple markets started making moves) you could usually capture a substantial portion of those profits and over-deliver in terms of portfolio performance. Big moves meant big profits, whereas small moves and choppy markets meant losses.

As mentioned, one of the keys to our long term profits was to follow automatic trading rules that determined clearly defined entry and exit points for all positions, and which eliminated all emotions from trading. While timing models and trading rules were important, a great deal of our outperformance came from applying very strict money management rules. In particular, our performance was greatly determined by asset allocation rules that put us into the big market movers for the year. Good money management and asset allocation rules, rather than buy and sell systems, almost always dominated the performance of our portfolios, and I find this principle to be true with most every fund manager I have looked at. You live or die based on the excellence of your money management systems.

Speaking frankly, when there is a big trend then most every decent trend following system will make money for you if you are a trend follower. Since you cannot predict the performance of individual trend following systems, you cannot anticipate which system will be the most profitable for you in a market, but if there is a strong trend they will all tend to make money. It is the large strong trends that make you most of your money in a year. Therefore, being in the right market is usually the most important thing to making the big money because you could have 97 markets that did nothing significant in terms of price movements all year long, and 3 markets that made large moves no one could even imagine! Having more money allocated to the 3 markets which made the big moves of the year would definitely separate you from all the other fund managers who were also using trend following rules, too, so your asset allocation had a bigger effect on your overall performance than the actual rules you used for trading. Generally speaking, how you manage your portfolio through your asset allocation and money management rules will have a bigger impact on your total profits than the accuracy of your individual trading systems, especially when you use several systems bundled together to trade separate markets.

If you have a large allocation to gold or oil in your portfolio and either makes a big bull run that year, you will usually have a fantastically profitable year compared to funds that gave them just a mild weighting in their portfolios. The same goes for stock portfolios that heavily invest in the best moving stock sectors of the year. That's the power of superior asset allocation. It always pays to be in the biggest movers with the strongest trend strength, but the question is how to determine which ones will be best that year. You cannot put all your bets on just one asset because if that market suddenly turns you could lose a significant portion of your funds. The best strategy is to have significant positions in the best performing markets, but you also want the diversification of having many other positions, too.

The investing approach of Boucher's elderly European friend had similarities to all this in that it basically used a version of "momentum investing," or relative strength investing, to secure positions in the strongest moving world stock market leaders. In momentum investing you are looking for an asset that is already strongly increasing or declining in price, and then you enter a trade that rides the coattails of that trend in hopes that the move will continue. The assumption is that any market movement will have continuing momentum or inertia that pushes it in the same direction, and you want to capture a good portion of those profits if you can. In short, you are basically hoping that a market surge, once identified, will persist long enough for you to make money by the time you get out. You cannot capture all the profits of a trend from low to high, but if you can capture just 30-50% of the trend, and do this over and over again, you can end up looking like a genius. Baron von Rothschild is famous for saying, "You can have the first 30% and the last 30% of any move, just give me the safe 40% in the middle," which captures this idea precisely.

The problem with momentum investing, which is betting on a trend to continue, is that it doesn't always continue. You might get in too late and you might get out too early. You must also often eat lots of little whipsaw losses, too, which are short trends caused by temporary volatility spikes that never turn into big moves. You must also try to keep as much of the profits you make from big trends as possible, rather than always lose them through sudden trend reversals that might take away most of your gains. In the aforementioned gold market, it was typical to slowly accumulate profits for months and then see them all suddenly erased in a single day when gold made a spikey move in the opposite direction.

Many markets are extremely volatile like this, especially with today's large price swings triggered by automatic trading robots. These sudden moves can kill an investor who overtrades with too much leverage, and who is not risk balanced with a number of diversified positions that helps dampen volatility. When these sudden moves happen, it's hard to tell anymore if a price drop is due to deteriorating fundamentals or just artificial market manipulations. You need clear exit rules to get you out of positions under both circumstances otherwise you face the potential of catastrophic losses.

For instance, one of my best friends, an experienced investor, had all his retirement funds invested in Citibank stock which had climbed in price for many years to make him a millionaire several times over. Without an exit rule, however, he just could not pull the trigger to get out of his Citibank holdings as the stock continued to decline throughout 2007 and 2008. After every drop he would say to himself that his long term winner was sure to go up again, so he kept holding onto his position. After all, how could Citibank possibly go bankrupt? Every time he got ready to bite the bullet and sell some shares, Citibank's stock price would suddenly collapse causing yet another round of waiting in hopes he might liquidate at a better price. He eventually lost 95% of his savings when Citibank, previously a $55 stock, fell to its floor and entered penny stock territory at $3-4 a share.

If a market advances slowly through a solid trend, as in this case study, you can make money on that trend *as long as you exit before prices suddenly collapse and eliminate all the accumulated profits.* "What the market giveth slowly, it quickly taketh away." When a particular market moves just a little, then you probably won't make any money at all on that investment and it would simply have been better to put those funds in some other investment that was moving more strongly. Momentum investors always try to put their money in the strongest trends, but they use explicit rules to define those trends and their entry and exit decisions.

The best type of momentum investing tries to sort out which trends are not flukes, but genuine movements with strong fundamentals that are therefore likely to continue. You don't have to get in at the bottom or out at the top of a big price trend to make substantial money. You do not have to pick tops or bottoms. All you must do is just capture a great enough portion of a trend to make money. Most of the time you cannot capture even 50% of a stock trend, and yet you can still do extremely well capturing a small fraction if the move is large enough. The key is to make money without risking too much and by minimizing losses when you are wrong. Since you can never predict how much you will make from the markets, you try to make as much as the market will give you (without risking too much) and minimize losses when they occur.

When will a moving asset stop moving in the same direction? It will keep moving until it stops moving. That's all we can say. Nonetheless, people use all sorts of methods to try to forecast the end of market movements. There are technical methods like cycles analysis, Elliott Wave analysis, and even seasonal analysis, but no method is consistently reliable. In short, no one ever knows for sure which market will be the biggest mover of the year, and when a trend will definitively start or end. A market could stay in the doldrums for years, or keep marching upwards well past anyone's expectations.

To get around this problem of the frequent uselessness of forecasting, in momentum investing you simply get into an investment after you identify that prices are making a trend and then hold that investment until some rule determines that the trend has significantly changed. Between getting in and getting out of the investment, you hope the trend continues long enough that you can make some exceptional money. Whenever the trend moves against you, you also must have rules to manage (adjust) your risks and profits so that they don't all suddenly disappear.

In this case, our European money manager never entered into investments simply because they demonstrated upward price action. Before investing in some foreign stock market, he always insisted that there was *some fundamental reason* behind its upward advance and for stock market fundamentals he focused on interest rates. Because he was investing in stocks, seeking that fundamental reason meant that he was always looking to see that there was a *favorable interest rate environment to support the bullish trend.* The underlying monetary conditions served as his confirmation indicator!

As we have already seen in discussing market timing models, over the long run the interest rate models are among the best you can use to tell if the stock market environment is fundamentally bullish or bearish. You can come up with sentiment models, economic models, valuation models and all sorts of other models to help time the market indices. However, except during periods of financial extremes called "end games," interest rate monetary models tend to best decipher the underlying fundamental forces moving stock markets and separate conditions into bullish and bearish environments. Hence, seeking a fundamental reason behind a stock market advancing trend, the interest rate explanation is what our expert European money manager chose to rely upon.

If a country's stock market was performing well—meaning it was above its 40-week moving average—this money manager assumed that it would continue to do so as long as there were fundamental reasons behind the advance. Thus, he was looking to invest in world stock markets that were already moving up *and* which also had a favorable interest rate environment, which he monitored by looking at a 40-week moving average of the bond and treasury bill (short rate) prices for each market. If a country's stock and bond markets did not have these two characteristics, he didn't even consider it as a possibility for his investments.

As with our earlier interest rate model, any time a country's stock index fell below its 40-week moving average, it was eliminated from his consideration. Anytime the bond and bill (short rate) prices for a country both fell below their 40-week moving average, he also eliminated the market from consideration as an investment. Both the market trend and interest rate trends had to be favorable to consider something a possible investment. This highly secretive manager combined these basic rules in the following model which he then used to achieve his exceptional returns.

THE RULES:

First, he kept a 6-month relative strength table of world stock market indices that compared as many global markets as possible. He also produced a 6-month relative strength table of world interest rate trends, too. If some country's stock market was trading above its 40-week moving average then its trend was considered bullish, and bearish otherwise. This trending signal helped insure that prices were moving in the right direction. He only looked at rising markets to construct his table.

As to this world interest rate table, he created a 6-month world relative strength table for all 10-year bond markets and all 90-day short rate prices, and then averaged the two indices together for each country to come up with one final composite number. If 10-year bond prices were going up for a country (if they were greater than their 40-week moving average) it was considered bullish because it meant interest rates were falling. If short term interest rates were falling (if they were less than their 40-week moving average) it was considered bullish as well.

After constructing a relative strength table for all the world's stock markets and interest rate markets, he only considered investing in markets where *both* the stock trend *and* the interest rate trend were favorable. He was basically sorting all the world's markets into an "A" pile and "B" pile. The "A" pile contained stock markets that were already going up where the interest rate environment was also favorable. The "B" pile contained markets where this wasn't happening, and so you wouldn't even consider those markets for investment. You were going to invest in the "A" pile candidates and avoid the "B" pile markets because an upwards trend wasn't there or the monetary environment (interest rate) fundamentals weren't there. Thus, your asset allocation strategy was to invest only in some subset of the markets currently advancing that also had strong fundamentals. You also avoided the "B" pile candidates which represented the potentially negative consequences which Warren Buffett would denote as representing "catastrophic risk."

By looking at this table that evaluated as many world markets as possible, this European manager could compare all possible markets at one glance to see who was doing better or worse than everyone else, and then position himself in several of the top markets. By always investing in the top tier of favorable stock markets, he was hedging his risks by practicing international diversification. By investing internationally, this also gave him the chance to outperform everyone else who was just limited to investing in their home nation.

You can immediately realize that the idea of international diversification would allow him to find some country in the world where the stock market was moving up when others might be declining. This methodology capitalizes on your ability to put your money in widely different markets. As the story of my Nicaraguan college classmate illustrated, this ability to move your assets to other countries is sometimes essential to *preserving* your wealth rather than just increase it.

Remember that this money manager was not only looking for a positive momentum trend in each foreign stock market, but was looking for confirmation of a favorable monetary environment in that country by referencing the interest rate trends – his "fundamentals." Thus this method taps into my professed preference for combining technical and fundamental information together. Once he had the two relative strength indices, he then combined the stock market and interest rate relative strength index into a single index for each country, ranked them all in order from highest to lowest, and only considered investments in markets at the top of the list. Those were the markets already doing better than everyone else in terms of price movements and interest rate fundamentals.

With his massive relative strength table finished, now came the time for asset allocation. This manager simply took the top five markets from this list and put 20% of his money in each of those markets. If there were only four countries on the list, 25% of his investment funds would be allocated to each market equally. If there were only three countries on the list, 25% would go into each of the three markets, and 25% into T-bills or money markets to collect interest. If there were only two countries on the list, 25% would go into each of those two markets, and 50% would go into T-bills or money market funds. If there was only one country on the list, it would get 25% of his funds, and 75% would be put into T-bills or money markets.

If there were no countries with an advancing stock market and favorable interest rate environment, this ultra-successful money manager would simply park the funds in T-bills to collect interest until one or more advancing markets showed up. He put his money in cash, and this allowed him to sidestep large drawdowns during bear markets, which were usually accompanied by the unfavorable interest rate trends that his model had aptly captured. He never tried to get a quick gain in a market, but simply said that if the conditions were not right or the opportunities were not promising, he simply wouldn't invest in a country's stock market. Whatever the market would return him, after allocating his money to the strongest investments, that's what he would earn.

Every six months, on January 1 and July 1, he would then rebalance his portfolio to include the new top-ranking countries from his table. If he found that a country had dropped off from his combo relative strength table list, he would simply re-allocate those funds to another country that was now in the top tier rankings. Which country? To one that had the highest rank of any he wasn't already invested in.

These were his basic investing rules, and with the computational power of modern computers that is now available, there are lots of ways someone could try to improve on these results after doing some intensive research. He basically followed this simple plan with persistence and in time he achieved an extraordinary rate of return that harkens of Warren Buffett. The method was opportunistic in that it identified the best opportunities in the world and pursued them to the exclusion of all others, banking on the persistence of momentum when there was a fundamental support for the bullish move. He also diversified himself through asset allocation so that he was always protecting himself by hedging his bets.

Most momentum investors are usually perplexed as to when they should exit a market, but the periodic re-evaluation and then rebalancing of his portfolio made sure this happened automatically. Study after study shows that rebalancing a portfolio usually increases returns and reduces risk, but it requires discipline to do this. Rebalancing is equivalent to taking some profit off the table when a market has moved much higher, and re-allocating those funds to assets not performing as well. It forces you to take profits on a portion of your position.

In the commodity fund management arena, many funds are also designed to do automatic rebalancing, too. Many fund managers liquidate positions to harvest some profits when market volatility increases, and this procedure tends to reap far more gains than simply holding long term positions until their trends turn. The fact that you secure some degree of definite profits—by cashing out a portion of a strong position after extreme price moves send the volatility skyrocketing—ends up making you more money than if you are simply a pure trend following investor. Even William O'Neil who studied the largest market winners of all time, and famous stock trader Dan Zanger, both said that you should consider selling 20-30% of any new position when a stock moved up 15-20% from a breakout point because you never knew if the trend would falter and turn down again. Thus, the regular rebalancing of your portfolio from such enforced selling becomes an essential element of incredible outperformance and long-term investment success.

While the 6-month rebalancing period for this methodology might not be optimal, only testing can determine what rebalancing period would perform best. A 4-month or 3-month rebalancing period might be even better, but you'd have to perform extensive computer simulations to find out. The longer the holding period without rebalancing, the more you are exposed to risks that rebalancing normally helps to eliminate. Then again, the longer you hold a position, the less likely you will be prematurely thrown out of a truly advancing market because of temporary volatility. In any case, this manager also had a number of other strategies that also helped him cut potential losses, boost his performance, and achieve consistent results with very low risks.

There are lots of different ways to possibly improve upon this basic technique, and now that you know the general methodology, you might end up using some form of this strategy in the management of your own funds.

For instance, S&P analyst Sam Stovall came up with his own version of this basic relative strength methodology which you can find in *The Seven Rules of Wall Street*. He would invest in the top ten industries that exhibited the strongest trailing 12-month price performances. He would rebalance his holdings at the end of every month, removing those which fell out of the top ten, and then buy the new candidates that came into the top tier. Over the last twenty years you would be swapping three industries per month on average, which is a lot of turnover but quite doable. There are lots of things researchers can test that might improve upon the basic method, and many principles revealed in this example about how to achieve *both consistent and magnificent* multi-year returns by internationally investing in world stock markets.

First, you want to follow a large number of potential investment vehicles, which in this example were the international stock markets. Today you might also add many more country, industry sector, commodity and currency ETFs as well as various no load mutual funds to your list of investment candidates. Having a larger list of investment options increases your chances of finding bull markets (or bear markets) to invest in, and the more markets you consider helps with the task of minimizing risks and diversifying your positions. Next, you want to produce a mega-list of all these candidates ordered by their relative strength and fundamentals.

It is easy to rank markets in order of their relative strength to determine the runaway markets moving the fastest at any point in time. Thus it is very easy to determine who is currently strongest in terms of current price movements. You can go to a website such as **ETFscreen.com** and do this immediately. The problem lies in figuring out which relative strength leaders have any *fundamental power behind them* because it is always fundamental "fuel" of some type that helps to insure a trend's strength and reliability for continual advancement.

In stocks, traders often try to get at this idea of *fundamental fuel* by determining if the volume is increasing in the direction of the trend, or if company insiders are buying shares. Some Wall Street houses go so far as to build complicated models for each stock, market segment or sector to estimate their bullish potential. Others screen stocks for various criteria to see if there are various fundamentals behind a breakout, such as quarterly sales accelerating at a pace of 40% or more, a return on equity of 17% or more, annual earnings up 18-20% or more, and continual quarter-over-quarter sequential expansions of company earnings and revenues. These are all examples of screening criteria that look for potentially explosive stock situations.

Rather than just getting into a stock, market index, ETF or other asset because the price is going up, you must remember this rule that *there must always be some type of fundamental fuel, or fundamental causation, behind the market advance for you to safely get into that investment vehicle.* Otherwise, you open yourself up to the potential of losing all your money by investing in some type of empty bubble. The Dubai real estate property bubble, the internet stock bubble, and various short lived collectible trends are a few examples that come to mind of upward price moves that had little fundamental strength behind them.

Our European manager looked for his fundamental support by referencing interest rate trends in every country he considered, and this determined the safest and most profitable periods for investing in those countries. He always wanted to be in stock markets when yields were falling for as we have seen, lower interest rates typically power strong stock market advances. In any case, whatever you choose to rely upon as your fundamental reason to invest, you must make sure it truly indicates that there is substantial, growing buying power behind an advance.

In individual stock trading, we already know that earnings increases and increasing trading volume are two types of reliable indicators which suggest some lasting power behind advancing stock prices. However, another indicator for trusting superior relative strength is that there are also *other leading stocks in the same industry group* demonstrating similar strong performance as well, which then suggests that the advance is an industry issue. A stock's price momentum is usually driven by the performance of its industry or sector rather than by the particulars of the stock, so when multiple stocks in a sector also outperform, this suggests that the trend is more reliable. However, this does not identify the actual fundamental fuel behind the advance. The big principle to understand is that you always need to insure there are valuations or fundamentals behind leading price movements and surging relative strength when using this particular momentum investment technique.

If you can restrict your investments in only the top performing (high relative strength) markets that have growing fundamental support, this is wisely concentrating your money where the top opportunities lie. Many of those investments will often turn into runaway markets that are likely to keep progressing into the far future. If you use asset allocation and money management rules on top of this to further diversify your risks, and periodically rebalance your portfolio to keep the monies concentrated in the best performers (and away from losers), you have the basics of an outperforming investing technique. These are the basic ideas behind this 19% per year system.

Quite a few researchers, including Ned Davis Research and AQR Capital, have found that simply partitioning stocks into large quintile, quartile or decile groupings based on relative strength rankings consistently differentiated the best performing from the worst performing stocks of the year. In other words, relative strength rankings definitely differentiate the best from worst stocks! This partitioning of stocks into a sliding scale of high to low relative strength rankings has become a staple of the investment community, and the idea has been incorporated in the famous Value Line rankings, IBD (*Investor's Business Daily*) rankings, and VectorVest rankings, among others. When you use ten deciles for ranking purposes, the higher relative strength groupings have always performed better than the lower in consecutive series; the top decile performs better than the second best, which performs better than the third best and so on. That's what you want to see if there is truly some fundamental relationship behind some particular investment technique.

Many research studies have shown that buying the top tier of stocks with the strongest relative strength rankings, and then selling those stocks when their rankings fell far enough, would greatly outperform the market. There are studies showing that portfolios that give their greatest exposure to high momentum stocks significantly outperform those with the lowest levels. When momentum (relative strength) is combined with stock valuation, the results are particularly beneficial because the two strategies are negatively correlated. When value stocks, for instance, have been long term losers but then move into high relative strength territory, they usually go on to outperform in spades. We will later see that this was one of the factors to the Walter Schloss value investing system.

Some relative strength research going all the way back to the 1920's (Mebane Faber) has shown that buying the top performing stocks can outperform the buy and hold benchmark in 70% of all years, and simple adjustments to the basic idea can improve drawdowns and volatility dramatically. Other research (Tom Hancock) has shown that a momentum stock selection strategy outperformed a broader market average by nearly 4% per year from 1927 to 2009, which is an incredible difference since it is both significantly large and consistent. James O'Shaughnessy found that using relative strength as a criteria for stock portfolios added an extra return of 4% per year as well. Another study using rolling 10-year time horizons, starting in 1940, showed that relative strength investing outperformed buy and hold portfolios in 100% of the time periods. From yet other studies we also know that these relative strength outperformance results hold when applied to various other asset classes, sectors, and international stock markets, but rarely for short time horizons. Strong relative strength performance can continue over weeks or even months due to inertia, so the most common profitable strategy has been to hold assets ranked highest by their relative strength and hold them until their ranking falls to some pre-determined level.

Another big lesson you should derive from this, besides the idea that relative strength rankings identify which markets are probably *the best movers of the year* that will possibly continue to outperform (so that relative performance often leads to absolute performance), is the idea of *international asset diversification* once again. If your worldview is consumed solely by U.S. equities, you dramatically cut your potential for superior returns. This technique and the experience of history both strongly suggest that you should always broaden your investment horizons to include international assets. "It's hard to set up different brokerage accounts to do international investing" is no longer an excuse to international diversification because the availability of ETF funds for all sorts of markets, asset classes and sectors now allows you to tap into foreign markets with ease.

Remember that relative strength, or momentum investing, is not a contrarian or value investment strategy that identifies an undervalued asset, takes a position and then sometimes waits years for it to go up in value. Relative strength ranking systems lock onto the correct side of the major leadership trends that are already moving. They are momentum-based strategies that are always invested in the best movers. What they are usually missing is the extra requirement that those asset movements are strongly supported by fundamentals, and yet even without that condition the various studies consistently show that this methodology still works wonderfully. Our European money manager's extra requirement for strong supporting interest rate fundamentals separates his methodology from a simplistic relative strength strategy of always investing in the market leaders until they fall out of the top leadership tier, and with these extra precautions this strategy is still an outperformer. You should therefore always look for a fundamental reason behind an advance, if you have a means to do so, because it helps put the odds in your favor that the trend is safe, reliable and will continue.

In *The Hedge Fund Edge*, Boucher stated that he performed extensive research on this basic system to determine various ways to make it better, and I'm sure you can see there are many things you might want to test. Today you can monitor the relative strength of many markets using websites like ETFscreen.com that indicate who's performing best at any moment in time. It's only the interest rate information backing each stock market that is difficult to find and match with the relative strength numbers so that you can easily duplicate the technique. However, on individual stocks the proxy for interest rate relative strength might be earnings relative strength, and that information is available from sources such as IBD which also publishes *industry* relative strength figures.

MORE RELATIVE STRENGTH (MOMENTUM) INVESTING RULES:

If you just want to invest based just on price momentum alone, then you might wish to follow the lead of Gerald Appel who has created a quarterly (rebalancing every 3-months) momentum investing strategy that rotates between just five basic ETFs: a large cap value fund (IWD), a large cap growth fund (IVW), a small cap value fund (IWN), small cap growth fund (IJT) and international stock fund (EFA). The rules of his momentum investing strategy are extremely simple, and detailed in *Beating the Market, 3 Months at a Time*. At the end of every quarter you find the total quarterly returns, including dividends, for each of these five funds. Then you place equal amounts of capital in the two funds which have performed best and hold that allocation until the next quarter. Without making any predictions, the relative strength rankings use the past performance of the funds to tell you what you should hold for the next upcoming quarter. You do this simply because you expect the momentum to continue, and you expect it to continue because that is what usually happens.

From 1979-2007, this simple strategy returned 16.2% per year compared to a 11.5% CAGR for the S&P index, and you got that return at nearly half the drawdown! The basic rule, when we apply it to a larger universe of investment candidates, is to simply rank all available funds or ETFs (in the universe you want to consider) at the end of each quarter based on their *total* previous quarter's returns, and then invest in the top performers for the next three months. This is similar to our European fund manager's winning formula with the caveat that he added the extra stipulation that we had to see a positive interest rate environment for each stock market investment.

Thus, if you just want to use just the price momentum (relative strength) rankings themselves as the basis of your investment strategy—because you know that relative strength investing performs successfully in both bull and bear markets even without knowledge of the underling fundamental reasonings—you now have yet another simple way of outperforming a buy and hold index strategy. Don't let Wall Street firms fool you with their slick promotional campaigns. It really is that simple.

The only big problem with momentum relative strength investing is that individuals who want to use it tend to be bad at applying the strategy effectively because it is emotionally difficult to execute, and thus they often lack the discipline to stick with it. You must buy the strongest assets and ruthlessly cut those that become weak. The turnover can also be large because trends don't often continue, and so whipsaw losses become the same volatility curse we mentioned that afflicts tend following traders who time the commodity markets! Rotating in and out of an ETF or other fund often means buying high and selling low, which is very difficult for some people since it entails realizing losses. Not only do emotions and personal bias often interfere with this process, but it also becomes difficult to track many individual investment vehicles if you want to consider a wide asset universe for your investment candidates. As you go from industries to sectors to asset classes, the larger groupings make the strategy easier to execute.

You can apply relative strength analysis to assets classes and international markets, and then sectors or industries all the way down to individual stocks. While most humans are not emotionally equipped to execute the strategy, such as being mentally equipped to track hundreds of investment vehicles on a regular basis, the superior returns are often found by doing what no one else wants to do or is able to do. For instance, many determined stock pickers cannot accept the idea that simply following a strong trend can produce better returns than making investments after a time consuming valuation analysis. Therefore many analyst style investors avoid this proven approach because they just don't believe obtaining superior returns can be that simple … in spite of the historical track record. As I said, you have to choose an investment strategy that matches your personality and style, otherwise you will not use it.

RELATIVE STRENGTH INVESTING PROFESSIONALS

The best course of action if you believe in relative strength investing is to therefore find professional money managers totally devoted to relative strength momentum investing and who can execute the strategy in a disciplined fashion that avoids the problems of emotions. For instance, Vellum Financial (San Luis Obispo, CA) and Dorsey Wright Money Management (Pasadena, CA) both have relative strength investment funds that based on disciplined, tested, systematic investing rules.

Vellum Financial runs an impressive relative strength portfolio that offers daily redemptions, which is one of my requirements, and monitors countless assets. It partitions its major momentum fund into ten sectors such as domestic stocks, international equity, precious metals, utilities, commodities, bonds, and so forth. Each sector receives an equal weighting of portfolio capital. In the Vellum relative strength SAM portfolio, each of these sectors then considers dozens of different candidates for investment including specialized mutual funds or ETFs for each sector. In total, over 2,600 different investment vehicles are monitored so that you won't miss any large bull markets in the world but will certainly capture the real outperformers in world market movements. The top performing asset within each sector always becomes the main investment vehicle and is swapped out for another once it falls out of the top tier of contenders. During the 90's, the backtested fund returned 20.1% per year on average compared to a 12.2% CAGR for the S&P500, and during the "Dead Decade" of 2000-2010 it returned 21.9% per year compared to the S&P's 2.5% CAGR. All of these numbers match our European money manager's 20% track record, too, but with far less exposure and volatility.

The record for disciplined relative strength investing speaks for itself.

You are *not* constantly changing your bets every time a new horse takes the lead in a race, but through a disciplined analysis select a strong leader within the pack and stay with it until it falls a bit too far behind the other leaders. If you stay with it—because it will usually finish at the top or near the top of its sector—and do the same thing for several different asset classes, this disciplined methodology usually ends up securing you great absolute returns that beat the market. It is not guaranteed to work but surely tends to do so, and in fact tends to outperform many other investment techniques. You can argue against it all you like, but the facts are that the long term track records of outperformance are there for many versions of the basic technique just described.

Relative strength investing is the principle of investing in the winners who are already outperforming their peers … if they have some kind of fundamental force behind their advancement … and staying with them until their rankings drop significantly … but all the while giving them just enough leeway that they can falter a bit without being immediately kicked away for not remaining number one. The key is determining what type of relative strength measuring system identifies the best investment candidates, what rules you should use for getting into and out of trades, and if possible, what type of fundamental information can verify the price movements if possible. Some versions of relative strength investing, of course, don't use fundamental confirmations at all.

As general investment principles, you always want to be in a market when the trend is in your favor, you want to ride that trend for as long as possible, and you also want to concentrate your capital in the largest gaining markets deemed safe. If you have the requisite research capabilities, many asset allocation systems can be developed along these basic ideas or you can just park your money with a momentum-based fund that has a good track record in managing investment funds using this technique. In strong bull markets, the practice of momentum investing has a good chance of outperforming other investment methods if you always have some winners who continue to stay at the top end of the outperformance table, and that's what tends to happen. But you need some type of disciplined methodology to identify those winners, because you can never know for sure who will truly outperform. No system or method can tell you that.

Our private European manager was always investing in the markets of the industrialized countries when their economies were growing and interest rates were falling. At present the BRICs (Brazil, Russia, India and China), N-11 countries (Bangladesh, Egypt, Indonesia, Iran, South Korea, Mexico, Nigeria, Pakistan, the Philippines, Turkey and Vietnam), and "New Tigers" (Poland, Turkey, Peru, Columbia, Philippines, Indonesia, Ghana) or MENA countries (Middle East and North Africa) are replacing Japan, the United States and Europe as the countries with growing manufacturing sectors, rising middle classes and the greatest economic potential. Because the prosperity trends are moving into these nations, these are the countries you should be investing in.

These are the markets of hope with the greatest potential for truly stellar returns into the future, and this relative strength momentum methodology offers an extremely powerful way to select investments in these markets over the long run. There is more than 80 years of supporting evidence that relative strength investing performs well across many different markets, and the real time track records indeed prove it works! The returns from momentum investing are even negatively correlated to those from value investing, so a perfect match is to split one's funds and use both investment approaches together.

JACK DREYFUS AND HIS STOCK PICKING SECRET

Despite all this evidence for the success of momentum investing, you might wonder whether this European story of investing in fundamentally sound, high relative strength (momentum) stock markets was a fluke. Yet another story comes to mind that sheds some interesting light on these same principles. It concerns the investment technique of Jack Dreyfus, who is famous for founding the Dreyfus Fund. The Dreyfus Fund returned 604% from 1953 to 1964, as compared with 346% for the Dow Jones during the same period, and beat the next best fund by 102 percentage points. We met Jack Dreyfus earlier in a story about how he astutely got out of his stock positions after listening to bridge party discussions, and he is the one individual widely credited with bringing the public into the stock market because of his approach to mutual fund marketing.

Like our skillful European, Jack Dreyfus was considered perhaps the best fund manager in the late 1950s with performance often twice as good as his competitors, but no one knew what he was doing. William O'Neil, founder of the business newspaper *Investor's Business Daily* and the stock brokerage firm William O'Neil + Co., was an avid student of Dreyfus when he was young. In order to discover the investment strategy that was behind his stellar performance, O'Neil would study all his quarterly reports and examine how his stocks were purchased. After marking all the purchases on price charts with red ink, O'Neil discovered that unlike the usual fund management strategies at the time, most all of Dreyfus's stock picks were purchased at new highs!

In other words, Jack Dreyfus was not achieving his outperformance by buying stocks at their lows, or through buying shares at some special price that was arrived at through some complicated value computation. Rather, he was buying them when they popped up on the radar screen because they were making new price highs! Actually, this is a derivative form of momentum investing which simply uses a new price high as the buying trigger. This is not the same as buying leading stocks that are relative strength leaders, but there is a parallel here because a new high also telegraphs to the world the fact that a stock is moving significantly. With some further digging, O'Neil interestingly found that almost all the stocks Dreyfus bought had recently had strong increases in their quarterly earnings reports. Hence, we now have the fundamental tie-in we're always seeking (that our European manager had specified through interest rates) which explains the fuel behind an advance. As "slaves to earning power," stocks tend to go up as earnings go up, so this sort of requirement was the equivalent to making sure that a stock market had a favorable interest rate environment to fuel a bullish continuation.

Hence, Dreyfus was buying stocks via a philosophy similarly adopted by our European money manager in the sense that buying stocks making new highs was like investing in the markets showing the highest relative strength performance. Secondly, Dreyfus was also only buying the stocks if the fundamentals warranted it, which meant if the companies had earnings increases. For our fund manager, this translated into favorable interest rate trends. There may have been other criteria which Dreyfus used to select his stocks, but this was the big secret which William O'Neil discovered. By following this strategy, Dreyfus was conquering every one of his competitors who followed a "traditional" approach of fundamental analysis that was basically buy low, hope it goes up, and then sell high.

WILLIAM O'NEIL'S CANSLIM

William O'Neil, who discovered Dreyfus's secret criteria, also went on to perform another study of the greatest stock market winners of all time. As a result of all his various investment studies, he eventually developed the now world famous CANSLIM investment methodology which he revealed in the book, *How to Make Money in Stocks: A Winning System in Good Times or Bad*. If you want to become a great stock picker, it is essential that you buy this book and read it. The CANSLIM system is another investment methodology for stock picking that provides solid guidelines for investment selection, tries to keep subjectivity to a minimum, and which combines both fundamental and technical analysis into one system once again.

The CANSLIM methodology basically tries to find future large stock winners by using knowledge about the characteristics of all past exceptional stock winners, including what their trading patterns looked like before those stocks surged in price. Just as market climate studies look at past history to determine the conditions when stocks might advance or decline, CANSLIM looks for stocks that match the characteristics of the greatest stock winners of all time. That's pretty smart and is the type of analysis I like. Before we get into the specifics, let's see how this idea has historically performed.

An independent study by AAII showed that the CANSLIM stock picking methodology was the best of 50 different trading systems tested for the 12-year period from 1998 to 2009, and showed an average of 35.3% per year gain versus 3.3% per year for the S&P500, and a cumulative return of 2,763%. If you want to be a *stock picker* and try to trade your way to wealth with a portion of your funds, this is one of only a handful of systems I recommend for picking stocks in bull markets, but you must really work hard to learn it. Although it has not been confirmed, some accounts say that O'Neil, who has become a billionaire from his companies *and* by using this investment technique, has averaged an annual investment return near 40% over nearly half a century (1962 - present), which is a better long term track record than almost anyone else, including the famous George Soros and Warren Buffett.

Can his CANSLIM methodology be duplicated? Can his methodology be learnt and then replicated by private stock pickers like yourself? It has indeed been mastered by numerous people, many of whom have won public trading contests using the technique and who have gone on to write books about the method. For instance, Chis Kacher was an O'Neil protege who used CANSLIM to achieve a 18,241% return over seven years (from 1996 to 2002 at approximately 110% per year) which he documented in *Trade like an O'Neil Disciple: How We Made 18,000% in the Stock Market*. His co-author, Gil Morales, achieved a 10,904% return in the stock market from 1997 to 2005 (80% per year for 8 years). Many others who have mastered the methodology have also achieved extraordinary returns during great bull market runs.

As stated, the basic CANSLIM stock investing methodology once again combines both fundamental and technical analysis in an interesting way. In terms of the fundamentals, the *method requires that the companies whose stocks you buy must be showing strong fundamental growth conditions*. With CANSLIM, you also only buy stocks that exhibit a special technical price pattern, but they must be "solid" because they have strong fundamental conditions (with good annual growth rates, good quarterly earnings per share, and other strong fundamentals) that match what has historically been found in the biggest stock market winners. Stocks are only considered investment candidates company annual earnings are up 25% or more in the last year (or each of the last three years), and the annual returns on equity should be 17% or more. The company should also be involved with a new product, service or idea that is fueling that earnings growth.

These requirements represent the fundamental "fuel" that can power a stock blasting off to new heights. They are essential prerequisites on CANSLIM software screens. For further details of all the CANSLIM rules, you can easily crack open one of the many books written about the technique, which you will have to do anyway in order to study and master the necessary price patterns you are required to identify for the technique.

CANSLIM looks for stocks *before they make price advances*. It does not find stocks already outperforming and then try to justify an investment through fundamentals. It first filters the stock universe by some particular fundamental criteria it wants to see in the company, and then looks for a special consolidation price pattern that often occurs right before a stock explodes upwards. That's the technical analysis aspect of the system. If the stock passes the filter criteria, makes the consolidation pattern and then moves upwards, it becomes an investment contender.

When the stock starts advancing briskly, the question is then how to keep most of the rising profits before the trend reverses. If you just get into a new position, the emphasis is on preventing catastrophic losses. To prevent losses, the CANSLIM methodology uses strict money management rules including a 7-8% stop loss that is applied to all investments without exceptions. Rather than a 7-8% stop, super trader Dan Zanger (who used a derivative of CANSLIM to make his own investing millions) said he would be very quick to get out of stocks if they returned back to his trend line or breakout point, and would never risk more than a $2 stop loss. That's extremely tight because in traditional CANSLIM trading the stop loss is more lenient. You cut losers when a stock starts failing to make new highs once out of a chart cup with handle formation and then drops 7-8% from your purchase price. It is probably just coincidence that the 7-8% stop loss is our long run expected annual return rate for the stock market. Like Warren Buffet, with CANSLIM you also never average down in price or add to losing positions.

The CANSLIM rules also tell you to take some profits when you are up 20% to 25% in a winning stock. There are many rules for when to sell a position, and the enforcement of these rules is part of the reason this becomes a superior stock trading technique. The rules ensure that you minimize losses when wrong and lock in profits as they rise (which helps prevent greed from turning a winner into a loser). Successful CANSLIM users report that the major reason most people fail to make money with the technique is that *they don't apply these important money management rules.* In other words, it doesn't work for some people because they don't follow the system! They want to buy stocks, but they don't want to follow the rules that require them to take losses when the trends don't materialize that they hoped for. If they are not following the rules, they are not following CANSLIM but something similar that doesn't work.

O'Neil not only has made a personal fortune publishing the helpful investment newspaper IBD (*Investor's Business Daily*) and using CANSLIM for his own investments, but he was kind enough to share it through investment seminars all over the country. A cynic might say he shared in order to increase the sales of his newspaper and other services, but he did indeed share his research results and subsequent methodology, derived from studying price history, holding nothing back. We have all benefited by it. Twenty years from now, even fifty years from now, people will still be studying the basics of the CANSLIM methodology and adapting the basic insights for their time. If you are a stock picker and like studying charts, mastering his technique will help you build your trading and investing skills, especially for momentum investing.

Many books (and websites) have been written about the CANSLIM investment methodology, making it readily available to anyone who wants to learn it. Since an incredible amount of information is readily available, we can therefore leave its many rules to elsewhere for those who want to master the technique. While its mastery usually requires hundreds of hours studying stock charts, the important thing is that you know this methodology exists, know its potential return, know that other people have also mastered it and duplicated those exceptionally high returns themselves. For the right people that want to remain stock pickers rather than invest in index funds using market timing models or give their money over to disciplined momentum fund managers, this may be the one technique you are looking for to build a comfortable retirement or financial legacy that can be passed onto your children. However, it definitely takes a lot of study time to learn this technique thoroughly, which seems to work best in bull markets. Therefore you should start your learning phase well before a bull market period commences to get the most out of it. You should study the various chart patterns of past CANSLIM winners so that those patterns become easier to recognize when you are finally ready to trade it, and during your learning phase you can paper trade the various techniques to get used to the ins and outs of the methodology without worrying about losers.

While CANSLIM is extremely successful during large bull markets, the caveat is that during sideways markets and bear markets you will often find few candidates that satisfy the bullish selection criteria of this technique. Regardless of what people say, the size of the *overall bull market* you are riding to some extent determines the potential success with the system. It is one of the best stock selection systems possible in a bull market, but not in a bear market despite advertisements to the contrary. Without a bull market, it doesn't do so well because there are fewer large winners or continuing momentum. However, relative strength rotation strategies continue to perform well throughout such periods. Thus we must once again remember Boucher's relative strength rotation rules for finding investment opportunities, or the market timing models we discussed that might tell you when you can profit from CANSLIM the most.

Because of the tight stop loss, many CANSLIM traders suffer frequent whipsaws and small trading losses during sideways markets. This eats away at their capital and demoralizes them so that they stop using the technique while waiting for a sustained bull run. Then, as its proponents warn, they commonly miss the bull run and fail to achieve the returns of others who have mastered this stock trading technique. The potential for small whipsaw losses is therefore the price to bear if you want to engage in momentum trading of some form or another.

Many investment newsletters advise you to only buy stocks that are already going up, and they define "moving up" by some criteria such as a 50-day moving average crossing a 200-day or 40-week moving average (and vice versa for shorting). With CANSLIM you are looking for a particular chart pattern that has historically been found in the biggest stock market winners right before they blasted off, and you verify those potential purchase candidates using a checklist of other fundamental conditions that have signified outperformance in the past.

If you are not in a mega-bull market then international diversification, such as by investing in different asset classes via relative strength rules, can help you grow your funds when a domestic bull market just isn't there offering any opportunities. CANSLIM cannot appreciably help you during a domestic bear market. As the example of Japan's "lost decade" shows, a stock market can stay in the doldrums for a decade or more, so you must have a variety of investment techniques available for all sorts of market conditions if you want to consistently grow your assets over the long run and not miss any major opportunities.

In today's world you can buy ETFs on international stock markets, stock sectors, industry groups, interest rate vehicles, precious metals, foreign currencies, commodities, and more. The ETFs open up a whole host of possibilities for someone seeking better returns when their country is experiencing a devastating bear market that can last for years. If those losing years can be turned into positive periods of growth, we've found a way to continue our climb upwards to achieve the goal of accumulating great generational wealth.

O'Neil does not actually consider the CANSLIM strategy as "momentum investing" because you are identifying companies with strong fundamentals (big sales and earnings increases that suggest new products and services) *before* those stocks make a big momentum move upwards. Also, he does not buy stocks because they have been big movers, but because they make a special chart pattern that is typical of the largest movers *prior* to their advance. However, many do consider this in the category of momentum investing because you are trying to capture stocks with the greatest potential for forward momentum, so it is simply a matter of definition.

Let's not argue about it. To me, it doesn't matter what we call it. We are just looking for any superior proven methods that will help us outperform the 7-8% CAGR of buy and hold over the long run. What's important is that for those who want to be stock pickers and manage their own funds, this is a methodology promising exceptional returns for the stock pickers who learn to master it. It is perfect for those with the right temperament who are disciplined enough to learn its rules and follow them exactly without meddling with them or trying to alter them for every situation. Through the CANSLIM system you do indeed capture many momentum movers during bull markets, but you also invest in such a way that you cut your losses quickly when you are wrong, and you force yourself to lock in some profits through disciplined selling criteria that prevent the emotions of greed, hope and fear from destroying all your gains.

Those who become the most successful with CANSLIM typically share a common characteristic. They become wedded to it, absolutely living and breathing it. They become such big fans that they spend hours studying stock chart books to embed the triggering price patterns in their subconscious. If you don't have that type of commitment to master the technique, and if you start out during a bear or sideways market, you will probably fritter your money away trying to master the technique. If this methodology doesn't match your personality, you will probably lose thousands of dollars trying to master it.

Once again, one of my cardinal principles for success through investing is that the investment methodology you choose must match with your personality, which is why we are presenting several widely different techniques. If this methodology does not match your personal style, you will surely deviate from the method and lose money. Therefore, don't try to kid yourself into thinking you will readily master a method such as CANSLIM or momentum investing that goes against the grain of your personality unless you are willing to put hundreds or even thousands of hours into retraining yourself. It can be done, but few are ready to apply that many hours to learning some new technique that goes against their grain even if the target is wealth accumulation. People can indeed master it, just as they can master almost any skill after 10,000 hours of practice (as mentioned in *The Talent Code* by Daniel Coyle), but it certainly takes a lot of time and commitment.

Incidentally, O'Neil also had a very interesting opinion about the topic of "market timing," which is the nature of many of these investment techniques we are discussing. In his book he said, "Don't ever let anyone tell you that you can't time the market. This is a giant myth passed on mainly by Wall Street, the media, and those who have never been able to do it, so they think it's impossible. ... The erroneous belief that you can't time the market—that it's simply impossible, that no one can do it—evolved more than 40 years ago after a few mutual fund managers tried it unsuccessfully. They relied on personal judgments and feelings to determine when the market finally hit bottom and turned up for real. At the bottom, the news is all negative. So these managers, being human, hesitated to act."

We have already seen that simple seasonality rules give you a way to time the market, and simple models that technically time fundamental information give you a way to time the market and achieve superior returns. There are many complicated timing models we could have gone over that trade the market rather well, but if they are not available to you in real time then for all intents and purposes they are worthless. That's why didn't go into even better models you could not duplicate.

You might also say that a market climate, market environment, or market direction model are market timing models, but I'm not worried about semantics. All these various models tell you when you should be fully invested in stocks using index funds, specialized ETFs or mutual funds that might outperform during those periods. You can even combine their indications with something like CANSLIM to tell you when you should be using this individual stock picking technique.

If you don't want to be market timing a single index, then you can turn to relative strength (momentum) investing that has you taking positions in a diversified portfolio of the currently strongest market winners. Yet for an even more powerful stock selection method that works extremely well through *both bear and bull markets*, we must turn to picking undervalued stocks rather than momentum stocks, which is our next super investing topic for the hyper-compounding of your investment wealth.

6
SUPERIOR VALUE INVESTING

Most people know of Warren Buffett, who is often considered one of the most successful investor of the 20th century and who has been consistently ranked among the richest people of the world. The investment methodology he follows, which I strongly advise from among these top five methods, is based upon the value investing philosophy of Benjamin Graham.

When people dream of becoming rich or even amassing generational wealth through investing, Warren Buffett is one of the primary role models that always comes to mind. Rather than envy or criticism, a great appreciation arises in people's hearts when they learn of his pledge—already being instituted while he is alive—to give away 99% of his accumulated wealth to philanthropic causes. The monies will all go to current needs rather than endowments, thus avoiding the trap of foundations that lose their rudder over time. Foundations often end up becoming controlled by individuals and organizations (including intelligence agencies) who deviate from the founder's intentions, and end up using their vast funds to support questionable goals.

When pledging his wealth, it is interesting that Buffett actually wrote that good luck, or fate, played a great role in the making of his riches. Most people don't believe that fate plays any role in wealth accumulation, but Buffett basically admitted that it does. As he mentioned, had he been born in another country or at another time, he might never have had the opportunity to use his particular skills in the investing arena. Thus, along with applying principles of value investing and relying on the role of compound interest, those strokes of fate played a critical role in his becoming one of the richest men in the world through investing:

My wealth has come from a combination of living in

America, some lucky genes, and compound interest. Both my children and I won what I call the ovarian lottery. (For starters, the odds against my 1930 birth taking place in the U.S. were at least 30 to 1. My being male and white also removed huge obstacles that a majority of Americans then faced.)

My luck was accentuated by my living in a market system that sometimes produces distorted results, though overall it serves our country well. I've worked in an economy that rewards someone who saves the lives of others on a battlefield with a medal, rewards a great teacher with thank-you notes from parents, but rewards those who can detect the mispricing of securities with sums reaching into the billions. In short, fate's distribution of long straws is wildly capricious.

The reaction of my family and me to our extraordinary good fortune is not guilt, but rather gratitude. Were we to use more than 1% of my claim checks on ourselves, neither our happiness nor our well-being would be enhanced. In contrast, that remaining 99% can have a huge effect on the health and welfare of others. That reality sets an obvious course for me and my family: Keep all we can conceivably need and distribute the rest to society, for its needs. My pledge starts us down that course.

The fondness and admiration which people hold for Buffett contrasts sharply with how people felt about another of the richest men of all time. I'm referring to Marcus Crassus, a colleague of Julius Caesar who is often considered the wealthiest man in Roman history. The story of Crassus is quite instructive as to the perils of ambition and being greedy for wealth and fame.

Crassus's biography offers many admonitions regarding the folly of those who have definite virtues, but who are also faulted with the particular vice of excessive greed and avarice. Greed may spur you to accumulate stupendous wealth through business or investments, but it is also greed that may cause you to lose everything, including your life and legacy. The lesson from Crassus's life is that wealth is something you should not accumulate at the expense of personal character, ethics and behavior, and that the drive for wealth and fame can actually be your undoing. Once dead, you certainly cannot take all that money you have accumulated with you and as for fame, who knows how you will be remembered? After you die, everything that you have ever accumulated in life may disperse with the winds leaving you with no legacy at all, so you must think carefully about your life purpose and ambitions. Fortune and fame, wealth and power cannot be controlled but one can remain steadfast in adhering to ethics.

Crassus made his wealth through a variety of diversified businesses such as managing silver mines and buying slaves, training them, and then re-selling them. He accumulated most of his gargantuan wealth, however, by employing the basic rule of another individual also once cited as the "richest person in the world," namely J. Paul Getty, who always told people to *buy assets for less than they were worth*. Crassus would buy real estate assets for cheap prices when they were extremely undervalued, which is the basic idea behind value investing, and then fix them up so they increased in price. However, it was the method by which he obtained those great deals that made Crassus hated by many, for he accumulated much of his wealth through public calamities and by refusing to lend a helping hand to those in times of need.

One method Crassus used for buying real estate at cheap prices is that he would greedily buy the land and estates of "proscribed citizens" at knock-down prices during the rule of Sulla, a one-time dictator of Rome who used proscriptions to get rid of his enemies. A proscribed citizen was someone declared to be an enemy of the state, and was *ipso facto* stripped of his citizenship and excluded from all protections of the law. No person could inherit money or property from a proscribed man, nor could his widow (or widowed daughters) remarry after his death. If you killed a proscribed man you were entitled to keep part of his estate while the remainder went to the state, and thus the proscribed commonly lost both their lives and fortunes. Anything could make you an enemy of the state, particularly your political views or the fact that you were wealthy or had too much personal power, prestige or influence.

History shows time and again that the way for the wealthy to protect themselves in dangerous political situations is by spreading the money around so that no one considers you an enemy but everyone considers you a friend and benefactor. I know of one wealthy Chinese banking family that actually preserved itself and some degree of its affluence during Mao's Communist Revolution because it had always taken this approach of charitable public giving on a vast scale. This same strategy of generosity to the public also saved various nobles during the guillotining stage of the French Revolution. If you use your wealth to do great things for the people rather than just engage in conspicuous consumption, you will not only benefit the public by returning those funds to the very source of your money, but help protect yourself from calamity as well.

This is one of the lessons for being able to accumulate riches across the generations, especially in difficult countries and unstable political environments. You must spread your wealth among the people and often among government officials as a form of insurance or protection. On the positive side, the Eastern religions say that a policy of generosity and being charitable is like storing up merit in heaven, and even maintain that your charitable deeds will earn you great good fortunate karma in the future. Whether this is true or not, it is often a good strategy for influence or self-preservation.

Plutarch, in his *Lives of the Noble Romans* (which I always encourage the young to read in order to absorb its lessons of history and character), records how Crassus would also increase his fortunes by purchasing houses at prices well below market value because they had caught on fire. He would also buy homes in the immediately surrounding neighborhood whose owners, seeing the imminent danger, would often be willing to sell at a discount. When a house caught on fire in ancient Roman times, it would usually burn to the ground and then become entirely worthless, so there was a great incentive to sell a property if fire threatened it. Since a fire would also often take neighboring estates with it, it is understandable that many owners would often sell at emergency prices in those situations.

As soon as Crassus heard that a house was on fire, he would immediately arrive and then negotiate to purchase the doomed property for a modest sum. While a private firefighting brigade of five hundred workers stood standing by, Crassus would not offer any help in putting out the fire. Rather, he would only employ them to put the fire out, before much damage had been done, if a purchase deal could be struck, and every minute of delay during the bargaining led to lower price offers by Crassus. Through this means, and other less than ethical methods, it is said that the greatest part of Rome came within his hands, and he eventually established himself as the richest man in the country. He basically grew rich through the general strategy of buying assets for less than they were worth.

After becoming rich, Crassus still desired more. Now he also wanted fame and political power, much like the business billionaires of today who, after achieving their wealth, aspire to win a seat in the Senate thinking they are now somehow qualified for leading the nation. For some reason, many rich people automatically believe that their wealth proves they are now qualified as wise statesmen and political leaders for the populace. They believe that the very fact they have become rich somehow proves that they have the requisite wisdom required for politically representing the people, deciding what is in their best interests, and guiding the nation. In any case, to help his political fortunes (and help protect himself), Crassus therefore started trying to influence the courts of his day. He also provided interest free loans to powerful politicians or gave them support for their political campaigns, thus indebting those individuals to him.

When Spartacus launched a slave rebellion against Rome, Crassus had accumulated such immense wealth that he volunteered to equip, train and lead an army of two legions at his own expense to defeat him. When a segment of his army fled during the battle, abandoning their weapons, Crassus revived the bloody ancient practice of decimation. Decimation meant executing one out of every ten soldiers as punishment where the unfortunate victims were selected by drawing lots. In this way he demonstrated that he was more ruthless and dangerous to his troops than the enemy, and eventually prevailed over Spartacus and his rebellion. When the slave rebellion was finally defeated, Crassus ordered six thousand of the captured slaves to be crucified along the Appian Way. Their bodies were not taken down after death but were left rotting on the crosses to dissuade others from defying Rome in the future.

These incidents provide some insight into the type of man Crassus was. Working his way up the Roman political system, he became a Roman consul and was eventually appointed to govern Syria, which promised to be an inexhaustible source of wealth to any who governed it. But in addition to wealth and political power, Crassus was now greedy for military glory. He therefore decided to cross the Euphrates River to conquer Parthia, which had never done the Romans any harm. As he was passing through the gates of Rome to march on Parthia, it is said that the tribune Ateius Capito called a curse down upon him for his intended war *nulla causa* ("with no justification") that was motivated by ambition. Due to poor military decisions, Crassus finally lost his life in a small skirmish with the Parthians, and Rome's engagement with Parthia ended with one of the costliest and most humiliating defeats in its history. This story of a "war without justification" should cause us to reflect.

How is Crassus known in history? You have just read his story, so whatever your own reactions are in reading his tale indicates how he is now known. He certainly became richer than anyone else of his day, but as an cautionary tale, that avarice also destroyed him. Even the fate of his corpse tells a tale. It is said that the Parthians poured molten gold into his mouth to symbolize satiating his thirst for more and more wealth. It's also said that his skull was later used as a prop in a play. What a strange fate to a life of vast wealth, power and fortune!

The reason for these stories? To help you crystallize your own ideas about the ultimate purpose behind the pursuit of wealth and to help you think about what is really important in life. On this road you must reflect upon the fact that the road for becoming wealthy also involves preserving your life, health, relationships, virtue, honor, ethics, and reputation as well as your wealth. Doesn't it? Since we are talking of pursuing value investing, we should pause to ask ourselves what are the true values for life in general. What are you ultimately after in life other than just pursuing money? What are you doing it all for?

Another interesting story is that J. Paul Getty, another of the richest men in the world often cited, once agreed to pay only $2.2 million when his grandson was kidnapped, the amount being the most he claimed could be deducted from his taxes as a loss due to theft. He lent the rest of the $3 million ransom to his son, the teenager's father, at 4% interest. Perhaps this was a public relations stunt to dissuade future kidnapping attempts, in which case we might consider it a very wise strategy, but the particulars should cause us to think deeply on the situation. This is the behavior of a man whose estimated worth was roughly $1/900^{th}$ of the entire U.S. economy, which at today's value of $160 billion, would come to more than four times Warren Buffett's net worth.

I have known men who surrendered their entire multi-million dollar fortunes to prevent the death or imprisonment of their families during the Marcos reign of the Philippines, and were happy for the chance to have escaped calamity. I have known men who left absolutely everything behind to escape Communist China, and others who abandoned everything they had ever accumulated to escape bloody regimes. This is always a possible future when the politics of a state, for whatever reason, become subverted over time.

While most people want to become wealthy, you must think carefully on these things to decide for yourself what is truly valuable in life. For instance, it is said that Confucius once returned home one day and found that the stables housing his horses had been destroyed by fire, but the very first question out of his mouth was whether anyone was hurt. People came first; the loss of the property and the expensive horses was only a secondary concern. If you do not have this type of empathy for your own kind over property, what can we say beats inside your chest?

J. Paul Getty had five marriages and five divorces, which proves nothing at all. But he also had five sons and missed every one of their weddings due to business. The richest man in the world, he installed a pay phone in his house so that guests might use it rather than make long distance calls for free. Confucius would censure such a man who time and again showed he could readily open his pocketbook to pay for a piece of expensive art, but who could not his open his heart for the richness of human relationships. Should one not cultivate consideration of one's own kind over material things?

In what Andrew Carnegie, Bill Gates, Peter Cooper or Warren Buffett might criticize as short-sidedness, lack of wisdom, or simply the masking of greed, Getty once said, "If I were convinced that by giving away my fortune I could make a real contribution toward solving the problems of world poverty, I'd give away 99.5 percent of all I have immediately. But a hard-eyed appraisal of the situation convinces me this is not the case." Hence, when he died he left most of his money to an art museum rather than philanthropic causes that might help the world in a substantial way. Inspired in part by Andrew Carnegie's *The Gospel of Wealth*, John Rockefeller chose an entirely different route in establishing a very active philanthropic foundation meant "to promote the well-being of mankind throughout the world," and his many business excesses and personal faults have actually often been overlooked because of his charitable legacy. While I have written this book with my hopes to help you accumulate great generational or legacy wealth for you and your family, my hope is that you also do something with it that truly improves the lives of many people rather than simply spend it or, in the face of great human suffering, leave it all to something as unproductive as an art museum.

Incidentally, as an interesting anecdote we should note that Getty, like Buffett, also recognized the great role that fate had played in his wealth accumulation. "In building a large fortune," he once said, "it pays to be born at the right time. I was born at a very favorable time. If I had been born earlier or later, I would have missed the great business opportunities that existed in World War I and later. I suppose it takes a long time and it takes extraordinary circumstances to be born at the right time and have cash money available at the right time. I was fortunate due to my father's foresight and my good luck. In the Depression I did what the experts said one should not do. I was a very big buyer of oil company stocks." Some success in life are indeed due to fate, and if it is indeed fate that brings you into great wealth through business, investing or inheritance, you should carefully consider how you might use that luck for greater good tidings rather than just compound it for no reason at all.

Turning again to the topic of value investing, we must note Warren Buffett gained his wealth through this very road of value investing that we are discussing, and so it makes sense to see if we can emulate his basic investment principles to capture such returns ourselves. Most people know that Buffett studied the value investing ideas of Graham and Dodd, encapsulated with the book *Security Analysis*, which became the initial foundation of his value investing technique.

Graham also published *The Intelligent Investor*, which Buffett has called the best book ever written about investing. It puts forth the idea that investing and speculating are quite different things. When you conduct a thorough analysis of an investment and then buy that investment if it promises you a safety of principal and an adequate return, that is investing. Everything else, Graham says, is speculation. The idea Graham espoused is that you should not be frivolous with your money by entering into investments with the gambler's attitude that it is okay to lose. You must do your homework and be well informed about the worth of a business before you buy its stock. He said that if you pay too much—even for the best businesses—you will lose money.

Graham additionally put forth a principle that has become synonymous with the Warren Buffett style of investing. The idea is that whenever you buy a stock you should consider yourself as an owner in the business, and if you have enough cash then you might even consider buying the whole company so that you become the sole owner and can keep all the revenue flows. Because the proper mindset should be that you are buying a business and becoming the sole owner, before you buy a stock investment you should be looking for certain ownership (selection) criteria. You should try to buy *great companies at fair prices* rather than fair companies at great prices, and then you will avoid many management problems or great losses in investment values. You want to buy great companies because you want to avoid catastrophic risk and you want those businesses to keep spinning off profits for a very long time, even if idiots were eventually to come to run them. As Warren Buffett advised, "Buy into a business that's doing so well an idiot could run it, because sooner or later, one will."

Buffett feels that you should look for businesses with favorable long-term prospects that exist because of durable competitive advantages. You should invest in companies whose managers think like owners, and you should invest with a *margin of safety* that exists because the business is undervalued. The price you pay and the time period for which you hold a stock are two of the most important issues for succeeding as an investor. If a business is sound, he said that the favorite holding period is forever because it will continue to throw off profits and cash flow while gaining in value. Once you buy a sound company, thereafter you need not be too concerned with the daily fluctuations in stock market prices and their incredible volatility. Because you are buying a company rather than engaging in stock speculation, you should only concern yourself with the long term growth in the value of your business because that is why you bought it. These are just a few of the many basic principles that Buffett derived and built upon from initially studying Graham and his methods.

Many people try to duplicate Buffett's investment methodology on their own, but in actuality, this is a full time job that few can replicate. His exceptional track record proves that his investing methodology is certainly sound, but unless you are a full time investor who has the time to devote himself fully to value investing, it would be hard to duplicate Buffett's judgment or returns. What seems more reasonable, especially if you are looking ahead ten to twenty years, is to seek out value managers like Buffett and to park your money in funds they might manage. For instance, in a 1984 speech to the Columbia Business School, Buffett revealed the investment track records of several other value investors like himself (Walter Schloss, Tom Knapp, Bill Ruane, Charlie Munger, etc.), all of whom had beaten the S&P500 index year in and year out through all their years of investing. It is a simple task to find similar investment managers, since they are mentioned in popular magazines and financial newspapers all the time, and give them some of your money to manage.

If you wish to try to duplicate Buffett style investing on your own, consider the process you must replicate. Let's just focus on one small section of his methodology, which is to try to find great businesses with a competitive advantage called a "moat" (a broad defensive ditch surrounding a castle meant to hinder intruders from entering it). Finding companies with moats means searching for companies with strong competitive advantages such as brand name products that consumers are likely to prefer buying, products that represent high switching costs to the consumer, products or services that involve difficult to obtain regulatory licenses, patents, and so on. While it is true that such companies can often earn a return on capital of more than 20% per year, which is certainly better than what most money managers can achieve over long periods of time, finding those firms is not as easy as it sounds.

Once you find such a company, the next step is that you must value it correctly using some valuation formula. If it is overvalued you should not buy it, and so you must wait for a better time and start looking elsewhere for a new investment candidate. If the stock is undervalued and you want to become a buyer, now you have to decide how much of your investment portfolio you should allocate to that company by taking into account all sorts of factors. After you do indeed buy shares, your work isn't done yet because now you have to stay up-to-date on what's happening with the company by reading news stories, analyst reports, quarterly reports and so on. If you get any of these valuation steps wrong along the way then you are facing the prospect of losses rather than profits, and you must remember that you will be doing this for multiple companies in your portfolio. You must buy at a discount and then monitor those investments. There are many complications involved with value investing and to do it correctly, it's a full time job. Benjamin Graham originally taught Buffett and others that this is what they had to do to properly select and manage investments. However, near the end of his life, Graham said that there was a far easier way!

What most people don't know is that months before his death, he gave an interview, published by *Medical Economics* in September 1976, called "The Simplest Way to Select Bargain Stocks." During this interview he updated the ideas from his book, *The Intelligent Investor*. Incredibly, those new ideas seemed to overthrow most of his earlier emphasis on the detailed stock analysis for which he had become known! In the interview Graham said, "I have lost most of the interest I had in the details of security analysis which I devoted myself to so strenuously for so many years. I feel they are relatively unimportant, which, in a sense, has put me opposed to developments in the whole profession. I think we can do it successfully with a few techniques and simple principles."

After years of strenuous analysis aimed at determining the value of stock investments, Graham's new favored investing approach—which he extensively tested—chose stocks according to a very simple formula that required very little thinking or analysis at all. If a stock passed the simple hurdle criteria of his formula, he might buy it without doing all sorts of other complicated analysis.

THE RULES:

In this "Simplest Way to Select Bargain Stocks" interview, he revealed this new stock selection criteria for identifying undervalued companies. He felt these simple criteria would outperform his original work and average a return of 15% a year or better on your total investments, plus dividends and minus commissions, over the long run. Here is the basic investing technique he discovered:

First, create as large a list as possible of common stocks currently selling at no more than seven times their latest (not projected) 12-month earnings. While Graham said to select shares with a P/E of less than 7, he explained that he arrived at this criteria because he wanted a earnings-to-price ratio (the inverted P/E ratio) was at least twice the average current yield on top-quality (AAA) corporate bonds. Today we might use a P/E criteria of 10 or even 12. In any case, the low P/E requirement tends to be the first sieve that helps you select underpriced stocks selling at a discount.

Once you have those initial candidates, you are looking to select a portfolio of at least 30 stocks (at a minimum) that not only meet the P/E requirements but also have strong balance sheets.

You don't just want a low P/E but also want companies that are financially strong because they have a satisfactory financial position. His only screening criteria for this condition was that a company should own at least twice what it owes, so its debt should be less than half of its assets. How can you measure this? You can look at the shareholder equity/total assets ratio to get an idea of debt levels. If you look at the ratio of stockholders' equity to total assets and the ratio is at least 50 percent, the company's financial condition can be considered sound.

Now for the selling rules. After you buy such a stock, you would sell it after it appreciated by 50% or after two years went by, whichever came first, and then simply repeat the process when funds became available and new stocks met the tests.

In other words, Graham said we should look for companies with a strong balance sheet where the shareholder equity/total assets ratio was greater than .50, *and* the stock was trading at a bargain because it had a low P/E that was no greater than 7. While today we would certainly use a higher P/E, the selection formula is that simple. The stock must have a low P/E (the level to be decided by market factors) and the company's stockholder equity to assets ratio had to be 50% or better. This means that if the company was trading for $20 then we would have the potential to be paid $10 if it sold all its assets. When many stocks pass these criteria and you have several contenders to choose from, you should select the ones with the highest ratio or select them using other criteria you might favor.

Today we can do computer studies that might help us tighten these two criteria through additional measurements such as free cash flow, the return on equity, profit margins, minimum market capitalization, earnings growth rates, or even industry. For instance, we might employ Buffet's rule of avoiding high tech stocks or financial stocks, or sectors Buffett would say were "bad bets" because they were too volatile. We might also try to eliminate companies from consideration that might go out of business because of declining sales over consecutive years. Free cash flow is also important because that's what a company can use to minimize its debt in times of trouble. Anything that might help determine if a stock would be a takeover candidate would be helpful as well. Even trading volume can be a criteria if we are concerned about liquidity.

Through computer simulations you might even test whether adding some type of earnings growth, cash flow, profit margin, EBITDA or return on equity criteria to Graham's basic rules might help determine even better candidates. There are all sorts of additional requirements one might test to determine if a stock is financially sound, as well as underpriced. In addition to adding a quality measurement to its selection criteria, one might also see how the methodology performed under different economic models that identified the market environment. These ideas, however, are just possible improvements on something that already works superbly. With only two ratios, Graham's preliminary selections were finished.

The basic Graham criteria are simple and sound and actually mirror similar criteria that billionaire investors, growth oriented CEOs and private equity firms use to rate takeover candidates. The methodology actually finds stocks using the same basic criteria which private equity firms and other groups who buy companies use to determine what companies to buy as acquisitions. Buying companies is how other larger companies grow, and these criteria often get you in front of all the buying activity because they find strong companies at a discount that buyers usually want to snap up.

Now these very simple valuation rules determine which stocks you might get into, but when do you sell them? In terms of selling rules, Graham's rules were simple and crystal clear, even more so than CANSLIM. These rules are another key reason why this strategy works so well. Graham said that as soon as an undervalued stock goes up by 50%, sell it. If a stock hasn't met this price objective by the end of the second calendar year from the date of purchase, then you should also sell it regardless of its price. Thus, you sell when a stock increases by 50% or two years pass by ... or the company gets bought ... or the stock splits.

How did Graham come to his conclusion that this basic method could make about 15% per year? Graham and a team of assistants spent two years back-testing this method for the fifty years between 1925 and 1975, and they found that the return not only more than doubled the return of the Dow Jones average but stood up to any of the tests they would make upon it! Joel Greenblatt, founder of the Gotham Capital hedge fund (that achieved a 50% annual return during the ten years it was open to investors) and author of *The Little Book that Beats the Market*, also tested the formula for a period between April 1972 and April 1978, which included a severe bear market and market recovery, and found it beat its relevant index by over

10% per year! This is an incredible alpha over a simple buy and hold strategy.

More recent computer simulations, starting in 1965 and running through to 2010, show a 14.3% compound annual growth rate for the simple Graham strategy versus a 6.1% CAGR for the S&P500 index. This was once again far better than buy and hold and safer because buying assets for less than they are worth has tended to somewhat protect you during market crashes. Thus it has worked extraordinarily well over 45 years, and that's *without* using any leverage at all! That's simply amazing. Just as Graham and Greenblatt found, this simple method did much better than the entire market but with far less risk for the investor. It did better than the market as a whole, protected capital during bear market years, and it's incredibly easy to duplicate on your own simply by using Google Finance to search for companies satisfying the basic two criteria.

One extra source for those who wish to duplicate this investment technique is found in the Inevitable Wealth Portfolio (IWP) newsletter, which was founded by editor Charles Mizrahi to pick stocks according to this technique. The *Hulbert Financial Digest* has tracked his portfolio returns over time and found them soundly beating the indices, once again adding another analyst to the list of those who have confirmed the validity of this simple Graham technique.

Why does this methodology work so well and why is it such a good candidate for wealth accumulation over the long run? One of the reasons behind its success is that *it forces you to sell and take frequent profits of sufficient size*. The selling rule *forces you* to take advantage of any opportunity that realizes a definite sizeable gain in your investment rather than to keep holding onto a stock and possibly see that gain whittle away. You are forced to realize a profit when it is adequate, and then put your money into an entirely new fresh opportunity.

The formula certainly doesn't know anything about a company, such as the requirement that the company creates new products or services as demanded by the CANSLIM investment criteria. You also don't need to evaluate the future prospects of a company at all or keep up with news on the corporation. Once it gives you the targeted 50% rate of return, you are forced to get out and rotate your monies into a new candidate with fresh potential. You must liquidate at either a profit or at the two year mark and reallocate your funds to another potential winner.

If we delve further to fathom the reasons behind the astounding long term success of this technique, the formula basically identifies companies that have been doing fine and then suddenly fall off trend. Good stocks become an undervalued situation when prices become severely depressed because of high doses of pessimism or uncertainty about the company's immediate future. You may have heard of irrational exuberance, but there is also such a thing as irrational pessimism which is a case of extreme negative expectations that have gone too far. Negative emotional extremes can often hit stocks hard and depress share prices more than they should. These simple Graham valuation criteria help you find those situations where stocks become cheap but the stocks themselves represent good companies, so they *basically identify solid dollars selling for pennies*. Since some of these companies are very troubled, not all of the stocks identified by these criteria turn out to be good bets, but that's the case with all investment strategies. You just want to see if you *consistently* come out ahead in aggregate if you religiously follow this strategy for a large number of stocks, and that the method generally works throughout all types of different market environments.

Basically, a portfolio of such good companies—which is why Graham insisted on at least thirty companies or more—represents a good bet on true values eventually reasserting themselves as companies resolve problems and their futures become clear. If the future turns out better than expected, the depression pushing down any stock's prices would be lifted, and that stock would then go up significantly like any other case of mean reversion. *Buying a basket of such shares insures an additional measure of diversification so that you are buying value with a sufficient margin of safety.* Buying a basket of such stocks also helps prevent self-destruction because with Graham's method, only a portion of shares outperform the market, so it isn't necessarily a good stock picking system for extreme outperformers. It simply creates a portfolio of undervalued stocks whose prices currently incorporate negative expectations about the future, but buying them cheaply represents a good bet that, given enough time, produces an overall great aggregate return.

A common argument against this technique is the fact that just because a stock is cheap doesn't mean it won't get cheaper. Hearing of the methodology, investors always worry about how you can protect yourself from a further drop in prices for all these companies. After all, CANSLIM protects you from catastrophic loss by using a tight 7-8% stop loss, but there is no stop loss here. Since most investors have heard they should cut losses early and take small loses to prevent big ones, the lack of any such protections worries some investors even though historical testing shows little chance of catastrophic risk. In this case, it turns out that you are protecting yourself by the fact that the downside is already limited because shares have already fallen so much in price. The downside is limited by the fact that prices have already fallen a lot *for a good company with little debt.*

You are also protecting yourself via the diversification strategy of buying many such stocks, each a "good" company and each at low value-based prices. These are not showy, high flyer companies but just good, basic, salt of the earth companies. In describing these undervalued companies, Walter Schloss mentioned they were mostly secondary rather than top grade companies, usually had little sex appeal, and were usually just struck with trouble at the time of purchase. They were not flashy, but you were buying good companies cheap. Warren Buffett liked buying *great companies at a discount,* so his basic strategy is to only buy a few of those companies and to wait a long time for such opportunities. This strategy is for a more active investor who buys many more opportunities that are *good, but not great,* and so it needs the protective power of more diversification. That is the difference between this method and Buffett's method of betting deeply by concentrating his funds in only a few holdings.

Since poor future expectations or recent bad performance were already reflected in the low share prices when a stock was initially identified as an undervalued candidate, it just turns out that investing in those already depressed prices does not hurt you much in downturns (because most of the price drop has already been factored in) while a turnaround to good performance will produce amplified returns. If more negative expectations turned out to be true, history shows that the stocks selected this way would only turn down a little more, or not at all. Since the downside was therefore somewhat limited, you simply needed a long term time horizon, which Graham found to be two years, to wait for the initial pessimism or uncertainty to be resolved, at which point the share prices would bounce back due to mean reversion.

With this valuation methodology, you are basically identifying stocks that are *good solid bets.* You are not using a methodology that requires a precise prediction of a stock's present value or future value. You are not making any predictions or forecasting anything at all. You are just trying to select a basket of good companies that have already experienced some negative expectations about their future (which are perhaps overly pessimistic), and because you are buying them cheaply together with a basket of other bargains, it turns out to be a good bet in aggregate. If we look at the technique with dispassionate simplification, the basic idea is that if you have some way to figure out what something is worth and pay a lot less (J. Paul Getty's rule), then it doesn't matter what the market does in the meantime. Just give yourself enough time for a mean reversion return to higher values, and you'll make money. The proof is that *after testing the idea over fifty years, it works over the long haul* even though the ride can be bumpy at times.

The importance of having an adequate holding period and the fortitude to withstand periods of adversity cannot be overemphasized for the long term value investor. As Buffett might say, volatility is not the same as risk when you use this type of investment methodology, and since your methodology is to buy value at depressed prices, you must take advantage of an exceptional bargain situation regardless of market volatility. Even Greenblatt found that his own "Magic Formula" strategy, which evaluates stocks using just the two metrics of earnings yield and return on capital, often produced a bumpy ride. His own cheap and good stock strategy, developed after analyzing Graham's work, was down five out of every twelve months on average even though it showed a 30% annual return over seventeen years.

In his book *How to Be Rich*, billionaire J. Paul Getty also said, "It is possible to make money—and a great deal of money—in the stock market. But it can't be done overnight or by haphazard buying and selling. The big profits go to the intelligent, careful and patient investors, not to the reckless and overeager speculator. The seasoned investor buys his stocks when they are priced low, holds them for the long-pull rise and takes in-between dips and slumps in stride." Volatility, it seems, is something to be generally ignored if you can buy an asset for less than it is worth. An incredible number of mega-wealthy investors understand this principle, and so they eschew the quick "get in, get out" mentality of traders because they invest their monies in undervalued assets for the long run and never worry about short term market volatility. As many popular books have recently pointed out, millionaires differentiate themselves from poor people because of many characteristics, and one of these characteristics is the fact that *they tend to think long-term.*

Many people have investment time horizons that are far too short for them to make money with this two year technique, or they hold stocks far too long and then lose all their gains as in our Citibank tale. Thus, you need patience and discipline to succeed with this highly recommended methodology. In settling for less—just a 50% return if you can get it—and then recycling that money into a fresh new opportunity, you end up going home with more money than you do by searching for large winners. As long as a country's economy doesn't self-destruct while you are holding these value investments (as long as we assume the nation avoids implosion or destruction), the basic Graham methodology predicts that the market will eventually recognize a greater value for your undervalued shares and reflect that through higher share prices.

This strategy reminds me of one story about John Templeton, founder of the Templeton Funds, who like Buffett also became a billionaire through his personal investing strategies and investment management services. The Templeton story is that he bought $100 of every stock trading below $1 on the NYSE stock exchange back in 1939 when Germany was at war with Europe. Protecting himself by buying a basket of shares, he ended up buying 104 companies for a total of $10,400. Even though 34 of those companies went bankrupt, this strategy turned his initial sum into $40,000 four years later when U.S. industry picked up as a result of the war. Hence, diversification is one means of protection which Graham worked into this methodology since not every stock picked this way is a winner.

Incidentally, John Templeton is another individual who can be juxtaposed beside Crassus. Duplicating the philosophy of Getty to "buy when everyone else is selling and hold until everyone else is buying," he attributed much of his success to his ability to *think independently and avoid the herd, buy when there's blood in the street (good values), stay disciplined, avoid stress and stay happy.* His philanthropic activities have totaled over $1 billion, causing him to be named one of the most influential people in the world for the good his wealth has done. Templeton, like Buffett (Carnegie and Gates), proved beyond the shadow of a doubt that great wealth could be put to great good use for the world's betterment.

With Graham's system, buying companies at depressed prices (because things look pessimistic) is to some extent duplicating Templeton's ideas of buying when "blood is in the street" or "everyone else is selling." Graham's rules also put into practice the words of John Neff who said, "Buy stocks that look bad to less careful investors and hang out until their real value is recognized." As Warren Buffett once noted, if a business is worth a dollar and you can buy it for 40 cents, something good may eventually happen. Thus you now have a methodology to weigh the value of potential holdings, and can accumulate a portfolio of good bets where the criteria suggests there is a gap between price and value. Then you must simply wait to sell. It's like a pawn shop that buys marketable assets for less than they are worth so that they can later be resold at a profit when a buyer is eventually found. You are only hoping for a 50% profit, but in two years' time at the max.

The bonus factor to this methodology is that it was tested throughout all types of bear markets and it still performed great under the very conditions you would most be worried about. As a long term method for capital appreciation and gaining wealth, this one is therefore a winner! At the very least you are buying good assets for cheap (at prices less than their fair value), and history shows the tendency of a mean reversion to fair (or better) prices in your favor whenever you give those investments enough time. Our next chapter will show some simple criteria which might even be used to improve the selection mechanism of this basic technique, but it's already exceptional as is.

Famed investment manager Mario Gabelli, whose own investment methodology also involves searching for undervalued assets, also employs Graham's two-year time horizon, and this is possibly a rule that in various forms might be applied to many other investment strategies if it increases their performance. If a stock has not moved up in two years time of waiting then perhaps it will continue to go nowhere. Thus you should then re-allocate your funds into a new stock that has a fresh chance to appreciate.

As for Graham's 50% selling rule, it is also favored by famed value investor Walter Schloss who achieved a 15.7% CAGR over the 45 years from 1956 to 2000 (compared to the market's return of 11.2% per year), which also puts him in the ranks of the best investors of all time. Nearly rivaling Buffett's return, Schloss said he chuckled at those who were reluctant to buy Buffett's Berkshire Hathaway stock because it never produced dividend income. If you grow your assets as much as Buffett did, he said, you can just sell some shares to get any income you need, but some people lose sight of the big picture because they are overly focused on dividends. We should remember this remark when we come to the topic of dividend investing.

Schloss's personal value investing method was to keep an eye out for companies making new price lows (especially a three year low) where management owned the stock. His screening criteria also included looking for stocks that didn't have a lot of debt and were selling for less than their book value. Such criteria are the crux of being selective. Schloss once summarized his approach saying, "We want to buy cheap stocks based on a small premium over book value, usually a depressed market price, a record that goes back at least 20 years ... and one that doesn't have much debt." Incidentally, stocks also often get bought out when they trade at significant discounts to their book value, too.

Schloss always strove to *buy assets at a discount rather than to purchase earnings* because earnings were unreliable and could change dramatically in a short time. Basically, he wanted to buy stocks that were depressed in price but where the company was not going broke. He preferred value over popularity, and like Buffett preferred to stay away from industries outside of his circle of competence. Since he noted that very few people become millionaires buying bonds, Schloss always avoided bonds (even though they pay a guaranteed return) since they limited your gains while inflation reduced your purchasing power, and their guaranteed return was rarely positive after inflation. Bonds simply sacrifice the potential of higher returns for lower volatility. Hence, he was similar to Buffett who said he "would always pick an investment strategy that over five years could give him a 12% compounded annual return, but that was volatile over one that promised a stable 8% return annually."

Like Buffett, Walter Schloss also said to ignore the overall economy and the market with its gyrations, and never made forecasts or predictions. Because he did not like forecasts, this is another reason why he always preferred buying assets at a discount to buying forecasted earnings. It is very hard to predict the future and whether a company's good fortunes will continue, so when a stock he purchased achieved an exceptional rate of return he simply banked the profits, ignored whether that stock went much higher, and then tried to do it again. If he didn't own it anymore then he put it out of his mind.

Once you start creating factor seasonal charts, you will see that they can often help you with all these forms of value investing. Whenever you generate a list of stocks that satisfy Graham's valuation criteria, you can simply *find the companies at or near their seasonal lows* (perhaps adaptive seasonal lows or factor seasonal lows), and consider investing in those over others since the seasonal low explains a portion of the price drop. Stocks that suddenly meet Graham's valuation criteria exactly at the time of an expected seasonal low or right before a seasonal climb is due, often quickly rebound to higher prices. A seasonal chart can also help you determine when you might want to risk holding stocks for the possibility of a little more return, or when you might get out early because you are just shy of the 50% gain but heading away from a seasonal peak.

Perhaps the most interesting point about Graham's methodology is that *it seems to turn the entire field of detailed stock analysis, which he started, on its head!* Graham is one of the grandfathers of the entire field of detailed stock analysis, and thus directly responsible for the existence of thousands of stock analysts all over the world who try to pick superior stocks, and yet whose mutual funds rarely beat the market return. Despite helping to launch this field, near the end of his life, he wrote the following in *Common Sense Investing: The Papers of Benjamin Graham*:

> I am no longer an advocate of elaborate techniques of security analysis in order to find superior value opportunities. This was a rewarding activity years ago when our textbook "Graham and Dodd" was first published; but the situation has changed a great deal since then. In the old days any well-trained security analyst could do a good professional job of selecting undervalued issues through detailed studies; but in the light of the enormous amount of research now being carried on, I doubt whether in most cases such extensive efforts will generate sufficiently superior selections to justify their cost. To that very limited extent I'm on the side of the "efficient market" school of thought now generally accepted by the professors. ... I favor a highly simplified approach that applies a single criteria or perhaps two criteria to the price to assure that full value is present and that relies for its results on the performance of the portfolio as a whole—i.e., on the group results—rather than on the expectations for individual issues.

In this book, Graham once again revealed the methodology we have reproduced here. At that time he preferred a P/E ratio of 7 times the reported earnings for the past twelve months, but mentioned you could use other criteria such as a current dividend return above 7%, or price no more than 120 percent of book value, etc. These parameters are something you must test using historical simulations to improve upon. Nonetheless, all the various value investing methods he developed consistently grew assets at 15% per annum or better, which was twice the performance of the DJIA for a fifty year period! That's fifty years, which satisfies my criteria for a long term positive track record for a simple system that is objective, easy to duplicate on your own, and fundamentally sound. He discovered a clear, manageable investing system that diverts your attention away from things that aren't important while focusing you on the things that are the most important for your long term success.

An even better method than this, he once mentioned, earned 20% per year over three decades of testing, and involved buying common stocks at less than their working capital or net current asset value (giving no weight to the plant and other fixed assets and deducting all liabilities from current assets). Unfortunately, this type of opportunity is scarce and therefore doesn't have the wide applicability of the method we have gone over, but illustrates how powerful a value investing strategy can be even when it is incredibly simple.

All in all, you should definitely consider using value investing to manage a substantial proportion of your stock portfolio. You can do it yourself using Graham's rules as they are very simple to use, and just studying his investing principles can revolutionize your investing style. You can also find a portfolio manager with a good track record who is devoted to undervalued opportunities (value investing) like this and park a portion of your funds with them for the long run. Better yet, you can divvy up a portion of your funds into several units and park those monies with several such managers. I am convinced that quiet value investing, rather than chasing after the high flyer stocks touted by Wall Street, should be one of the cornerstones to the growth of your wealth.

A caveat is in order when selecting fund managers, however, because while many claim they are value investors the truth is that most are not. A study by Lakonish, Shleifer and Vishny examined 1,300 pension funds and scored them as to the various rules of value investing. They found that *while many claimed to be value oriented, the vast majority of their portfolios were no different than the broader market index, and only slightly weighted toward value investing.* Fund managers commonly say they are value investors, but are simply not! Thus it is easy to see how managers deceive themselves into thinking they are doing something they are not, and easy for you to see why the professionals have a difficult time beating the market.

If you aim to duplicate this strategy yourself then whether you increase your leverage or not based on the market climate, analytical fundamental models or other analysis methods, and whether you write options on your stocks to collect extra premiums so you "get paid" while waiting for them to be sold (which we'll discuss in the next chapter), this is the basis of a outperforming investing technique that any investor can use. You can even go on to manage a fund based on these principles. These principles exploit the cycles of pessimism and optimism (irrational exuberance) of the public that undervalue and then overvalue securities. As history shows, you can use that bobbing back and forth between emotional extremes to your advantage.

7
DIVIDENDS OR OPTIONS

This fifth and final section on growing your wealth is not just about another system for managing your investment portfolio. It focuses on what you should *avoid doing* and avoid focusing on in order to get a greater return on your money. It entails how you can increase your portfolio returns by using either dividends or options to supplement your portfolio's income, but you must do this in the right way. In this chapter we will offer specifics and also generalities because learning how to buy and sell options safely for consistent income is a topic that requires a larger discussion than can be covered in this one chapter. If you learn *what not to do with options*, however, you will save yourself tremendous sums over the long run, and those lessons can be easily communicated.

While people often make arguments that you should not focus on market timing, market climate, trend measurements or index funds to grow your wealth over the long run, we have seen proof positive through real life track records *and* historical testing records that this just isn't true. Market timing methods play a definite role in investment management. Many ordinary people eschew all these methods because they think the road to investment profits is to become a strict buy and hold investor who ignores market volatility and invests in solid stocks *that pay high dividends*, but these dividend investment funds have never performed as well as most of the techniques we have covered. This is due to their construction. There are many reasons why you might think that traditional dividend investing is the best way to grow your wealth, so we shall first reveal some of the common errors surrounding this approach so that you can avoid these errors and grow your wealth as safely and as quickly as possible.

Individuals often cite statistics showing that reinvested dividends are the true source of most stock returns over the long run, or account for a large majority of those returns. This is absolutely true. Then they argue that dividend investing must therefore be the sure way to build a "legacy IRA" which accumulates so much wealth that excess monies can eventually be passed onto your children who can continue that style of investing and grow the legacy to even greater heights. While my purpose has always been to give you some foundational methods that might help you accomplish this goal of generational wealth if you have enough compounding time, dividend investing has never been proven to be the way anyone can accomplish this objective.

To be sure, dividends account for an incredibly large portion of the stock market's total return over time. Professor Jeremy Siegel (author of *Stocks for the Long Run*) has even published historical evidence that high dividend yielding stocks, when the dividends are reinvested, accumulate more total return than growth stocks or index mutual funds. The proportion of total returns contributed by dividends will change depending upon the date from which you start your analysis, but he found that roughly three-quarters of the real return from the stock market came from dividends while only one-quarter came from capital gains. Unfortunately, his calculations did not account for the negative effect of taxes on dividends, which would make the returns lower, but this negative could be easily counteracted today simply by buying dividend stocks in a tax shielded vehicle like a trust, IRA or 401(K). Tax avoidance is a crucial key to most forms of wealth accumulation, and you certainly want to be putting all these investing methods to work managing portfolios that are tax protected inside IRAs, 401(K) plans, trusts and other sheltered vehicles.

While you can certainly point to various academic studies which show the superiority of dividend investing over the long run, when reality faces theory you cannot find any dividend fund managers, or anyone especially devoted to dividend stock investing, who has produced superior long run returns from any basic version of this technique. No fund manager has *come up with a systematic method, or systematized way, to do dividend investing and used it over the long term to consistently beat the market in a way you can easily duplicate.* The implication for private investors is that to grow wealthy through investing you should not wed yourself to the typical ideas bandied about for buying dividend stocks, namely to only select from the companies which have steadily increased their dividends for several years or more. There might be some way to do dividend investing that outperforms the market, *but not according to the approaches we typically see used in dividend investing.*

Where the rubber hits the road, we have found academic studies but not fund managers who have consistently beaten the market using some type of dividend investing. On the other hand, momentum (relative strength) and certainly value-based fund managers have solid, proven track records of outperformance. You can find fund managers who have done well selecting large cap stocks, most of which paid dividends, but hardly anyone with an outstanding track record who had specifically set out to maximize dividend income. I have only discovered one tested solution where an investment researcher and fund manager, James O'Shaughnessy, found a system that selects large cap stocks that pay high dividends, but we cannot say that the method is specifically aimed at maximizing dividend income even though it tends to do so. Nevertheless it does capture much of what we are looking for, so we will cover it in this chapter.

Dividend stock investing will offer much greater potential if someone can come up with a systematized technique which maximizes your dividend income while having great selling rules for the underlying securities to protect them from loss. However, in terms of absolute returns, nearly every dividend investing system I have ever seen underperforms the best systematic investing methodologies we have mentioned. We have mutual funds like WisdomTree's Large Cap Dividend ETF (DLN) or Vanguard's VIG fund that requires stocks to have increased their dividends for ten consecutive years, among other criteria, before they are included in the fund. This is the sort of typical criteria (continually increasing dividends) which people use to select dividend stocks. However, funds built this way simply don't have the great track records of value-based investors like Buffet, Graham, or Schloss *and* they cannot match the outperforming track records of various momentum investing approaches.

I am not entirely negative on dividend investing strategies because I am always seeking high yield investments myself, especially on resource stocks that are primarily assets (mirroring Schloss's value investing approach). The point is that if you want higher absolute returns on your investment funds then the logic says to use the best systematic investing methods with proven track records. These options don't normally include dividend funds. Since you want to use superior investing methods to outperform the market over long periods of time, and you can always cash out a portion of an outperforming portfolio, you don't need to search for that exceptional return by requiring dividends on your stocks.

You can indeed "produce a higher return per unit of market risk" through dividend investing, but what you actually want are *higher absolute portfolio returns* that beat the market, otherwise why go to all the extra effort of using some specialized investing technique? Unfortunately, no dividend strategist has been able to produce a track record like the value investors who have consistently achieved as much as 20% annual returns from portfolios that are actually safer than the market. Momentum (relative strength) investing typically produces better returns, too. There are various reasons for this and if those problems can be solved then some form of dividend investing may morph into one of the best portfolio strategies of all time, and so far O'Shaughnessy's method comes closest to providing this basis.

Everyone likes the idea of a portfolio throwing off regular cash through dividends or any other means possible, which is the emphasis of this chapter. As stated, one of my personal preferences is for high yield investing strategies that work for resource stocks (timber, coal, uranium, fertilizer, mining shares, oil and gas royalty trusts, master limited partnerships, Canadian income trusts, etc.) since these asset plays tend to go up in value in addition to throwing off cash. I believe that the next decade or more will belong to the resource, asset and inflation investor because the demand for resources is going up, their supplies are dwindling, and the central banks of the world are trying to flood all their economies with inflation. This will help push prices up over the long run. In the meantime, all of us are still looking for some version of a basic dividend stock investing system *now* that has excellent stock selection rules, lower risks than the market, and incorporates scientific selling rules that rotate you out of stocks when appropriate so that you will prevent losses and maximize your returns.

It is an extremely compelling idea that you can build your retirement funds and possibly a "legacy IRA" by purchasing strong stocks that pay dependable and growing dividends. This is everyone's dream, which is to identify stocks with both appreciation potential and dependable growing dividends, buy them at attractive prices, and then reinvest those cash dividends for even greater returns. If you could find a way to do this, you would surely create a "compounding machine" that would produce both steady income and capital appreciation over the long-term. Warren Buffett tries to do this but he goes about it in a different way than by chasing dividends. He pursues cash flows. He tries to buy cash flow revenue streams that let him further accumulate yet more cash flow acquisitions and their potential capital gains.

If we use Buffett's returns as our target objective, no one has come even close to getting near his rates of return through dividend investing. While I do think it is possible to come up with a variety of better screening criteria for dividend stocks that pay impressive yields and which will also go up in price, so far the track records along this line cannot match the *many* exceptional track records of value investors. This failure is probably due to the fact that you must focus on three things rather than one—both dividends *and* value *and* exit rules (to protect the capital or liquidate at a profit). Most dividend strategists primarily focus on just the dividend streams while value becomes the secondary consideration, and protective exit rules or profitable selling rules are left unclear but determined on an ad hoc basis.

A *logical, enforced selling rule* is one of the pivotal rules for success that we saw in both value and momentum investing. When people buy a dividend stock, however, their first thought is that they will hold it for a long time, so selling rules don't normally even enter their mind. After all, they are buying the stock at this price for its dividend and yield. They plan to keep it. They selected what they believed was a "safe" stock whose dividend was high and had been steadily increasing, so they don't normally think of selling if prices drop because they believed in the stock from the start and had already locked in a great yield. As you know, that refusal to sell opens you up to the risks of severe loss which is the weakness of overly focusing on dividends rather than capital. Thus, you must have selling rules to prevent a situation where a dividend stock goes belly up.

Bethlehem Steel, for instance, produced steady dividends you could reinvest for years, and then the company went bankrupt. At what point would you have gotten out? Would it depend on whether the company cut its dividend by a certain amount, or whether the price of the stock fell, and if so by how much? Various selling rules seem to go against the very premise (primary assumptions) of dividend investing in the first place, but they are necessary if it is to outperform. Most investors who get into dividend investing usually end up suffering severe capital loss during bear markets, but don't know what to do about the situation since they lack these tested rules.

WARREN BUFFETT'S ACTUAL
INVESTMENT METHODOLOGY

Dividend investing is such a seductive idea because it makes great sense to periodically collect cash like interest, and then continually reinvest that cash for greater returns. In the Graham and Schloss value investing methods we covered, you must periodically sell your stocks and then reinvest the funds in new opportunities to achieve the compounding results we are after. You are already buying those stocks at low prices, so are not particularly worried about selling rules other than Graham's two year holding period limit. A critical key to the success of these techniques is also the fact that you are forced to sell your stocks when they appreciate, and then try to repeat the process all over again. This is the basis of their success at compounding returns.

Some people understand that this principle of compounding is how Warren Buffett actually accumulated his great wealth. After you spend a lot of time analyzing Buffett's investments in detail, you will find that Warren Buffett's real investing system involves many strategies (rather than one) that buy companies for their revenues so he can hyper-compound that money by reinvesting it over and over again. Buffett tries to buy businesses for a discount that spin off good cash flow, and then uses that cash to buy other cash flow businesses when they are also at a discount. In this way, he keeps using his increasing stores of cash to buy other great businesses that spin off further revenues, and thus the value of his overall holdings increases over the long run. That's his secret ... buying cash flow (as compared to dividends) at a discount that he can further compound by doing the same thing over and over again.

In other words, Buffett finds great businesses that throw off consistent and growing cash flows, and which have competitive advantages or "moats" that help protect those cash flows and the value of those underlying businesses from degrading. He likes companies that offer products that never go obsolete, which have little competition, and that people always want to buy so that the sales, and thus cash flows and earnings, will be protected and grow over the long haul. For instance, the Burlington Northern Sante Fe railroad is one of his newest purchases whose (semi-monopolistic) revenues will most likely continue to grow for decades as America's West coast trade with Asia increases. Buffett doesn't buy tech stocks because he sticks with what he knows and understands, and he has no way of knowing if the products (and thus profits and cash flows) of a high tech company will quickly become obsolete since the field changes so fast. Instead he prefers stable, solid, predictable cash flows and earnings that are sure to grow over the long run but with little risk that his asset will depreciate in value. This is a businessman's style of thinking, which is to prefer security over speculation.

Buffett has a first year hurdle rate of a 15% return that he is always trying to make on his capital from day one with any new investment. He insists that when buying any new stock or business that he must get that first year return! The price he pays for the investment has to be such that he is sure he will definitely get his 15% targeted return by the end of his first year. In other words, he won't buy a stock unless he is absolutely positive that he will get a 15% return on his capital in the very first year of his investment. If the investment looks like it will make less, he just doesn't buy it.

This is a very simple target that he is after, and there is nothing fancy about his analysis. He doesn't use any complicated discount cash flow models to value businesses. He doesn't use complicated spreadsheets or forecasts. One of his biographers said he is like a horse handicapper who isolates the one or two factors that determine the success of a business, and then makes his decisions by relying solely on the company's historical figures—without any projections or models of the business—to see if he can get his return. He just wants to make sure, from day one, that he will get that 15% return *with a big margin of safety*, and then he wants that investment to grow from there.

Any business he buys also has to be "excellent" from the start, rather than just "good," and that's why he doesn't worry about selling rules that dividend stock investors must worry about. If the business is seen as having any type of catastrophic risk, he doesn't even consider it as an investment. He just says "pass." Once he decides a possible investment has catastrophic risk, he's very realistic and never tries to talk himself out of the "no" decision. He just walks away. By asking the catastrophic risk question first, he saves himself a lot of time and energy because then he doesn't even have to do any other analysis work once he says "no." If there is the potential for catastrophic loss of his capital, he doesn't even try to determine if he can make 15% in his first year of owning that stock.

This is a totally different attitude than that mindset of the typical buy and hold investor and another example of how his mental perspective sets him apart. Even Sir John Templeton, founder of the Templeton Funds, explained from his many decades in the business that it usually took five years for a stock investment to work out because of how he selected them, but Buffett would never get into those types of stocks. Templeton said that during the first year there was a 50:50 chance that the investment would be losing money. By the second and third year of the holding period, it should move into the black and the fourth and fifth years were the time when you should expect that the real profits would be earned. That's a totally different expectation than the one used by Warren Buffett who looks for an immediate 15% return in his first year and growth thereafter as well.

Buffett only buys businesses at discounts or "fair" prices that can give him the return he wants, and after buying these businesses, he lets the cash they throw off accumulate so that he can buy yet more undervalued assets that also have reliable growing cash flows. As stated, he is therefore *more of a businessman rather than an fund manager*, and it just so happens that you can buy his holding company as a stock. He is not like most investment fund managers who buy stocks hoping to later sell them at higher prices, but buys entire businesses that will spin off cash (and also increase in value), and he uses the cash from his many other businesses to acquire them. If he does buy a stock knowing that he will just hold it for a temporary period (rather than buy an entire business with the intent of owning it forever), it is usually because he estimates that the earnings growth is currently selling at a discount and he can buy cash flow and price appreciation at a bargain. He bets that the market will eventually recognize the true value in the future so that he can later liquidate his investment at a premium over his purchase price. Once again he tries to buy assets or cash flows at a discount, and then waits for a mean reversion where the market eventually recognizes a higher value to his holdings. In the meantime, he wants to collect money from that investment while he waits for the market to recognize his determination.

In short, while he says that the perfect holding period of a stock is forever, he is not a buy and hold investor but rather, a businessman who uses every dollar of free money he can get to buy more cash flow and earnings through any sound strategy that makes this possible. He wants to hold investments as long as they will continue to throw off cash and increase in value. This is why his returns are so consistent and high over the long run. Everyone else is out there trying to pick stocks, but Buffett is out there *trying to buy complete cash machines, namely entire companies with earnings and cash flow that will spin off yet more cash, which he then can use to buy more companies that spin off more cash ad infinitum* .... If he buys the entire company then his optimal holding period is forever, but if he only buys a portion then he is just like every other investor and only wants to buy it as long as some subset of the cash flow, earnings, dividends and value are increasing.

In terms of cash flow, by owning entire insurance companies like GEICO he also gets access to their "float" and uses that free money to buy more companies. Float is the money insurance companies collect in insurance premiums that they have available for investment before claims come due, which is usually in two to five years time, and Buffett uses his access to that capital to buy other investments. Buffett is always trying to *buy free money* in any reasonable way possible, which he can then use to compound his investment growth. This is the basic idea behind his many different strategies.

With insurance holdings and other companies, Berkshire Hathaway (the conglomerate holding company managed by Warren Buffett) generates enough cash that it becomes a bank for the businesses he owns, and one of the first things he tells his acquisitions is that they should fire their banker because he is now their banker. When you have a company that has a lot of equity and is sitting on a big pile of cash that it likes to compound, it's actually a bank masquerading as a business! This is the real secret behind Buffett's success rather than the fact that he is a "value" or "growth" investor. He buys cash flow and uses that cash flow to buy more cash flow, but of course he only buys assets and their revenue streams at a discount or at fair value and only if those underlying assets will safely grow in value. That's why he doesn't worry about market fluctuations.

If you truly understand this, it should produce a radical transformation in your understanding of long term investing. Buffett buys cash flow that he reinvests in more value and cash flow, and thus his overall portfolio grows in value. He is not a gambler buying stocks he hopes will go up, but a businessman buying cash flow and value. Most people buy dividend stocks with ideas related to Buffett's perspective, but because they select stocks in the wrong way they cannot achieve his returns. Furthermore, when most people think of investing they imagine that they will buy the next highflying

Apple, Walmart, or Microsoft stock and that the super stock will skyrocket in price shooting to the heavens. Therefore they are always chasing after the next Wall Street darling whereas Buffett never pursues this. The common investor's dream is the equivalent of playing lottery tickets, or hoping to win the big jackpot in a casino. Yet except for the track records of a few CANSLIM investors who have done well during raging bull markets, few of the investment managers who have achieved fantastic long term track records have done so by finding the "super stock market winners" that most people dream about. Think about that! No one has made the big money this way even though this is what is commonly touted on television and in financial publications. Check Warren Buffett's track record, for instance, and you won't find any highflyers at all. You'll only find just good solid stocks, which are often valuable assets with near monopolistic returns, and which have little chance of economic collapse.

Most of the superstar investors, including Buffett, have all been businessmen executing strategies similar to what mega-rich oil baron J. Paul Getty recommended. His advice was to consistently buy good businesses (or assets) at cheap prices, and then wait for those discount prices to either return to normal or overshoot to some degree of optimistic, exuberant overvaluation. You buy an asset for less than it is worth, and then you wait for a mean reversion that will return its price to fair value or some degree of irrational exuberance. Then you liquidate your investment at a hefty profit that was achieved very safely. Whenever you see value, you go in and suck it up. Graham's method, for instance, has you buying good assets at a discount, and when you make a 50% profit on the stocks in less than two years time, you automatically liquidate your shares. It doesn't matter what happens after that. You are not trying to hold your stocks for 200%, 300% or 700% gains. You're like a pawn shop owner who buys an asset for cheap and doesn't want to hold it forever but immediately sells it when any customer comes in who will buy it at a large enough premium that has earned you a sufficient profit ... and you do this over and over again! I call this, "Wash, rinse, and repeat." Walter Schloss also mentioned that he couldn't care less if a stock continued to double, triple or even quadruple after he sold it. This should be your attitude as well.

Even CANSLIM has rules telling you to liquidate some shares at a 20-25% profit point, so the idea of selling at a decent profit, and then reinvesting your money in fresh stock, is one of the "secrets" to long term *systematic* trading success. In commodities trading, this idea of enforced selling after a price run-up, and then reinvesting your monies in a rebalanced portfolio, is also one of the necessary keys to risk control and profitable success. When you simply follow time-tested rules that tell you when to get in or out of a stock or market, following such rules in a disciplined fashion removes your emotions from the investment process and that's part of the necessary formula for success, too. As an example, the most successful real estate investors never fall in love with a property, but unemotionally look at each property in terms of the numbers—the cash flow and profitability figures—in order to mercilessly determine what and when to buy or sell. In the end it all comes down to the numbers rather than the love for any specific property. It's a numbers game.

In Buffett's case, when you buy an entire business you get to keep all the earnings it spins off, whereas if you are just a partial owner who buys stock shares, you only have access to what they pay you via cash dividends or distributions while also sharing in the appreciation of stock value. By keeping all the earnings for a company you own outright, you can keep reinvesting the profits in other projects and continue compounding your results. Since you can use actual cash in hand any way you like when it becomes yours, the most profitable way to use it is to buy other steady cash flows (if you are not likely to lose the money you invest and you can buy those cash streams at a discount) and then you can continually compound your funds in this manner.

If we take See's Candy as an example, we will find that Buffett bought the company for $25 million and *it's paid him around $1.3 billion in revenues since then*. It threw off that much cash over time and yet was an extremely modest investment. Buffett doesn't normally buy stocks with the idea to flip them at higher prices, but typically wants to get access to their revenue generating capabilities. This is his radical difference. As of this writing, Berkshire Hathaway has nearly 50 companies spinning off cash for Buffett, and this number does not include all the companies that have been acquired and rolled into each of those individual operating units.

When people ask how Warren Buffett made his money, you can now tell them it was by *buying cash flows for discounted sums, and using that money to buy additional growing cash flows at discounts when he could find them*. Of course he also wanted the net worth of the companies to increase in value, too, but he was buying valuable businesses at a discount because they gave off cash flows and he could use those revenues to buy more valuable businesses, which is just like reinvesting dividends in more dividend producing stocks. He has used other investment techniques, too, and part of his success has been due to using many methodologies rather than being wed to just one particular value investing method, but that's the main idea in a nutshell. He has always been very risk averse and will never buy a firm that has catastrophic risk where he can lose his principal. He also never tries to talk himself out of a "don't buy" decision after he see it involves potential catastrophic risk. He basically goes after bargain stocks that can increase in value without ever suffering the chance of severe decline (bankruptcy), and which are also like high yielding CDs where the interest rate will increase over time. They aren't highflyers but just good, solid companies.

Buffett always measures the value of a company by its historical ability to generate earnings and revenues over the years, and like Schloss *doesn't depend on forecasting.* For acquisitions he targets successful businesses that have competitive moats, excellent economics, excellent management, and don't require a lot of reinvestment. This way he is sure to keep getting his returns, doesn't have to use a lot of money for reinvestment, and rests secure that his asset will likely retain its value even during bad times. In addition to the steady or growing earnings requirement, he also expects to see an increasing value over time which he can buy right now at a reasonable price or discount. He never advocates the idea of blind dollar cost averaging because it involves buying stocks regardless of how overvalued the market might be, which is an idea he doesn't subscribe to.

If you can buy the increasing revenues of Coca Cola, Gillette or Wrigley when their stock prices fall to a discount and their situations still promise continued high earnings, and when you can do this over and over again with reinvested sums, you have a strong formula for success. If you do this over enough time, the value of your holdings will certainly grow immensely. It's just a natural result of the law of compounding through reinvesting. While Buffett has seen his money grow over 45 years at a CAGR greater than 20% because of reinvestment, the problem with dividend funds that try to do the same thing is that the monies are reinvested in stocks at full value rather than selling at a discount, the stocks aren't necessarily the highest quality companies, and you cannot actually count on the dividend streams always continuing if you don't look at the underlying quality of the companies as Buffett does. John D. Rockefeller is noted for saying, "The only thing that gives me pleasure is to see my dividend coming in," and the risk for dividend investors is just that—that the company might one day cut the dividend, which then often crashes the price of such stocks. Buffett invests for cash flow knowing that underlying value will also increase if cash flow (earnings) does, so he tries to rules out this potential from the start by only buying excellent businesses.

High dividend stocks are typically not the companies which have the quality "moat" protections required by Buffett that would help insure the continuation of their revenue streams and dividends, as well as help maintain the underlying value of the companies as investments. They do not necessarily offer a potential for much higher capital gains either. Additionally, most dividend funds do not have any specific selling rules that help protect against value losses as well. These are just some of the many reasons why dividend funds have worse track records than those from value investing.

If you could continue to always purchase safe, growing dividend streams from undervalued "moat" stocks that also went up in price, and you had a disciplined mechanism for selling them when they became overvalued or fell in value, then you might be able to duplicate Buffett-like returns. However, most of dividend investing strategies concentrate more on selecting dependable, growing dividend streams for purchase than they focus on other criteria such as company valuations and possible selling rules for those investments. Selling is typically handled on an ad hoc case-by-case basis. Thus, few managers have specific selling criteria such as those exactly specified by Graham or CANSLIM. Capturing yield is important, but defending capital with appropriate selling rules is as important as well!

Since dividend stocks aren't always purchased when they are undervalued in price, a real killer to performance is buying dividend stocks that are too costly and which then often drop 30%, 40%, 50% or more during market corrections, or when the board of directors suddenly votes to suspend the dividends. Such companies usually cannot maintain their value because they were not companies having a competitive advantage "moat" from the start. Vetting companies by Buffett's "moat" strategy would help guarantee both the sustainability of the dividend stream and appreciation potential for stocks, which is why some funds now do this, but then you are usually sacrificing the large dividends you want for value and you don't know which of these two criteria will maximize your returns. You can certainly try to buy these stocks at a discount using seasonal analysis to purchase shares near seasonal lows, which is a revolutionary technique for dividend investors who have never seen the idea. You can also purchase shares after a market collapse temporarily pushes prices down before mean reversion returns prices to normal, but then you might as well buy value stocks at that time since the value strategy has a superior proven track record!

Nevertheless, we still have people who are set on buying high paying dividend stocks where there has been an unbroken stream of increasing dividends for many years. Thus we have the S&P list of "Dividend Aristocrats" and the Mergent list of "Dividend Achievers" which have increased their regular cash dividends annually for the past ten or more consecutive years. There is no guarantee that these companies will not cut their dividends in the future, and so to parallel Buffett's or Graham's tactics, a dividend investor would want to buy these companies at a discount if they satisfy certain value criteria. *Adaptive and factor seasonal charts might also scientifically help you with this goal,* but if you learn to *write covered calls against your positions,* you can also increase the cash you generate from these stocks through yet another way to help your portfolios return far more than from the dividend cash return alone. This can help cushion against any capital losses during market declines you already have several timing or climate models that tell you when writing call options is most favorable because the market usually goes down.

Investing in companies that will not only consistently pay high dividends but increase them over time sounds like a winning strategy, but which mutual fund has done this to consistently beat the market over the long term? The problem is determining the right stocks that also offer capital appreciation, but that's the problem with all stock selection methods! No one escapes this dilemma, so why would you apply so much effort to an investment methodology that has inferior returns as compared against methods proven to have much higher and consistent returns? Now you've made your job harder by adding the extra criteria that you want increasing dividends from those investments as well. Here you must determine whether a stock is safe and will grow (rather than fall in price), whether the dividend is safe and will grow, you're also seeking a high current dividend yield, and you are going by the seat of your pants for the most profitable selling rules.

Once again, all I can say is that if you are fixated on dividends because they provide you with personal income, remember that you don't need dividends to live off your investments. You just need profits! You can always liquidate a portion of your investments and use that for cash. Until a fund manager comes up with something better, the records clearly show that you can more safely secure investment profits through the capital gains achieved by value investing rather than by chasing after dividend stocks. If you want to get rich through investing, you should not overly focus on dividend stocks, at least not in the way most people pursue them! If you are looking for much higher returns than the market, disciplined relative strength investing and value-based investing strategies are certainly better options because of the superior track records.

Dividend investing, as normally done by the public, is therefore not in my set of top choices for a safe road to riches, even if you can find the best buying opportunities by scanning for seasonal lows. A recent study by James O'Shaughnessy even showed that you could outperform the market by purchasing stocks based on many value criteria other than the dividend yield and do much better. Selecting stocks based solely on their dividend yields ranked at the bottom of his list for the best value-based selection criteria that might deliver investment outperformance. He did come up with a dividend related investment strategy that returned approximately 15% per year, and this tested strategy, with its well defined rules, is the only one I would consider as a dividend investor.

THE JAMES O'SHAUGHNESSY VALUATION MODEL

Who is James O'Shaughnessy? James O'Shaughnessy is rather famous in the field of quantitative investing because of all the research he has published. His initial path breaking book, *What Works on Wall Street: A Guide to the Best-Performing Investment Strategies of All Time*, included backtested results for how well competing stock-picking approaches have worked over the four decades from 1951 through 1994. In every new edition of this book, he has reported on new research results that continually update his recommendation of the best investing techniques to use for superior investing performance. According to the fourth edition of *What Works on Wall Street*, a new "Trending Value" stock selection strategy he discovered has outperformed the market with an annual compound growth rate of

21.2% over the 46 years period between 1964 and 2009!

This latest model uses an aggregate composite of valuation measures—six of them in fact—rather than the single P/E ratio most often used to value stocks. It combines the price-to-book value ratio, price-to-sales ratio, price to free cash flow ratio, P/E price-to-earnings ratio, earnings, and shareholder yields into a single composite number. As he explains, "Each stock in the universe gets a score of 1 to 100 for each of these factors. The final value score is an average of these scores. The Trending Value portfolio narrows the investable universe to the 10% of stocks with the best score based on the value composite, and then selects a concentrated portfolio of 25 stocks based on trailing six-month momentum."

In other words, the winning investment strategy that returns over 20% per year ranks all known stocks by percentile for each of six separate valuation measurements. The stocks having the worst of a particular valuation metric got assigned a value of 1 for that metric, and those with the best value got a score of 100. For example, stocks with low P/E ratios are considered cheap and represent a good investment opportunity. Hence, if a stock has a P/E ratio that is in the lowest 1% of the investable stock universe, which is good, it gets a P/E value rank of 100. This type of rating scheme is similar to the SAT test score reports for high schoolers which would tell you that you scored better than X% of the population.

To rate a stock, you perform this type of ranking for each of the six individual valuation factors and then add up all six valuation ranks, divide by six, and arrive at a single value composite rank. The stocks in the top 10% band (the top decile) of this composite value rating have historically averaged a compound annual return of 17.3% over time. Wow, that's impressive if it's the CAGR over several decades! So you use six different valuation rankings to come up with one single value metric, and once you have a single composite rank for each stock, you are only going to consider investing in the top 10% of all valuations. You are only going to invest in stocks which belong to the top decile (10% tier) of the composite value rankings. These are the stocks likely to outperform the market because of their value as measured by some average score of different types of valuation metrics.

How do you then choose which ones to buy? Now we come back full circle to our secretive European money manager's rule, which in its own way combined fundamentals with relative strength (technical analysis) to get some idea of trend strength. What we do next is also reminiscent of John Hussman's approach that combined relative strength investing with valuation metrics. The answer is that you also sort the top 10% of stocks, as scored by the single composite value ranking, using their six-month relative strength ranking! The top tier stocks are the only stocks you are going to consider buying, so you then sort them by their relative strength. Then you buy the 25 stocks with the highest six-month relative price strength for your portfolio.

By adding this one extra rule, O'Shaughnessy's portfolios achieved an annual compound growth rate of 21.2% instead of just 17.3%. O'Shaughnessy's methodology borrowed a principle from Hussman's market climate model in that it does not just get you into stocks based on a composite valuation figure, but produces about 4% more per year *because it adds a trend strength measurement* (relative strength rule) to the selection criteria. When Tom Hancock studied the long term track record of momentum investing from 1927-2009, he also found that relative strength investing outperformed a broad universe of stocks by this same bonus of 4% per year. It appears that adding that type of rule correctly, if it's appropriate, seems to give you about a 4% extra boost to your portfolio return on a yearly basis. Because the relative strength rule was also used by our secretive European money manager, I believe you can start to see how all of the superior investment systems often share some similar methods with each other, and these common rules become part of the reason why they end up outperforming everything else.

While my own Wall Street experience predisposes me to prefer logical, tested strategies like this method that have been proven over the long run, I am always wary of complicated multi-factor models because of the high possibility of over-fitting past data. When a model has too many dimensions or calculations, you should always become suspicious. Even O'Shaughnessy noted this because he said, "If the math gets higher than algebra, it's pretty certain you will lose your money." Like Graham or Schloss, I prefer a basic simplicity that is fundamentally sound, has few dimensions subject to tweaking, and which has worked well over many decades. I like simple methodologies I can teach a high school or college student who can then use them for decades and then retire very well off. On the other hand, when you start constructing complicated models you have to beware of a common data mining fault where you keep adding condition upon condition until you find something that seems to work, but not in real time conditions.

In other words, when you combine many conditions together to finally find a subset of characteristics that outperforms everything else, that elaborate subset of conditions rarely produces the anticipated high returns into the future. Graham's rules and philosophy, which are so simple, help protect against this potential fault of over-complication.

All this having been said, O'Shaughnessy's premise is still basically sound because all sorts of different combinations of valuation measures boiled down into one metric worked at building outstanding portfolios. The historically tested results for many different combo metrics worked so well that you can more than likely also use this one with safety. The real problem with O'Shaughnessy's multi-factor valuation model lies in the fact that you might not be able to do it in real time on your own. None of the individual stock screeners commonly available to the public have the capability of running all the screens demanded by his complex criteria, so the only way to independently find these stocks is by subscribing to different databases and using a lot of computer power to collate and combine all the results together. O'Shaughnessy used Compustat PC Plus, Research Insight and the FactSet Alpha testing application to screen and test his various stock strategies. Alternatively, you can sign up with O'Shaughnessy Asset Management (Stamford, CT) to get access to the results of this approach. At least with the simple Graham investment system, which performs extremely well with less complexity, you can readily find the data using Google Finance and its free stock screener and do everything on your own without much trouble.

The reason that this new *What Works on Wall Street* strategy was brought up within our dividend discussion was not because I wanted you to have another value investing methodology, but because it once again emphasizes the fact that many other strategies are superior to the public's fondness for buying dividend stocks rather than using better strategies that have been proven to grow your wealth greater with more safety and certainty. Shortly we will examine what I call O'Shaughnessy's "dividend strategy" which invests in large cap stocks that all pay good dividends. It is a value strategy which requires that a stock pays high dividends, but represents a far better approach than simply picking stocks because they have had steadily increasing dividends for several years or currently offer a high dividend yield, which are the basic core to most "dividend investing" strategies. The best returns actually come from picking stocks using systems that prioritize other factors *ahead of dividends*, and then taking dividends into account secondarily. Throughout my lifetime I have seen that most investors make the mistake of doing this the other way around and then don't get anywhere near the performance that they wanted which will help them grow sufficient funds for retirement. This is why I keep emphasizing that they should use a better way.

In the past, O'Shaughnessy reported discovering that the price/sales ratio (PSR) of a stock was the best single predictor of future stock performance, and this ratio eventually became the basis of various stock selection systems. In his most recent version of *What Works on Wall Street*, he ran far more tests and found even better metrics you should use when selecting stocks. When you rank the compound annual growth rates achieved by stock portfolios constructed out of the top deciles of these various value metrics, O'Shaughnessy found their CAGR performance was as follows:

Enterprise Value/EBITDA: 16.58%
Price/Earnings: 16.25%
Price/Operating Cash Flow: 16.25%
Buyback Yield: 15.81%
Shareholder Yield: 15.56%
Price/Book Value: 14.53%
Price/Sales Ratio: 14.49%
Dividend Yield: 13.30%

When we look at the list of preferred metrics you might use to build stock portfolios, along with their historical long term CAGR performances, we can certainly see that selecting stocks with the highest dividend yields was definitely a way to outperform the market return, but this was the worst of the *simplest best ways* to try to outperform all the superior methods he tested. Other researchers (Barry Ritholtz and Jeremy Schwartz) have also confirmed that buying the highest quintile of dividend players outperformed the overall S&P500 index by more than 2.5% per year since 1957, and this was just by blindly buying the highest yielding dividend stocks. The strategy is up there, but the returns are still volatile and surpassed by other techniques. Nevertheless, the results show that there is definite potential with this technique, which is why the idea of dividend investing is so enticing to many individuals.

Incidentally, it is interesting to note from this list that the EV/EBITDA ratio was O'Shaughnessy's newest best single metric for selecting outperforming sock portfolios. This ratio measures the value of a business and is often used as an alternative to the P/E ratio. In fact, it is the primary valuation tool used by investment banks and private equity firms when they are selecting takeover candidates! O'Shaughnessy basically discovered that investing in companies having the metric which buyout firms typically use to rate takeover candidates ended up producing his best performing portfolios. Since the simplified but *outperforming* Graham and Schloss criteria also picked out many takeover candidates, and since Mr. Outperformance himself, Warren Buffett, can also be considered a takeover investor since he buys entire companies, this insight should lead someone to creating a stock selection system, using all sorts of value criteria, that basically picks out the most likely takeover candidates.

Remember that none of this says that dividends are not important. We just saw that they are, and they are part of stock picking methodologies that definitely outperform the market. This entire discussion is geared around correcting the common public error in picking stocks only according to consistently rising dividends, or just consistent dividends, or just high dividend yields. Most all versions of these basic but popular dividend approaches will put you at a disadvantage. O'Shaughnessy's results also lead to the conclusion that many other simplistic investing methodologies (based on different metrics) create portfolios that do far better than investing according to dividend yields alone, so why not use those instead when the difference was as much as 3% per year and they were also better protectors of your capital?

THE RULES:

Thus, finally we can turn to O'Shaughnessy's "Cornerstone Value Approach" which I classify as a more proper dividend investing strategy than what most people use even though it is actually presented as a value-based investing system. If you want dividends *and* capital appreciation, this is the sort of strategy you should basically follow. In his research, O'Shaughnessy found that high dividend yields were a great screen for selecting large cap stocks, but not for small cap stocks. He therefore came up with an investing system that selectively chose large cap stocks that also had a high dividend yield. These stocks are *not* the highest dividend yielding stocks. In fact, O'Shaughnessy found that simply buying the stocks with the highest dividend yield *often meant you were buying companies in trouble* who then did poorly in terms of price performance. If you instead first looked for "quality" stocks as determined by various quality criteria (which therefore addresses Buffett's concern to avoid catastrophic risk), and then afterwards sorted them by their dividend yields, and if you then purchased the top 50 stocks from this group with the highest yields only *after* they had passed these various quality criteria, you then had a winning dividend investing formula. With this type of stock selection process, dividends are required but their priority comes second, not first. That is why you can come up with a winning dividend stock formula!

The "Cornerstone Value Approach" restricts your investments to large cap stocks which are presumably quality issues, or "market leaders," by virtue of the fact that they have grown to the size of being large cap issues. To be quantitatively identified as a "market leader," the strategy requires that a company has a market cap greater than $1 billion, has more shares outstanding than the market average, and 12-month trailing sales must be greater than 1.5 times the market average. These are all statistics which just insure that a company is generally *bigger and better than average*, and these stocks are usually less volatile than the broader market. Many are the quality type of institutions which Buffett seeks to buy at a discount. Another rule is that the cash flow per share for these companies must also be greater than the market average as well.

If all these conditions are met (and the stock is not a utility company), only then are high dividend yields used to select the final set of large cap stocks to invest in. Usually about 350-400 stocks will satisfy these criteria, most of which will be recognizable names of large companies. When you take the top 50 stocks with the highest dividend yields (excluding utilities) that already satisfy the market cap, shares outstanding, sales and cash flow criteria, this type of selection method produces portfolios with outstanding returns. The large cap issues with high dividend yields usually outperformed other stocks during bull markets, and didn't fall as much during bear markets, too.

According to *What Works on Wall Street*, this strategy had a 15% CAGR from 1954 to 1996 compared to 8.3% for the S&P500 index, thus well outperforming it. Hence this is a great starting basis for even better performing dividend stock investment strategies, which O'Shaughnessy has developed, and the key is that it starts off with a value-based approach rather than an approach that first focuses on the consistency of increasing dividends or just high dividend yields. While the private investor typically selects dividend stocks this way, O'Shaughnessy proved that this "value first" methodology is much better so *this* is how investors should do it.

SELLING OPTIONS FOR EXTRA PORTFOLIO RETURNS

While O'Shaughnessy's value-based dividend investing technique is certainly attractive, the actual idea behind a fifth investment strategy was to find any simple investing methodology that would continually throw off actual cash you could reinvest, like dividends, but without turning to dividend investing. Reinvesting cash is certainly important to long run wealth growth as the rules of compounding have shown, as Buffett's methodology (of seek cash flow and reinvest it) illustrates, and as the long term importance of dividend reinvesting has shown. But other than adding in cash ourselves every year, *which we definitely should do anyway through enforced saving*, how else can our stock portfolios throw off extra cash that we can use for reinvesting?

The only avenue available for generating extra cash on a regular basis from your stocks is by *selling stock options*, such as covered calls, and then reinvesting the option premiums just like you reinvest dividends. If you do this for dividend stocks, then you have yet another additional way to add an extra 1-2% or more to your monthly returns. However, the problem once again lies in protecting your capital from price declines. Since dividend stocks can often fall 30-50% in price during market declines, you need tested selling rules to protect you from the loss of capital during severe bear markets. You must protect yourself from Warren Buffett's issue of "cat risk," which is the possibility of a catastrophic capital loss.

To learn how to sell options (covered calls rather than naked options) in the correct way would require another book in itself, just as does the task of learning to CANSLIM, but you should know that it can add many additional percentage points of return per year to any stock portfolio if you learn how to do it correctly. The major point is that if you are buying stocks because of some investment system, *you should also investigate the various ways you might be able to write covered calls on those stocks, without destroying that working system, to amplify your returns.*

Dealing with options can generate additional monthly returns for your investment portfolio, but it definitely requires training to prevent continual losses. You should normally consider options trading as speculation, rather than investing, when you don't follow any rules and especially when you are a buyer rather than seller. Option buyers tend to always lose money whereas sellers tend to make money, but even the winning sellers are only successful if they are selective about their timing. They must learn to only sell options when the odds are in their favor and never try to force the market into making them money.

To make consistent money at buying options, famed Elliott Wave technician Robert Prechter once warned that it's almost impossible because you must be right with not just one but multiple factors. You must have a correct expectation of the future price level of the stock, and even if you are right you can lose money. You must have a correct idea of the length of time that the move will require, too, so now you have the problem of getting the price direction and timing correct as well. You must time your entry correctly because option prices can swing widely during the day, which is a third criteria. You also must estimate the momentum (volatility) of the move correctly, and additionally should have investor psychology on your side. It is so difficult to get most of these five factors right when buying options that it is no wonder that most people who trade options lose money.

When we look back at the history of the world, we will find country after country, culture after culture, society after society, and religion after religion citing several common ways by which men and women often destroy their lives. Those common destructive activities include drinking, drugs, debt, and most of all *gambling*. The modern equivalents to gambling definitely include options trading and commodity speculation, both of which have caused numerous bankruptcies and broken families for those who get deeply involved. Hence, I rarely recommend that unsophisticated investors buy options.

Even so, the Motley Fool website (Fool.com) reports that many site users trade options and as many as 40% of those options traders do so in retirement accounts, so trading options is—like dividend investing—extremely popular. Nonetheless, once again my warning is firm that most people will lose money buying options, so you should avoid buying puts and calls and stay away from the seductive siren's call that they can bring you riches. As with commodities trading, time and again you will read stories of brokers, who later became fund managers, recalling that they examined the internal records of hundreds of client accounts and found that 95-98% of the options people purchased would expire worthless, and that most options traders also lost money. There is a 95-98% chance of this fate and no escaping from this statistic. *That 95-98% means you!*

I never casually recommend buying options to anyone when they are serious about growing their wealth. The mega-wealthy never get rich through options, so put that dream out of your mind. They are absolutely *not* the path to riches. While it is often wise to buy puts for portfolio insurance, buying options is something that only professionally trained individuals should be involved in, otherwise you will probably lose money over the long run. You always hear stories of one or two people who struck it big by buying options, just as you hear stories about rare lottery winners, but the majority of personal tales include the sentence, "I lost everything." On the other hand, the majority of people who accumulated wealth through investing did so by devoting themselves to some conservative proven investing method over the long term. They just stuck with it, and those super successful systems rarely involved buying options.

Since nearly everyone who buys options or who trades commodities (derivatives or futures contracts) loses money, once again the chances are 95-98% that you would probably be in this large group of losers, despite the great hopes, if you follow these avenues. You should definitely avoid these two activities if you are really serious about wealth accumulation. Most people become involved with them because they seek excitement, but as George Soros said, "If investing is entertaining, if you're having fun, you're probably not making any money. Good investing is boring." Excitement, such as the thrill of possibly making big money, is the real reason why most people turn to options trading and as George Soros said, this explains why few people make money at it. Speculating with options is the wrong strategy to use for the goal of growing wealthy.

There is no short cut to wealth through speculation. The proven road of getting rich *fast* is actually via *slow long term investing*. This requires cultivating a particular type of mindset and perspective that includes avoiding speculation. One of my best friends told me her mega multi-millionaire father, a legend in the financial field in his country, would have her sit on his lap as a child when he read his investment newspaper, and would at those times teach her how to invest. He always told her two hard rules she should never violate: only buy safe assets that would keep their value while having a good chance to increase in price, and *to never ever trade in commodities or options*. That, he said, was the key to becoming rich through investing. If you are serious about growing your wealth, you should also heed this advice and *stay away from buying puts and calls since most of them expire worthless*.

Once again, avoid *buying* puts and calls unless you are an expert devoted to this field, or are doing so for a purpose other than speculation. On the other hand, *selling* puts and calls is another story entirely because if 95-98% of option buyers are losing money, there are ways to turn that statistic around and become a seller who consistently makes money nearly all of the time. What you should learn in order to make more money on your stock strategies is how to scientifically *sell covered call options* in a risk adverse manner to consistently collect option premiums you can then reinvest for hyper-compounding without having your stock called away.

For instance, if you are already invested in some stocks for which you write call options, collecting those premiums will greatly increase your returns. If a stock you hold (in a tax deferred account) is called away because it meets the strike price, why do you care? You had set the option's strike price above the market at some level for which you were comfortable surrendering the stock, and you can always buy it back again if you wish with the only "opportunity cost" being a possible gap in price. Since you must surrender the stock at a price you felt was adequate when you sold the call options, you can then look for a fresh opportunity since the stock met your price criteria. Once again, as the shampoo bottle says you should "Wash, rinse, repeat."

By selling at a gain for which you'd be happy to lose the stock anyway, you're locking in profits as Graham and other system methodologists have recommended. There are a lot of technicalities here, but learning how to write covered options selectively is part of your fifth investment strategy for adding gains to nearly every type of portfolio. Once you learn how to write options that usually expire worthless, you can decide whether doing this can help boost portfolio returns on the stocks that you have already purchased by following some investing system.

Even Warren Buffett, who typically dislikes derivative products, has used the strategy of writing options in order to gain access to that cash for reinvestment. In 2007-2009, Buffett decided to raise $4.9 billion by writing put options that insured buyers against falls in the value of several large global stock indices, including the S&P 500 in the U.S., the FTSE 100 in the U.K., the Euro Stoxx 50 in Europe, and the Nikkei 225 in Japan. Up to that point in time, this was one of the largest deals he had ever made in his life! In the past Buffett has railed against over-the-counter derivatives such as options, describing them as "financial weapons of destruction, carrying dangers that, while now latent, are potentially lethal," so why did he make such a bet?

The basis of this strategy is actually the idea of selling naked LEAP puts against strong stocks, a method popularized by Dennis Eisen in his book, *Using Options to Buy Stocks*. The idea is to sell LEAP puts on strong companies with great long term prospects, strong balance sheets, and where the possibility of incurring a loss was remote. That "free money" could then be reinvested in buying other profitable investments. In effect, the strategy allows you to create cash although, of course, you assume the risk of loss. This entails the risk of being assigned the stock or suffering financial loss because its long term price falls in value.

Upfront Buffett got $4.9 billion in options premiums for his special deal, which was pure cash. His total loss potential loss, or exposure, is $37.1 billion if world markets fall to zero and he has to pay on the puts he wrote. If the trade goes his way and the markets are higher when the puts expire between 2019 and 2028—which he expects since over the long run he felt that stocks tend to rise in line with nominal GDP—all that money he collected (and the money this premium allows him to make in the meantime through investing) will be pure profit. In 2008, Buffett thought the stock market was very attractive because it was priced at 70-80% of GDP, so this gave him what he felt was a good margin of safety for the deal, one of his standard investment requirements. However, a possible problem with his evaluation is that equity returns and GDP growth (and GDP per capita), at least for emerging markets, actually have nothing to do with each other and are unconnected over long periods of time. Whether this basic assumption holds and his forecast holds that the U.S. economy will continue to march forward in a general line upwards (bringing equity prices with it) will determine whether he comes out ahead.

If his put option trade goes underwater, Buffett still has 10-20 years to invest $4.9 billion of money, which has cost him nothing, to bail himself out. If he invests $4.9 billion at a 10% annual return, then Buffett will have $12.7 billion after 10 years or $32.96 billion after 20 years. Of course his average annual gain is near 20%, which means his $4.9 billion could possibly earn between $30.3 billion and $187.9 billion in 10 to 20 years time if he kept up that rate of return. Even if he has to pay up some loss, the amount is limited and he has an excellent chance of earning more than it costs him. This is what he is counting on, and so he basically got a large sum of money for free that he is now using for growth compounding.

This is what Buffett does, which is look for "free cash" or cash flows he can get at a discount, and then reinvest them. In this case, his strategy definitely entails some risk (so it's not really "free" money—that's just a manner of speaking), but he got an immediate large chunk of cash through selling options that he could use however he liked. If you execute this type of strategy at the bottom of a recession and the market then moves upwards from there, your chances of coming out a winner go up tremendously.

Warren Buffett's case is also exceptional because he sold 10-20 year options to special counterparties and he doesn't have to post margin as the trades go against him. Hence, this is not something you or I can possibly duplicate. The best you can usually do is sell naked put LEAPS on individual stocks. This case only illustrates the fact that people can sell naked options for cash, and even the conservative Warren Buffett has done so while calling derivative related products "financial weapons of mass destruction." This was an exceptional situation, and you need to take the time to learn how to buy and sell options safely if you wish to duplicate a similar naked LEAP put strategy like this on your own.

LEARNING OPTIONS ON YOUR OWN

Learning how to write (sell) options correctly, which means selectively, takes study and practice just as does the task of mastering CANSLIM. Many courses teach you how to write covered calls and option spreads, for which you can readily use the change-in-trend (flex point) patterns predicted by seasonal forecasting. If you use the seasonals or other methods to consistently pick better spots for writing call options when that the underlying stock is unlikely to be called away, you can do this over and over again. The major risk is capital loss for holding the stock if it declines, but if you are getting into shares because of some system, presumably that system has rules for buying and selling. Therefore the risk in writing calls is for the stock to be called away. This may cost you some lost profit if the stock moves a lot, which is why you must learn to selectively know when you should use this strategy.

Something even better for those who like the strategy of consistently selling options to collect the cash premiums is the best course I have ever found on writing options as a business, available at the website url **www.MarketTimingResearch.com/optionscourse.html**. As the very famous Federal Express television advertisement used to say, this is "absolutely, positively" the best options course I have ever encountered for teaching you how to write index options *with limited risk* for the goal of consistently making money. When we first saw the materials in this course, my partners and I were dumbfounded and kept asking ourselves, "In all our years of trading, why haven't we encountered this before?" This video training course teaches you strategies for how to consistently write index options *as if it were a business*, manage those positions in any type of market environment (even when the market goes against you), and thus create monthly income streams using options. What's amazing is that it even shows how to adjust losing spread positions so that you can turn losses into profits, which is something I have never seen demonstrated anywhere else. Since the majority of options expire worthless and the majority of people buying options lose money, you are taught how to reverse the equation to become an intelligent seller of limited risk option situations instead. The principles within this course are the type of information I would want to teach my children so that they could master its methodologies rather than just play video games and learn nothing at all. The adaptive (similarity) seasonal forecasting technique increases your odds with this methodology even further.

Learning how to sell options is therefore another investing strategy that helps you earn a consistent return on your stock portfolio, and can actually be applied to most of these other investment techniques to boost their returns. You can even use it together with dividend investing and certainly should if you are keen on that technique. But as with CANSLIM, you should not try to write options if it's not your forte because if systematically selling options doesn't match your personality, you probably won't be successful at it. I would estimate that well over 95% of individuals should stay away from options trading of any type, including these methods just described, because they don't have the personality for it. I firmly believe you will *not* be able to make money using any investing technique that goes against your personality (unless you spend an incredible number of hours learning how to do it) or which requires incredible discipline since this is something most people lack but is necessary for options trading. These are my basic rules for trying to master any type of investment technique, which is why you now have a half dozen or so of the best types available to choose from to become a super investor.

With the idea that you can write options to further supplement your portfolio returns, we have now completed our five basic methods of super investing that will help you grow your wealth through hyper-compounding over long periods of time. Far and away the best means for becoming wealthy is the road of starting your own business, but if you choose the road of investing to help build your wealth, this is the best collection of simple, sound techniques I have found over my investment research career to help you achieve your objectives.

If you are young, I would suggest you get started at this right away because every extra year of compounding that you add to your time horizon adds to your chances of securing a multi-millionaire outcome by retirement. If you have kids, I hope this is the type of book you would give them to acquaint them with various long term investment principles and what they can do through the road of investing, and how to tread it.

As for yourself, it contains the very lessons and techniques that I personally wish someone had introduced to me when I was still in my twenties, and which you can certainly use today to help grow your investment funds at an accelerated pace. I firmly believe you have in your hands the best collection of simple techniques you can easily duplicate on your own for safely growing an investment portfolio as fast as possible.

The fastest way to grow rich is to do so slowly using techniques like this that are consistently applied over the long run, so don't let impatience rule you. Find one or more of these strategies that match your personality, start to master them or turn your funds over to professional managers who already have, and be prudent with your risks. I especially recommend *value investing*, and sincerely urge you to learn and employ some version of it. The mega-rich and wealthy appear to have commonly relied on value investing to grow their wealth more than any other technique.

8
END GAMES AND CONCLUSIONS

In my library there are several hundred books on economics, business, personal finance, investments, and trading. There is practically everything you want to know about picking stocks, creating long term investment models, and creating shorter term trading systems for all sorts of assets and markets. There are countless books on this or that way to make money through investments, but precious few that combine this pursuit with emergency survival strategies that might be called into play over a seventy to ninety year lifespan. Such factors—surviving a war, loss of national independence, political upheaval, food shortages, an economic depression, debt default, massive deflation, hyperinflation, or even the destruction of a fiat currency—will come probably into play at least once during your lifespan.

Anyone who lives a long life will go through countless recessions and economic booms, and possibly deep calamities. For our last "bonus" investing topic, we should discuss a little bit about what to do during chaotic times because "magical thinking" will not then save you. You need to learn how to preserve your wealth during such critical periods, at which time it might even be possible for the astute who are mentally prepared to make a great fortune. Those who survive great turning points do so because they don't panic but act with the conviction of history and therefore follow some basic principles.

Everyone knows of books like *Rich Dad, Poor Dad, The Automatic Millionaire, The Zurich Axioms, Beating the Street, Market Wizards, Multiple Streams of Income, The Millionaire Next Door, The Millionaire Mind,* and other books that mix investing principles with personal finance and lifestyle factors. They will correctly tell you to stop being sloppy with your finances, set aside 10-15% of your income for savings, and contribute monthly to some type of tax deferred wealth accumulation plan such as an IRA. They will tell you to make bi-weekly mortgage payments, make extra principal payments whenever possible, pay down your credit card debt, live within your means, stop wasting money on cigarettes and lattes, invest in no load mutual funds, insure against risk, and capitalize on the power of compounding. However, rarely will you find a discussion on how to safely preserve or grow your wealth through the economic conditions normally experienced during wars and major geopolitical or "end game" financial disasters. These books are primarily concerned with normal day to day situations.

It is unfortunate that we did not also go into an entire class of investment techniques that requires deep strategic analysis for decades long investing—such as Harry Dent style demographics investing methods, macroeconomic growth models, comparative advantage analysis, long term cycles analysis, and long term supply and demand investing. Demographics in terms of birth rates, the population of age groups within a nation, and "peak spending" years for each generation do indeed play a big role in the consumer spending trends within an economy. Population trends help determine real estate prices as well. The ideas of world competitive economics and comparative advantages, such as not investing in countries that produce what China is producing but produce what China needs to buy, can also help guide individuals in macro asset allocation decisions. An investment strategist, in advising wealthy clients for the long term, always tries to identify the bigger macro trends because this is where the mega-wealth is made, but few books successfully teach this type of analysis in a useable fashion. You typically only gain access to that type of analysis by buying into hedge funds which invest according to such strategies.

We also did not go deeply into the rhythms of history explaining in detail how countries become rich and then become destitute in connection with these trends, how the major industries powering long term Kondratieff cycles represent the great investment and wealth opportunities of each generation, and how even cities (such as Detroit) can become prosperous riding boom trends and then go bust if they have not diversified their economic bases by the time the trends end. Nothing stays the same forever, and the long march of history shows how favorable and unfavorable environments often dramatically change for investors. One of the absolute worst things a country can possibly do along these lines is lose its manufacturing and industrial base, and it is unfortunate that the U.S., at the behest of corporations loyal to no one, has spent its past few decades doing just that. When a consumption-based economy, financed by personal debt, loses its major means of wealth production, ruin cannot be avoided because the jobs of the middle class, which support that consumption cycle, are themselves exported away.

Various books such as *Probable Outcomes* (Easterling), *Unexpected Returns* (Easterling), *This Time is Different* (Reinhart and Rogoff), *Bull's Eye Investing* (Mauldin), *Endgame* (Mauldin), *Riding the Millenial Storm* (Vittachi), *Tomorrow's Gold* (Faber), *The Fourth Mega-Market* (Acampora), *The Great Boom Ahead* (Dent), *The Great Crash Ahead* (Dent), *The Fourth Turning* (Strauss), *Boom, Bust and Echo* (Foot and Stoffman), *Stock Cycles* (Alexander), *The Kondratiev Cycle* (Alexander), *Leading Sectors and World Powers* (Modelski and Thompson), *Long Cycles in World Politics* (Modelski), *The Grand Strategy of the Roman Empire* (Luttwak), *Full Spectrum Dominance* (Engdahl), *Resource Wars* (Klare), *Why Countries Fail* (Acemoglu and Robinson), *Currency Wars* (Rickards), *The Great Super Cycle* (Skarica), *Conquer the Crash* (Prechter), *The Real Crash* (Schiff), *How Rich Countries Got Rich and Why Poor Countries Stay Poor* (Reinert), *Breakout Nations* (Sharma), *Investment Biker* (Rogers) all have interesting offerings on this subject of macro trend investing. Macro investing is definitely related to the big picture of strategic wealth accumulation over the course of multiple generations, and if you want to create ultra high net worth generational wealth, these books contain the sort of insight you need to cultivate over time. To break into the mega-wealth category through investing, you must think strategically long term and invest for that horizon while simultaneously striving to preserve your wealth from losses, taxes and confiscation. An understanding of politics, geopolitics and human behavior therefore becomes necessary.

Some other related larger scale investing topics include Modelski long cycles of national supremacy; Schumpeter's economic cycle theory; Kitchen (40 month), Jugler (9 year), Kuznets (20 year) economic cycles; inflation cycles, climate and war cycles; debt supercycles; contrarian investing methodologies; Elliott Wave Theory; socionomics; the Austrian economic school explanations for the causes behind banking crashes; the histories of banking crises and stock market bubbles, debt defaults, deflations and hyperinflations; and the ways by which fiat currencies typically get destroyed. These are all important topics, especially when you enter a rare end game situation for your country.

All along I have emphasized the fact that the tried and true investing methods work as long as a country is in that golden period where it continues to march forward with steady GNP growth, which is something that can definitely last for decades. However, countries can also be suddenly destroyed by a war that completely erases the progress of many generations (Iraq and Libya), or be struck by plague or famine (Ireland), political revolutions (Cambodia and China), or economic catastrophes due to unanticipated world events (tsunamis) or government mismanagement. The assumption with all these techniques is that none of these types of things will happen to derail you from your super investing goal. However, to grow your wealth you must indeed be knowledgeable about such historical possibilities and be ready for all sorts of such contingencies, which brings us to our sixth "bonus" super investing technique.

Governments, like people, accumulate bad decisions over time which they fail to correct. They can certainly pursue policies that eventually lead to economic ruin and have done so many times in the past. It is a sad fact that sometimes a nation can only be restored by the terrible lessons of a catastrophe. Like individuals, as time progresses they usually end up spending too much and taking on too much debt. They borrow to overspend on military forays, grand domestic programs, and to buy voters. Historically speaking, in general empires have very commonly overextended themselves through excessive spending, unnecessary wars and various other efforts we can define as "imperil overreach."

The spending to support all these activities can last only so long before there is a final day of reckoning. If a government spends more than it collects in taxes then it must borrow ever-increasing amounts to pursue its projects and so that citizens can live a lifestyle that is beyond their means. When the eventual day of reckoning arrives because the debt servicing cannot be paid, an "end game" occurs where all sound investment methods often cease working for a short while. Many people put their heads in the sand thinking this cannot possibly happen, and that systemic collapses cannot possibly occur, but as John Templeton said, "The four most dangerous words in investing are 'This time it's different.'" I would like to add that four other very dangerous words are, "It can't happen here."

To grow your wealth, *you must stay on your toes and know of these distinctive possibilities.* You must keep history and typical human behavior in the forefront of your mind. You must know that all markets, including real estate, never keep going up forever jus as economies don't go up forever either. You must know what excesses and types of financial distress are eventually caused by banking systems, excessive debt levels and over-leverage, and what to do when they occur. Historically speaking, typically you will see economic hangovers arrive after huge debt surges in a country lead to inflated equity bubbles in stocks or housing. Overly permissive lending in an economy typically causes prices to rise above sustainable levels. With excessive lending the banks look more profitable than they actually are and economic growth appears greater than it really is until the boom ends and an "unanticipated" crisis arises where that debt becomes difficult to repay and defaults ensue. Banks always play a key role in these problems because they are the source of the excessive credit which causes the problems. Corporations may spend hundreds of millions in lobbying fees for favorable legislation and tax breaks in their pursuit of profits, but paradoxically they do not insist—out of self-interest—that the banks be policed even though history shows they continually put the entire system at risk with their actions and imperil the profits which corporations work so hard to attain. While in the past the banks personally suffered for any mistakes they made in risk taking, now they ask that the hapless taxpayer pay for their reckless creditor behavior, and once their problem are resolved they just repeat their errors again!

Carmen Reinhart and Kenneth Rogoff in their excellent book, *This Time It's Different*, wrote a policy guide for all future generations related to these matters. They examined the fate of countless nations which experienced various types of financial crises and charted out the typical patterns of distress. They examined internal defaults, external defaults, banking crises, exchange rate crises and inflation crises. They found that the unwinding of a financially caused boom usually entails a decline in real housing prices (housing usually declines 35% over six years or more), declining stock market prices (which typically decline 56% over 3.5 years or more), exploding government debt (which usually rises an average of 86%), falling economic output, rising unemployment rates, collapsing tax revenues and spiking interest rates. What typically happens as the unwinding pattern depends upon the type of crisis that occurs, but Reinhart and Rogoff found that banking crises typically lead to sovereign debt defaults (there have been 250 cases globally since 1800), and sovereign defaults typically lead to inflation (greater than 20% per year) and currency collapses. The tipping point when countries start seeing sovereign debt instability is when the debt/GDP ratio for a country hits 60% or higher.

These types of events happen so often in history that you must know how to protect and preserve your wealth during the various different types of economic breakdowns possible! The best you can say is that "it hasn't happened to us yet" rather than "it won't happen here." While Warren Buffett tries to protect himself by never buying investments open to catastrophic risk, and while other investing strategies use stop losses to prevent large losses, those precautions cannot save you from these situations that can result in universal carnage. What I am saying is that you have a high probability of entering into at least one economically and financially catastrophic period during your lifetime—at least one—and you have to know what to do with your money during that period should it occur. You must know what to do during deflationary periods where there are massive debt defaults, during high inflationary or hyperinflationary periods, during prolonged super recessions or depressions, during banking or stock market or currency crises, and you have to be cognizant of any political risks affecting your investments, too. In this section we will particularly emphasize hyperinflation and deflation scenarios.

After such catastrophes there is never an "end of the world" Armageddon but simply a period of structural readjustment when the pieces are put back together again. Then the whole multi-decade cycle begins anew with the lessons being slowly forgotten as time marches by. For instance, the repeal of the Glass-Steagall act in the United States, which eliminated a sound mechanism of financial stabilization (and opened up ways for banks to outplay financial regulators), is an example of the selective amnesia that always leads to a repeat of the folly which motivated the reforms in the first place. It was Franklin Roosevelt's banking reforms, Glass-Steagall, the establishment of the FDIC, and most importantly *personal penalties for financial crimes* that helped set the stage for the American century of economic growth. If you do not deter people with criminal penalties for financial crimes, the whole process repeats itself all too readily. The fact that financial crimes are not prosecuted always puts the entire financial and economic system at risk. As it is now, the system is set up that even if a financial firm commits a crime, the penalty is just a *fraction* of what the firm earns, so ethics have degraded and legal penalties have now become simply a cost of doing business. Doing the right thing no longer matters when profits are available.

The threat of criminal actions against personal financial offenders—rather than the fact that they might simply lose a job with a minor wrist slapping—is what helped keep safer banking measures in line for many decades in the U.S., but the public sees that large financial criminals are now no longer prosecuted while the little man is. "To big to fail" has become "too big to jail." Such clear observations by the public usually lead to social and political protests against the reigning powers since it openly appears as if the government has abandoned the populace and been bought by moneyed interests. Many of the problems within a financial crisis can ultimately be traced back to sheer criminality, or a deficiency in personal morality and ethics within a financial system that rewards the breaking of rules at the expense of the public. Even the watchmen policing the system can be "captured" or bribed. Troubles always ensue when the financial system imposes no penalties when risk takers are wrong, but troubles balloon when those who break laws are not punished. As long as banking, which always plays a pivotal role in these breakdowns, is run by individuals undeterred because of the lack of personal financial and criminal penalties for their misbehavior, the process will continually repeat itself.

Turning to legislative and economic management, countless examples from history prove beyond the shadow of a doubt that countries can make gigantic mistakes in their policies, and no country remains prosperous forever. For instance, Liaquat Ahmed's Pulitzer Prize-winning book, *Lords of Finance*, narrates the story of how four central bankers following misguided policies helped plunge the world into the Great Depression. Since the best and brightest aren't necessarily in the civil service (they are usually elsewhere because it pays a lot more money), you should always be questioning the course of a nation's economic and financial policies, especially when smart people are not at the helm and the trajectory of the nation can be usurped by political campaign contributions. The U.S. has a unique problem in that key government positions are now being filled by investment bankers trained over the course of their careers in greed. Specifically, they are trained how to make quick profitable transactions rather than decisions for the public good. They have never been policy makers trained to think of the long term interests of the country. Rather, they have been trained to think in terms of the profitability of financial transactions whether or not they are good for customers. They have not risen to high positions by being concerned about the prosperity of the man in the street. They have only been trained to think in terms of self-interest and the profitability of a firm that wants to take money from counterparties. They are intimately familiar with the concept of greed rather than public service so who would you rather have making policy for the good of the nation? Someone trained in making countless financial transactions, or someone trained to think about what slowly works out best for the long term growth of economy?

Yet another clear fact of history is that the leadership helm of the world has never stayed constant, and one's dominant position disappears as one's economic, financial and military power declines. That power declines as a result of bad decisions by policymakers, so the errors can be traced back to officials once again. Over hundreds of years in the West, the concentration of wealth or world leadership has passed from Venice and Portugal to the Netherlands, and then to France, Great Britain and now the USA. One could argue that Spain should be included in this list, but the point is that each hegemon lost its position of predominance in time due to a variety of reasons including foolish official economic policies or attempts at overreach similar to those which toppled imperial Rome. In the nineties, I was giving lectures at Chinese universities showing that the new leadership helm of the world was unequivocally heading eastwards because of bad Western policy decisions, and this is where we now stand. China stands next in line for the leadership helm because of errant American policies that politicians refuse to correct. Just as monies once left Britain for America as it rose, the best investment opportunities in the future will definitely be in the East as well as in the emerging markets as they develop.

Today we are also facing several simultaneous international crises brought on by a combination of misguided economic and financial policies. There are banking and sovereign-debt crises co-mingled with unwinding real estate and mortgage bubbles, financial derivative excesses, currency wars, trade imbalances, overreaching military commitments, massive entitlement spending obligations, falling tax revenues and high unemployment rates. All of these problems are connected to the trends of globalization, the offshoring of the manufacturing bases of richer industrialized countries to lower wage nations, and the limits of using debt to fuel consumption-based economies. At the same time, as Aaron Russo has mentioned in interviews, an endless war on "terror" has been declared without any real enemy (no definite enemy that can be pinpointed), and therefore it can last forever because you can never define having won or winning the battle. Endless billions will uselessly be spent pursuing fictitious terrorists, ordinary people rebranded as terrorists to abolish their rights or remove them from the system of due process, or small infractions previously considered "criminal" and handled perfectly well at that level. At the same time, as economies turn sour various governments will try to take away people's personal liberties, silence their dissent, and perpetuate fear in the public so that the citizenry subordinate themselves to everything the government wants them to do. People can become terrorized to the extent that they are willing to give up many of their freedoms in order to make a crisis go away and regain stability. Meanwhile, new measures will continue to benefit rich elites and special interests rather than the community at large so that the gap between the rich and poor continues to grow to levels that have historically resulted in social instability. These are all bad policies.

Other errant political decisions together with misguided economic policies have also finally caught up with many host nations. While all nations are now somewhat interconnected through their economies, the Asian nations are getting stronger and the Western nations are progressively getting weaker due to these problems reaching a crescendo, a perfect storm of collisions whose consequences can no longer be ignored. The Western elite, such as the Anglo-American alliance, believe they will still remain at the top and still control the whole mechanism through their cancellation of public liberties, but they are losing their levers of power and are doomed to fail unless there is a change in strategic direction. At extremes like this, any ordinary means of monetary and spending stimulus will lose its effectiveness, and one must await an inevitable climax of wealth destruction and social unrest although every trick in the book is applied to prevent it.

Let's look at America. With the American manufacturing base and jobs having been exported away, the usual stimulus approach for bringing America out of economic lethargy no longer works anymore and is like pushing on a string. However, the cost of that ineffective stimulus is an ever increasing level of yet more debt that must be serviced but doesn't produce a return. When a country reaches the point where its debt grows faster than its economy (the interest on that debt overwhelms the economic growth rate), either the country must *drastically cut its spending or taxes must be raised* (usually to ridiculous levels). Both of these avenues will hurt overall economic growth. If this isn't done, there will be a default and then "austerity" will occur by natural consequence rather than by plan.

In both cases of spending cuts or higher taxes, social programs will have to be curtailed, military forays will have to end because you can no longer print dollars to finance them, the national wage rate must come down, and an overall lower standard of living will ensue. This is what is facing America for its future unless various critical policy changes are instituted other than just devaluing the currency by printing more money. Unfortunately, the American government and Federal Reserve are involved with endless *tactical* market manipulations to hold off a collapse, and they confuse these emergency interventions with a grand strategy. They only know how to print cash, but if this really could work at changing the situation, why not simply stop taxing all citizens since you could conjure into existence all the cash you needed simply by printing it? If you could simply print money out of thin air to produce prosperity, every kingdom in history would have figured this out years ago. Governments can borrow to create debt but they cannot create wealth. Governments cannot always access money for everything to "take care" of everyone, and so the road of excessive taxation, debt issuance and printing money is unsustainable. Therefore there is an inevitable fate of future destruction for America on the current road of printing endless cash and monetizing debt, even if this strategy has the noble goal of trying to help everyone and prevent deflation.

The way democracies and election laws are currently structured, allowing debt to default and deflation to occur is the last thing that the government wants to let happen, so America will most likely take the common historical path of trying to inflate away its debt and deflation problems. The better course is to let the debt default, clear the decks, and then growth will start again after the pain as happened in Iceland. However, the parties most hurt would be the banks themselves who own the Federal Reserve and participate in determining monetary policy. Since no one wants to see their company lose money, their conglomerate broken up, or lose a high position of wealth, power and prestige, most of the individuals involved at the levels of decision making will most likely choose the path of inflation to try to clear away the massive levels of crippling debt threatening the system. Unfortunately, this will threaten the system in simply a different way.

Additionally, we must remember that American elected officials typically pander to the wealthy corporations, organizations and the powerful wealthy who donate to their campaigns—thus becoming subservient to the wielders of concentrated wealth—and will therefore avoid making any necessary economic, financial or regulatory changes that would hurt their powerful financial patrons even though those actions might save the nation. Therefore they cannot deliver the change America needs to avoid deteriorating conditions.

When democracy becomes a bribeocracy because of campaign contributions, capitalism then becomes a corporatocracy. Thus, the whole American ship is now in danger of going down for fear of harming a few patrons. In trying to satisfy the many competing agendas rather than trying to do the right thing which is also the smartest thing, what everyone wishes to protect and prosper may be destroyed because the entire house may lose its foundations. As Churchill once quipped, "Americans will eventually do the right thing ... [only] after they have exhausted all the alternatives."

The banking system always plays a crucial role in collapses of this sort, as do other vested interests who have fattened up from the trends threatening the country and who had established grips on the levers of power. Such forces are not easy to dislodge from the seats of power. No one wants their gravy train taken away so they will fight to preserve it even as the ship goes down. Greed and corruption usually end up playing a major role in determining what actions are undertaken to save a nation rather than wisdom derived from historical lessons and sound principles. Special interests are rich, powerful and ruthless in demanding that their myopic interests be served to the detriment of systemic health. As a military doctor once told me, refusing to correct some errant ways is like refusing to amputate an arm or hand to save the life of the body, but this refusal to change is what the powerful often choose in order to protect their vested interests. Just as the mortgage crisis was really a moral and ethical crisis (because banks made loans they would never keep themselves and thus relaxed their lending criteria), the issues actually come down to ethics and selfishness in the end rather than pure legislation or economics.

America has also evolved a system where political candidates—many of whom are not qualified for statesmanship positions because they do not understand economics, geopolitical strategy, and why it's necessary to prevent wars and their unintended consequences—now commonly spend *hundreds of millions* of campaign dollars (if not more) to win a $174K per year job so that they can, in turn, dispense *billions* in favors to their contributors rather than do what is right for the country. Elected officials must please their donors to secure their re-election funds as well, so the need for campaign cash, and faulty contribution laws, have overridden the wisdom compass. Lacking both wisdom and willpower to stand independent, career politicians in America end up rewarding their patrons with policies that are harmful for the nation in total. It is as the British say, "If you take the queen's shilling you do the queen's bidding." In fact, it has gotten so bad that the U.S. government now even ignores the misdoings of major political donors and refuses to prosecute them for obvious crimes, which history shows will definitely lead to social unrest, tears in the social fabric, and other negative consequences.

The Occupy Wall Street movement in the U.S. was a complete waste of time in light of such issues because it totally ignored two key hinges causing much of the trouble in the first place. First, elections can be bought and therefore politicians can be bought, and thus legislation which is not in the best interests of the Constitutional Republic can be purchased. In short, elected politicians have become compromised policymakers. Second, the laws and regulations we already have remain unenforced so that flagrant personal corruption among the financial elite now goes unpunished. History shows that a government's refusal to prosecute the elite who have committed crimes typically leads to yet further crimes and provokes civil unrest, but this is a lesson of history that the American government seems not to have learned.

Campaign contribution laws are also one of the few pivotal reasons why America's economic and social problems have grown to what they are today. A major fault lies in the ability of extremely rich entities *who are not citizens or even living entities*—such as corporations who owe loyalty to no one, special interest groups and PACs—to contribute to political campaigns and thereby influence politics to the public's detriment. Because of an errant Supreme Court ruling, a situation that our Founding Fathers (and our system of checks and balances) never intended can now only be corrected through a difficult to achieve Constitutional amendment.

This is what Occupy Wall Street should have been working towards— *campaign finance reform*. To protest about anything else is rather pointless because it doesn't correct any problem. Without this key point being fixed, the bad policies will continue, the corruption will continue, and the middle class will become impoverished while ordinary citizens become enslaved as serfs shackled to debt servicing. Corporations will continue to go offshore because of lower costs, taking jobs with them, and the Fed will continue to try to manipulate the markets to avert a collapse, but a collapse will eventually come. A monetary crisis of major proportions eventually happens to every fiat monetary system, every government that overspends without restraint, and every country which destroys the methods by which the public can police its abuses of power to protect the public welfare. The leadership helm has become controlled by individuals acting in a tribal fashion who have no social contract with the greater part of the nation, and thus will result in terrible consequences for the country if not corrected.

What has allowed America to engage in uncontrolled borrowing for so long is the fact that the U.S. dollar has been the world's reserve currency. Other countries have been willing to accept the dollar because of its reserve status while the inflationary printing press was running full steam. However, the firm signs are in that Russia, China and other countries are no longer satisfied with this status quo and clearly want to exit the dollar. They dislike America's ability to militarily bully other nations because of the dollar status. They are joining hands to defeat the dollar's status as the world's reserve currency, which would plunge the U.S. into the ranks of the third world nations due to chronic inflation, high unemployment, massive debt levels and low growth unless it takes other actions to make the dollar more necessary. Many investigative reporters in the field of finance have revealed that various countries are currently preparing a replacement to the dollar standard (partially backed by a basket of real commodities such as gold, oil and minerals) because they can clearly see a banking crisis becoming a sovereign debt crisis, and then a dollar confidence crisis and currency crisis. If the dollar becomes worthless and they have no alternative then they, too, will be hurt just as well so they are quietly preparing a replacement in the wings. A rich man may have a billion dollars, for instance, but his funds are all dollars. If the dollar goes bad, how much money is he going to have when they become worthless?

The Fourth Estate, or press, has been silent on all such matters of importance, and without its spotlight the errant ways are not corrected. Americans are now so ill-informed that they do not insist on necessary financial, economic, military and governmental changes. The frequent failure of the press to report on matters of supreme significance is due to the fact that numerous independent news agencies have been slowly agglomerated into just a powerful handful which now control the news which the public receives, and those in turn are under the firm control of even higher forces. The media is now controlled by larger interests that don't want people to think or know; these interests are not aligned with the people's interests and so the news agencies now keep silent on the most important matters which truly affect the fate of the nation. Journalists have even learned how to self-censor themselves by noting the quality of assignments they receive when they truthfully report on important sensitive issues. They report that they cease being able to gain access to important people when they start asking questions of any consequence, and thus they now leave the most important issues alone whose discussion might help save the nation.

Thus, a compromised press now commonly fails to report on government wrongdoing and serve as a necessary part in the checks and balance system needed by every country to keep its government honest, and to help preserve the social contract between governments and their citizens. Unlike in days of old, if any reporter speaks up on touchy issues or even questions the way things are now being run, they promptly lose their job and cannot find equivalent employment elsewhere, so no one challenges officials or reports on these big issues anymore. The press no longer analyzes and forewarns the public that some particular policy will make matters worse, but only reports of a blow up after it happens.

As an investor who must be prepared for crisis, you must particularly understand that if the U.S. dollar is no longer in demand as the world currency then the consequences for the U.S. will be enormous—all bad domestically as well as for America's ability to influence world policy. The press is not discussing these issues at all or even talking about how to prevent these trends. Even the ability to wage war will be hampered due to the lack of funds available through money printing. The world leadership position of America will be lost, and one will be able to trace the national disgrace back to the errant monetary policies of the Fed, greed of errant corporatists, and errant political policies that pandered to the elite while refusing to face reality. In the future, historians will describe this all in terms of larger economic forces and trends, but in actuality, it all comes down to a question of character, ethics and values in key individuals or groups of individuals within various circles of power and influence.

TOO MUCH DEBT AND GOLD PRICES

When countries accumulate too much debt, as we are currently seeing in the U.S. and Europe today, historically the usual course of action has been to try to inflate the debt away by printing more currency. Of course this just compounds the problem by kicking it down the road while it continues to get larger. For some reason, when economic difficulties have been created by too much debt, rapid money supply growth, artificial interest rates and asset bubbles, governments think you can solve the debt problems by placing those conditions on steroids. They want to take on more debt by issuing more bonds and printing more money rather than let defaults clear the decks. They try to solve the problem of too much debt by issuing yet more debt! When defaults are prevented while borrowing and spending are not cut, further money printing and inflation are the only two options available to over-indebted countries. From history we know that governments usually choose inflation to get rid of their debt problems, and then collapse always comes anyway.

Gold and other precious metals can shoot up during such periods because they usually hold their purchasing power during deflations. Roy Jastram's famous study (*The Golden Constant*) covering 416 years of gold prices found that gold's value was particularly secure during deflationary environments, as we are now seeing. He concluded that gold is used as a store of value (and money of last resort) during deflations, especially as deflations often involve the collapse of the creditors in the banking system. Matching the theory, more than two hundred years of United States history shows gold hoarding during deflationary periods when there was a crisis in confidence on the credit worthiness of the currency. At those times gold rises in dollar terms because holders of "suspect" cash rush for the exits, and they strive to preserve their purchasing power with gold or any other real asset available. With either deflation or excessive inflation (when there is currency/credit risk and a flight to safety), gold therefore often serves as a store of value or means of increasing one's wealth even though it does not throw off any cash flows. It is an asset without any counterparty risk.

When it comes to the precious metals, often a defining criteria for a bull market in gold prices is the presence of *negative real interest rates*, during which time gold tends to soar in value. When there are negative real interest rates, you can say that the economy is trying to steal money from savers, and so they must look for an independent means to keep their wealth intact. People turn to gold as a safe haven when a monetary system is at risk, which often involves a time of high inflation or negative real interest rates or default risks.

To understand what can happen without such an alternative and independent store of value, one need only note the historical example of Argentina when the central bank created so much money that foreigners holding the currency panicked, causing the currency to collapse, and there was both a deflationary credit crunch and massive inflation of import prices at the same time. That type of situation will skyrocket the price of gold if it ever happened to the U.S. dollar. The dollar is backed by the faith placed in the U.S. government entrusted to it by the world community. If that faith is shaken, and there are plans afoot to attack its status as the reserve currency, the dollar will be in trouble and gold will once again soar.

Individuals usually don't see the big picture in such issues. For instance, most people don't realize that the war in Iraq was not really about oil, religion, or weapons of mass destruction. It was about protecting the monopoly usage of the dollar in world trade. Whenever an important country like Iraq announced that it would stop using the dollar to settle international trade, the U.S. would quickly act by launching military invasions to ensure that the Petrodollar would retain its monopoly as the single currency used in the critical international oil market. Saddam Hussein, for instance, switched his oil sales from dollars to Euros in 2000. Libya was also overthrown not just for its resources but because its leader, Muammar Gaddafi, was circulating influential plans for African nations to create their own gold-backed "dinar" as the currency to be used for trade transactions instead of the American dollar as well. When he also asked for his 144 tons of gold held in foreign accounts to be repatriated back to his country, the powers that be could bear it no longer and struck.

The history of all this goes back to 1975 when the members of OPEC agreed to sell oil only in U.S. dollars, and since that time the U.S. has become economically and strategically dependent on this Petro-policy of dollars only in international trade, which it protects at all costs because the breakdown of the Petrodollar system would cause its destruction. Without the Petrodollar, the United States would be far less relevant in the world economy and would no longer be its center. It would slowly (or quickly) fall to the status of a Third World nation due to rampant inflation caused by the fact it will have to bid for international goods and services using whatever currency is required. Countries will drop U.S. Government bonds as a reserve asset, and the U.S. will have to devalue the dollar just to survive. A major portion of the dollar's value is due to its use in oil trade and if that monopoly falters, so will the value of the dollar.

Most people do not understand that protecting the Petrodollar (and aspects of the drug trade) is therefore a lynchpin of U.S. geopolitical strategy. It keeps the largest U.S. banks afloat and makes many other strategic hegemon programs possible. Without the Petrodollar status as the center of world trade, the United States would have to change all its tax, debt, currency, trade, military and energy policies. Foreign countries would dump the dollar for some new currency needed to purchase oil, and entire national banking systems would suffer shockwaves due to the tectonic consequences this would mean for global banking. The U.S. Federal Reserve would lose its ability to print dollars to solve economic problems, domestic interest rates in America would have to rise, adjustable rate mortgage holders would be crushed while real estate values plummet, businesses would collapse and massive layoffs would occur, import prices (especially on oil) would skyrocket, and asset prices would plummet. With inflation rising, Americans would quickly find themselves in Third World living conditions.

Without being able to finance its various policies and forays simply by printing dollars, the powers of the U.S. would be absolutely demolished, and economically it would probably experience a depression and then recovery at a far lower level of living standards. These issues are so large scale that the typical individual never hears of them in the news, but one is not really qualified to be a statesman if they don't know about these *real* issues. There is always an ostensible or apparent *surface reason* given which makes policies acceptable to people, and then there are the real reasons why certain things are done on the stage of world geopolitics.

As to the topic of excessive debt, when debt levels get very high in a country then a government can, of course, abandon further money printing and debt creation by cutting spending dramatically. Without sufficient money to spend, "austerity" then happens naturally because the country no longer has money to pay for all its programs and promises. Nations with too much debt typically implement austerity measures in order to stay solvent and even shut down essential services within a nation. If a government can do this no longer but declares a debt default instead and asks for a debt restructuring, at that time "cash" becomes the one item of most value until the restructuring is over. The question is where to hold the cash because even large "safe" banks suffer the risk of bankruptcy during such periods. Gold is therefore often suppressed by financial powers before these troubles because they want to deflect money away from going into precious metals. Governments want to see that cash going into bonds and cash instead because this helps the system stay afloat.

Throughout history, the usual course of governments which land in this sort of trouble has therefore been to print ever increasing quantities of money rather than default. They try to depreciate or devalue their currency. They try to postpone an inevitable correction by suppressing interest rates while in the process they accumulate even more debt they cannot pay. To do this during an end game period when a crisis becomes inevitable, a government must start stop reporting accurate economic statistics, blatantly lie and misrepresent and "cook the books" to hide its problems from watchful eyes.

Unfortunately, artificially low interest rates will eventually kill savers and the economy in this scenario so it is no solution either. Japan, for instance, has tried this for two decades rather than allow debt defaults, and it has not improved its situation one bit. Consumption falls off, and businesses start losing money. The artificial manipulation of the markets kills both the markets *and* the economy. When you don't have an honest interest rate because of excessive money printing, you tend to produce harmful speculative booms and then busts. At the end stages of cheap money due to artificially low interest rates, people load up on debt because they go out and buy cars, houses and other things that should not be purchased. These items end up in a liquidation sale when the rates rise or the borrowers lose their jobs as a result of the economic policies. Companies cannot make correct decisions without a true price of capital either. The artificially low interest rates accumulate many negative consequences of mammoth proportions, and defaults become inevitable when the artificially low rates must finally rise. So many things become entangled up in the manipulations necessary to keep interest rates low that a disaster usually ensues when things finally unwind. In all the possible end game scenarios, an enormous crash results at the end with massive debt defaults, deflation, bankruptcies, historically high unemployment rates, suicides, higher taxes, less public services, and lower standards of living. As a lesson of history, sometimes entire monetary systems must then be retooled.

Since a common rule throughout history is that *debts that cannot be repaid will not be repaid*, defaults will certainly follow when debt levels get too high. The question then becomes how and when a nation will default, but it will certainly default. If there is a debt default, an astronomical sum of money that the economy had assumed was there will suddenly be wiped out. An unforeseen problem is that this deflationary trend can even lead to hyperinflation, too, if the government then starts upon the road of excessive money printing, the populace loses its confidence in that cash, and then suddenly starts spending it frantically on real assets or to stockpile items for consumption. In Weimar Germany, for instance, the government unleashed the printing presses but the country saw no inflation until, like an unanticipated burst of wind, prices suddenly started jumping exponentially. Governments the world over are currently fighting deflationary forces with inflationary forces (money printing), and the end game will most probably be a currency crisis, trade wars, bond and derivative market melt-downs, and the transition to a new monetary system.

Will we see deflation or hyperinflation? I think we will see both in places because right now we are fighting deflation through inflation that has the danger of turning into hyperinflation, which will in turn collapse the economy and monetary system unless there is a new standard. Peter Bernholtz, author of *Monetary Regimes and Inflation*, found that most every case of hyperinflation he studied looked the same and was first caused by massive budget deficits that were financed mostly by money creation. The tipping point to hyperinflation came when government deficits reached 40% or more of *government spending* (not GDP). It is practically a surety when debt rises to over 80% of GNP and deficits amount to more than 40% of government spending, *no matter how a country got into that situation*.

The money to fund that growth in debt can initially come from people's savings but usually later comes from the massive use of the money printing presses, and it is this money printing that causes hyperinflation when it finally reaches a tipping point. The debt levels prior to hyperinflations sometimes grew as the result of some extreme event such as the loss of a war, regime change or collapse, rampant government corruption, or the fact that a country pegged its currency or ceded its monetary sovereignty to some type of foreign denominated debt. In general, hyperinflations were usually caused by the political mismanagement of legislatures that eventually spent far beyond their means and racked up a debt load that became disproportionately large. This is why governments across the world right now are undertaking fundamental reorganizational reforms, rather than temporary austerity measures, that end up altering tax codes, cutting military spending, reducing entitlement programs, and eliminating other excessive initiatives which they cannot pay for in the long run. Anyway you look at it, unfunded liabilities grow so much that even with severe budget cuts, governments can no longer tax their way out of the situation. Thus this will lead to more money printing and then inflation.

Even when the government is not at fault for racking up debt, if most of the debt in an economy is owed to banks and corporations who can exert more control over the government than the people can, the government will do everything possible to prevent bankruptcies from occurring so that these debt loads will never clear. They will ask the public to pay for the mistakes of these private parties who should solely suffer for their own errors. Along the way, governments will typically print up money and make loans to large politically connected entities such as the mega-banks currently in trouble. If the banks hold onto that cash (possibly using it for highly leveraged speculation) rather than use it to make loans that recirculate the funds in the economy, the money still won't get into the economic system despite government wishes (unless there was a public debt Jubilee), and then the government will end up printing even more money until there is eventually a massive loss of confidence in the currency and the government's solvency. The job of a government is to promote confidence, so it will misrepresent, conceal and lie endlessly during these situations using pronouncements that cannot be trusted.

If there is a loss of confidence in a nation's currency during such times, people will stop buying government debt because they run out of patience waiting for it to fix its finances and lower its default risks. They may not see it as holding value anymore, they may not see it as providing them a return higher than inflation, they may see it as a credit risk, or they might not be able to afford it simply because they don't have any savings left to buy it. The government will then end up printing lots more money to fund its own debt itself, entering the realm of Ponzi schemes, because it can find no buyers for its bonds. Governments in such circumstances rarely get their fiscal house in order, which would require a major restructuring. No one holding an elite position in the system wants to lose their power either, which would certainly be affected by any restructuring. It seems the only goal of a government is to make sure it always gets the money it wants to spend, so it will continue to print and spend rather than get its house in order. At a point of sufficient money induced inflation from all this money printing, a hoard of cash held by the public can suddenly come out of hiding to start buying real goods rather than more paper, in turn creating extreme inflation. At such times, businesses stop investing because of the uncertainty, unemployment skyrockets, and savings will often flee a country to other currencies if the government doesn't impose currency controls. Where does the money flee to? To whatever is deemed safe, such as the precious metals (gold and silver), and governments will do everything possible to stop this flight of capital.

The U.S. approach to its current debt problem is following these scenarios exactly because the big losers in a debt default would be large Wall Street financial houses and the very banks that own the Federal Reserve. All of these entities exert a tremendous control over the government and none are eager to see any type of financial losses unless *their mistakes* are paid for by the American public. Hence, they have received billions in government bailouts but refused to recirculate the money in the economy through loans because they are using the funds for speculation. The need for liquidity is just one of the reasons that the U.S. government is forced to keep on printing money at an ever increasing pace, devaluing the dollar in the process and setting up the economy for an inflationary bubble.

If a country keeps inflating its currency without limit, as already stated the danger is that the public will eventually lose faith and confidence in the currency when it discovers what's going on, and then there comes the possibility that no one wants to hold that paper currency (or bonds) any longer. Hyperinflation can then ensue where the national currency ends up becoming worthless, so deflationary forces can actually end up creating hyperinflation which will effectively end the life of that paper currency. You cannot keep printing money, creating inflation, keep interest rates low and have your currency stay strong forever. Eventually you get hyperinflation and high interest rates, which has happened again and again throughout history, and this is a type of implicit default that usually leads to larger political changes. The typical collapse scenario is indeed high inflation after the slow but then rapid progressive debasement of the currency through excessive money printing.

In ancient Rome, for instance, the money was never debased until the Second Punic War when the Carthaginian general Hannibal threatened Rome with his army. To finance a massive military effort against Hannibal, Rome began to debase the metal content of its coinage, thus inflating the money supply. The nation also started adopting a more militarist, expansionist worldview which eventually led it into becoming a dictatorship. Eventually the currency became so debased over time that it lost most of its value, and a tremendous inflation ensued. Alexander del Mar, in his *History of Monetary Systems*, wrote "The numerary system lasted for nearly two centuries, during which all that was admirable of Roman civilization saw its origin, its growth and its maturity. When the system fell Rome had lost its liberties. The state was to grow yet more powerful and dreaded, but that state and its people were no longer one."

Few people reflect deeply on historical events such as these, including how civil liberties together with class mobility and free enterprise make for a powerhouse of wealth and hope as long as they last. As these pillars crack, great wealth, power and good fortune flee with them. In the case of Rome, no matter how it exactly happened, these issues were tied up with the struggle to fund Rome's excessive debt. Similar lessons can be found by examining the histories of Ottoman Turkey, Bourbon France and Hapsburg Spain.

Such mega-changes happen all the time and are the meat of history. Sixteenth century Hapsburg Spain, for instance, in just over one hundred years went from being a near nothing nation to become a great empire, and then destroyed itself to become a nothing nation once again. The conquered gold and silver riches of Mexico, Central America and South American flowed into Spain, slowly dis-incentivizing national production and turning the nation into a consumption-based economy which imported opulent goods from all over the world. Government expenditures soon exceeded income, thus setting the stage for decline. This setup is similar to what has happened to the United States over the past thirty years as this is always a long term process. Because of its growing wealth, Spain also began to think of itself as supreme over all other nations, and through hubris started waging countless wars with other countries. However, it ran out of funds, flirted with bankruptcy, and eventually had to borrow money to stay afloat since most of its gold and silver had already flowed out of the country to buy imports. It had already stopped producing on its own, so this was inevitable. The fall of Spain was associated with a fiscal crisis where government expenditures eventually exceeded revenues and where the mounting costs of servicing government debt became impossible to repay. As stated, this pattern has been consistently been associated with many imperial declines. In 1543 nearly two-thirds of Spanish ordinary revenues were used for interest payments on government borrowings, and by 1598 the monarchy had to spend 100% of revenues just to service its debt, which essentially led to the country's collapse. The many parallels to the U.S. situation are once again striking, and we must remember that the case of Spain *reveals a consistent pattern of history*! As with Rome, the end way out for these situations is usually currency debasement and devaluation rather than outright default, which means inflation for the populace and lower standards of living due to mistakes of hubris made by national leaders.

A WORTHLESS DOLLAR?

As stated, in the choice between deflation and defaults or inflation and currency devaluation, countries usually choose the path of inflation for many reasons, including the fact that it tends to hide the blame of the parties responsible for the crisis. When the currency in question is the world's reserve currency and other countries no longer want to accept it because of its devaluation, every country in the world will certainly want to seek alternatives, such as gold. No one can really predict what will happen if we truly have a world currency crisis involving the world reserve currency, which is presently the American dollar. Wars typically become entangled with such extreme situations, and we cannot rule out depressions either.

The best thinking is that everyone will seek alternatives to holding the fallen reserve currency. They will seek any other currencies in the world that are still strong. The Euro comes to mind, but what if the Euro itself is weak, entangled with the dollar, or independently in danger of collapse? Money will then definitely flood into precious metals and other real income producing assets rather than more paper instruments. If another country tries to offer some type of new resource backed currency (backed by a gold standard for instance), the rush to that currency may destroy that nation's exchange rate by bidding it up excessively unless a large enough block of countries also join hands to do something similar at the same time.

The potential for the eventual worthlessness of the U.S. dollar is one reason that *many* Eastern foreign governments have awoken and are currently purchasing vast quantities of gold as an alternative store of value other than the dollar. They can more easily accumulate gold when prices are artificially kept low through manipulation, and through manipulation the Western powers also desire to prevent people from turning to gold as an alternative to the dollar. At some point, however, this type of manipulation must crack, especially in negative real interest rate environments. Basically, it is a *fact* that China, Russia and many other Eastern nations have definitely joined together in a hunt to accumulate more gold reserves rather than American dollars, and massive amounts of physical bullion are leaving the Western bullion vaults for the East. As the saying runs, "As gold goes, so goes the power;" the creditors call the shots. Unknown to the public due to the silence of the press which no longer reports and analyzes, Western central banks have been forced to ship tremendous quantities of their gold bullion holdings to Eastern countries who have said they don't want to be paid anymore in paper currencies that these nations can simply print up, and who are building up their gold reserves. China has also started settling its trade imbalances with other nations *directly* without using the American dollar as the intermediate medium of exchange, so the dollar is definitely being replaced in world trade because of U.S. strategic mistakes that have hastened this development rather than thwarted it, an example being the threatening of Iran. The status of the Petrodollar is now threatened. It is said that China is also preparing (partially) gold-backed short term credit facilities for a new trade settlement system (Letters of Credit that are gold trade notes) which, when in use, people will eventually realize are the same as a gold-backed currency. If so, then when in use this will sweep the dollar aside as the dominant vehicle used in world trade.

These are titanic changes. The U.S. simply cannot attack China militarily to maintain dollar hegemony, so the writing is definitely on the wall for the supremacy of the dollar. America doesn't want to go to war with Russia either. As it stands, the Gulf states will quickly join with China and Russia if the dollar collapses so the U.S. has several strategic options open to it that can help save the nation, such as becoming an exporter of petroleum products (which may preserve some of the international need for the dollar) or world manufacturer once again. These possible "grand strategies" to save the nation deserve careful thinking as the PR coming from the shale oil and gas industry misrepresents many issues as to sustainability. What you must know is that China and Russia, together with several other key nations, are jointly considering how to build a new reserve currency and trade settlement system to replace the U.S. dollar through a vehicle that may be partially backed by gold, oil, and the mineral wealth of the supporting nations. How can the U.S. compete if this happens? During a transition period should this happen, gold is more than likely to shine. For thousands of years, gold has always been used as catastrophe insurance that is always used to help avoid the impact of chaos, and as a prudent investor you should now view it as "central bank insurance." It is insurance against a lack of faith in or actual collapse of paper money, and thus the "money of last resort."

The bottom line to this and many other developments is that you will probably see the price of gold continue in a long term bull market until this end game is finally settled and we establish a new normal. During end game periods, either cash or precious metals become the preferred store of value. Gold, without counterparty risk, has served this purpose for thousands of years. If central banks ever allow gold to become a Tier 1 asset in banking, which would effectively make it a 100% cash equivalent once again, you can take this as a sign that major dramatic changes are about to happen, and should act to protect yourself. After any parabolic rise in price, gold (and silver) may also collapse after a new normal is reached, but the important point is that it will probably be one of the few assets able to preserve its purchasing power through a crisis adjustment period.

The economic end game of the debt super cycle we are presently within will involve multiple global sovereign defaults, a cash crisis, foreign currency wars, economic declines, lower standards of living, higher taxes, public demonstrations, violent public revolts and social demonstrations, efforts to curtail public freedoms, and possibly eventual hyperinflation. Holding *cash in hand*, having a *foreign bank account*, holding *real income producing assets or items of consumption* (money is worthless if you cannot eat), or *holding gold and silver* out of the reach of the banking system (silver actually has better demand fundamentals than gold) are the few options possibly serving as safety mechanisms through such difficult periods.

Those options once again are: **cash in hand**, a foreign bank account holding **strong foreign currencies**, **real productive assets** (such as farmland) or **commodities of consumption** (rice, flour, cooking oil, etc.), and **precious metals** (particularly gold and silver). Which one you should use to preserve your wealth depends on the crisis being played out and surrounding circumstances. When there is credit expansion and inflation in an economy then stocks and real estate tend to increase in price. When there is a war or political crisis, food often becomes scarce. When there is a deflationary crisis of economic and financial chaos because of defaulting debt bubbles, bankruptcies in the corporate, private and government sectors, pension plan failures, real estate crashes and derivative defaults accompanied by a collapse in world trade, you must especially look to gold because it becomes the most liquid asset without any counterparty risks. Whatever goes up in value is what you should consider. Remember all these various options should any of this happen, and that we are only talking of holding physical gold and silver (not numismatic coins) when it comes to precious metals. We are not talking about holding paper certificates claiming you own gold and silver held by the financial system.

As another word of warning, you must be careful of holding gold and silver mining stocks in foreign markets, especially Latin America, during a catastrophic financial period where gold and silver start rising dramatically. Those companies may be at great risk of renegotiated royalties, stricter environmental penalties and foreign confiscation if precious metal prices skyrocket, just as some countries ended up nationalizing oil companies for their important revenues. For normal times one can safely trade paper gold and silver stocks, options, futures contracts, and precious metals funds. However, during "end game" periods there is nothing superior to holding *the actual physical asset* in your own possession rather than storing it in "allocated accounts" held by banks and other institutions, or holding a paper claim to it by investing in mining companies.

Remember that during a period of chaotic adjustment, everyone pursues a store of value but the question is what it should be if the reserve currency itself is endangered. Bonds, since they represent U.S. dollars, will no longer be desired and will represent a default risk. When debt levels get too high there always comes a moment of recognition when investors and creditors (bondholders) start worrying more about the *return of their capital* rather than the interest rate *on* their capital. To compensate for the higher perceived risk of holding debt, bondholders typically start asking for higher interest rates. Pension funds stacked with bonds collapse in value as the interest rates then rise. Adjustable rate mortgage holders can no longer pay their mortgages due to higher rates and the real estate market subsequently collapses. As interest rates climb and bond values collapse, this also increases the government debt servicing load which further hampers a country's ability to pay off its debt, and defaults start ensuing in all sorts of sectors. This is why governments try to flood the financial system with liquidity and inflate the problems away with excessive money printing and low interest rate policies when debt levels become too high. Once they get into a zero interest rate (ZIRP) scenario, however, they back themselves into a hole they cannot escape, and that policy itself begins to destroy the economic system. It dampens commercial activity. The record low rates we are currently seeing are a sign of a coming financial apocalypse when bond prices will collapse as rates finally rise. It is not a sign that national leaders have been great stewards of the economy.

If and when interest rates start climbing upwards in response to all this, a special cycle that has repeated hundreds of times in history starts repeating once again as bond prices collapse. Interest rates rise while spending and consumption fall. Borrowers curtail their borrowing. Pension obligations cannot be satisfied because the funds, heavily invested in bonds, collapse in value. Taxes rise due to the need of filling the revenue gap and consumer spending drops. The country falls into a great recession or great depression; people lose jobs or secure employment at lower pay and cannot buy the goods and services necessary for survival. As interest rates become excessively high, there is eventually no lending anymore and people start parking their money in assets that will resist inflation, namely commodity essentials. Real estate buyers cannot get mortgage loans and so real estate prices tend to remain flat or actually fall. The falling consumer spending cuts economic growth and makes it ever more difficult to escape the destructive spiral.

After a nation passes through this type of crisis, it must reorganize its many fiscal, monetary and social programs. It must prosecute corruption related to banking and financial matters at the very highest levels of business, rather than just a few token cases, and then publicly champion ethical standards of conduct to restore the respect for law and order its asks of its citizenry that is necessary for the country to function. If the financial elites can get away with vast crimes which caused the mess at these times, the public will always ask, "why not us?", and so criminal prosecutions of great financial wrongs are necessary regardless of the complexity of the cases. Large banking (and other) syndicates must also be broken up to restore the system to many smaller diversified pieces which are more manageable and which can be more easily prevented from going to extremes in the future.

The nation must also undertake political election (campaign finance) reforms since patronage often greatly contributed to the accumulated problems and prevented their correction. Because of the negative domestic effects of globalization on employment that most modern nations have incurred, countries who wish to recover from debt crises today will also have to somehow bring their exported manufacturing sector back onshore once again, otherwise there will be no wealth generation mechanism to pay for the new normal required to propel an economy forwards again.

If you don't clear the deadwood of excessive debt, it is theorized that the only alternative for rebooting economic growth is a catalyst of *radically new technological inventions* or the appearance of untapped markets that can provide new investment opportunities and employment, thus leading to a new economic upswing. The opportunities must be so compelling that investors withdraw their money out of safer assets and put it into venture opportunities centered around the new technologies and the changes they will bring. The fields of commerce and finance must see there is something in these new technologies that is *so breakthrough and so encompassing* that they can lead to massive returns on investments. They need to see that they can get behind the new technologies with profitable investment financing and then a new cycle of economic upsurge will begin again.

Many have speculated that only the release of *suppressed technologies* long held back can immediately provide enough opportunities for a new economic upswing of the global scale required if something happens to the world economy due to a global economic meltdown. Will the powers that be release such new technologies? The vested interests owning the established capital base that becomes destroyed has always held back the introduction of new technologies and "black project" discoveries that threatened their investments. However, in an economic meltdown there is nothing left to protect anymore and asset values cannot climb back to the old levels, so new impulses are required. There is no longer any reason to hold back the breakthrough technologies that would have made the old capital base defunct, and so they offer hope for new beginnings. In fact, their release is part of the salvation necessary for the system.

New scientific breakthroughs and technologies might therefore be the saviors of promise that provide the new impetus for an economic wave upwards after a general economic meltdown. As the famous economist Joseph Schumpeter observed, economic development always arises out of the destruction of the previous economic order. Even so, a nation giving birth to such technologies will have to make sure that those technologies are *manufactured onshore*, otherwise the employment benefits as well as revenues will accrue to other nations once again, and all these problems will be repeated. A new control system of incentives must simply be established.

Looking for some store of value through the pain and chaos that ensues during end games, we have noted that smart investors sometimes turn to farmland that produces what people need during crisis times, namely food. If your life is at risk because you have nothing to eat, all money in the world is useless. Basically, whatever people ultimately hold as valuable during such times and turn to as a medium of exchange always depends on the situation. Individuals who flee countries threatened by hostile forces often turn to gold and silver if possible, and are blessed when they had been smart enough to have previously set up foreign bank accounts. But if those bank accounts involve a currency that is itself in crisis, you end up simply substituting one problem for another. Everyone looks to store their money in the one currency that is strongest of all and subject to the least problems, but who can say what it will be until you actually reach that situation?

During monetary crisis periods, you need to realize that domestic banks will often freeze bank accounts or limit the amount of money people can withdraw on a daily or monthly basis, and countries will sometimes confiscate or outlaw the possession of various items. Governments will often enact currency controls to prevent the outflow of money looking for value elsewhere, so forward looking preparation is essential to protect oneself. Strange situations can arise where governments are not only manipulating interest rates and commodity prices but have to get their money from somewhere, so will end up nationalizing various industries (such as oil or mining companies) to secure their revenue streams, or try to force people to invest their money in government bonds by decree. All sorts of desperate measures can be called into play.

If a country experiences a hyperinflationary crisis, which is not an uncommon episode in human history, every hyperinflationary period in history sees an eventual collapse in the country's currency. Then the country starts over again. Most hyperinflations have lasted less than three years in length, and none more than twenty years. Stock prices often increase, as they did during Weimar Germany (even though the economy collapsed), while bond prices collapse since interest rates rise and the government debt is seen to have repayment risk. If people rush to get cash to buy commodities to beat the rising inflation, there are situations where the stock market can also decline, rather than rise, as people sell stocks to raise that cash. What ultimately happens all depends upon the situation. During Germany's hyperinflationary period, for various reasons food became unavailable in the cities even though it was plentiful in the countryside.

While stocks went up during Weimar Germany's hyperinflation, due to different circumstances the equity prices collapsed during Chile's hyperinflation of 1970-73 as people sold assets to satisfy their basic needs. They cashed out of everything to buy basic goods for survival, and so they sold assets to get hold of commodities just as people are doing today in Greece because of its modern day depression. Hence, whether stock prices go up or down will depend on the circumstances such as the degree to which an economy is open and what options are available to the public. You cannot just blindly say that stocks, assets or even property prices will go up during a hyperinflationary period. Housing prices may fall while farmland prices may rise; it will depend on the circumstances. In the case of Weimar Germany, stocks paying high dividends (20%) increased in price until their dividend yield became very little (1%). However, who can say that this will be repeated in every hyperinflation?

The prices for food and fuel (near term necessities people need) usually do rise during hyperinflations, but real estate (housing and property) prices *can actually fall* because of the rise in interest rates and the fact that banks may refuse to make property loans. You can even have instances of both deflation and inflation at the same time—deflation in the price of some financial assets including real estate, and inflation for living necessities and commodities as was seen in Chile. Creditors as a rule get destroyed during hyperinflationary periods if people are legally allowed to pay off loans at any time and then do so, giving the creditors valueless currency.

The middle class also gets wiped out, but corporations which issued bonds simply pay off their debts using depreciated currency and get to keep the assets they purchased. In past hyperinflationary environments, those who were willing at its peak to *trade the commodities they owned for real estate assets selling at depressed prices (or who purchased asset-based industries like mining and chemicals at its peak)*, made a killing after the crisis ended! This is the key to wealth generation during a hyperinflationary crisis, which is to buy real assets at a great discount if possible. The crisis always ends with the establishment of a new normal and just takes time to get there.

Wise individuals who understand history have consistently advised that during such times it is best to have your money in the currency of another stable country. However, if there is no safe reserve currency as an alternative to the U.S. dollar today, the only major alternative is precious metals. Thus wise individuals today commonly advise *direct private ownership* of gold and silver, such as portable bullion coins or bullion that is safely stored out of the reach of government hands and the banking system. Right now many wealthy individuals have started holding physical bullion in the vaults of Asia (Hong Kong and Singapore are deemed among the safest locations) rather than in the declining banking centers of London, Switzerland, or the United States that are prone to manipulations and confiscations. You can also buy physical precious metal trusts that actually hold physical gold and silver instead of paper promises, such as the Sprott Gold Trust (PHYS) and Sprott Silver Trust (PSLV). Because they actually hold the physical metal, these trusts have the potential to sell at a premium to the spot price of gold and silver. They may even outperform paper silver and gold exchange-traded funds like SLV and GLD if they ever are found lacking the physical quantities of precious metals they say they are holding.

Gold and silver, as stated, are basically deflation, central bank and catastrophe hedges, which is why precious metals are an important option for a long term investor. If nothing else, at some point during your life the precious metals should be considered as *some form of insurance*, which is why people in many countries slowly accumulate them throughout their lifetime. Perhaps they will serve as prudent insurance in the case of a war, asset confiscation (since they can be hidden), hyperinflation, banking crisis, or currency devaluation. The precious metals tend to do well in hyperinflationary environments *and* they also offer protection during deflationary periods.

During deflations, most assets decrease in price and you must keep your finger on the pulse of the marketplace to see which ones are increasing in price when everything else is falling. There is not one single description that fits all the past cases of severe deflation or hyperinflation, which is why the hyperinflation circumstances of Chile under Allende were different than those of Weimar Germany. For your own reference, some people think that what usually does well during deflations are undervalued commodities that are used on an ongoing basis, such as water.

FIAT CURRENCIES ALWAYS FAIL

If you want to preserve and grow your wealth over a long period of time, you must become familiar with all these various possible end game scenarios and the possible strategies for how to deal with them. Flexibility is the name of the game when it comes to the issues of wealth preservation and/or human survival over decades. History shows that the average life expectancy for a fiat currency is less than 40 years, fiat currencies throughout history have had nearly a 100% failure rate. Since most have lasted no longer than an average human lifespan, you should expect to see a major currency failure that affects you during your life. While people may claim that the British pound Sterling is still alive from 1694, it has actually lost over 99% of its value, so we cannot even count that fiat currency as a success due to its devaluation. Given enough time, eventually all fiat currencies fail and therefore it is only a question of time and circumstances. Political systems always eventually abuse a currency, and a country always eventually pays the price.

A study of 775 fiat currencies by DollarDaze.org reported that 21% were destroyed by war, 20% failed through hyperinflation, 12% were destroyed through independence, 24% had to be monetarily reformed, and 23% were still in circulation awaiting one of these outcomes. Researcher Vince Cate researched the fate of 599 dead paper currencies and though he came up with different figures, every single one of the 599 paper money systems he analyzed disappeared. Cate found that 28% were destroyed by war, 27% were destroyed by hyperinflation, 15% ended through acts of national independence (the new states renamed or reissued new currency), and 30% ended through monetary unions or reforms (such as the creation of the Euro).

Even if you assume that a fiat currency will last forever, monetary scholar Edwin Vieira has pointed out that every 30-40 years the reigning monetary system usually fails in some way, and then has to be retooled to start again. There is always an eventual end to the crisis *because people absolutely need some form of money as a unit of exchange* (other than just barter, which they often turn to during a crisis). There is always an end to any turmoil and then a new normal becomes established. This is inevitable because society cannot operate without some stable form of exchange, and so it must move to a new one. The question is how to preserve your wealth through the period of destruction, and possibly how to even increase it because a crisis always represents opportunities. Whenever you can buy assets at a discount whose prices will return to fair values after the crisis, this is the way to most safely accumulate wealth over the long run.

The same error of *too much debt* (whether due to private sector spending, overextended entitlement programs, or military attempts at imperial hegemony), and *too much money printing*, has been a common cause in the downfall of many monetary systems and nations. When an honest interest rate, free of government manipulation, no longer exists in the marketplace because the government interferes too much to protect its rising debt load, it is only a matter of time before an unwinding occurs. The great game of printing money cannot be played without limits forever. When governments reach the point where they are heavily influencing asset prices through their money printing so that no one can accurately determine asset values anymore, then bubbles will indeed form and their subsequent collapses can destroy economies. One always hopes that such problems will unravel *after* one passes away, but for the goal of amassing a secure retirement fund and/or sum of generational wealth, you need to know of such possibilities *now* and the fact that *at least one or more major financial crisis, of some type or another, are likely to occur during your lifetime.* Therefore you must know what to do ahead of time. You are likely to live through one complete sixty year Kondratieff wave cycle with its decades of inflationary growth and then banking crises with deflationary destruction. Hopefully you can teach your children how to prepare for such episodes even though they may grow up in fair times and therefore tend to disbelieve in such possibilities. All sorts of situations are possible which have often happened in the past and continue to repeat themselves with regularity.

THE FREQUENCY OF CRISIS

One more final bit of wisdom. In terms of the possibility of debt deflation and massive defaults, people often forget that the United States has *already* suffered through *four* major deflations in its history and nothing prevents it from suffering that pain once again. This is how history rolls; mistakes are repeated because human nature stays the same. In terms of hyperinflation, the United States has also already experienced this *twice* in its history. The first instance was during colonial times and the second instance happened in the Southern Confederacy during the Civil War.

We also have the recent examples of hyperinflationary Brazil, Turkey, Argentina, Chile, Hungary, Yugoslavia and Zimbabwe we can study as well as dozens of other cases where the currency printing presses in a country were switched to overdrive. As a political warning, looking all the way back to the Russian Revolution we can ascertain that it was caused by overprinting money to pay for the country's war deficit, which in turn led to surging unemployment and eventually militias fighting and beating the national army, an event that created the USSR in 1922. Napoleon's rise to power accompanied a hyperinflation, and Hitler's rise in Germany was in part due to the economic destruction that its Weimar hyperinflation wrought. The warnings are there for the Untied States if it bothers to heed the lessons of history.

If we turn to just "banking crises" rather than hyperinflations, within the past twenty years alone we have seen banking crises in Finland, Sweden, Russia, Ecuador, Venezuela, and the United States. Just as you should remember the story of my Nicaraguan classmate, or the Jews having to leave their wealth behind to escape Nazi persecution in Germany, or the seizure of wealth that occurred when China became Communist, you should firmly understand that all great countries can undergo both political and economic catastrophes. Unfavorable political forces, for whatever reason, can take control of a country and destroy your wealth. I have heard countless personal stories of young men and women who had gold secretly sewn into their clothes when they escaped on foot or by boat as refugees to other countries to start all over again, so the benefits of foreign bank accounts cannot be understated. In times of trouble you should not care about yield or return but simply about asset mobility, liquidity and how to preserve your capital. A foreign bank account, in a safe haven, is called for.

When you are not in an end game extreme situation, the long term investor must still always be aware of the normal Madoff Ponzi-like investment scams in the marketplace, and refrain from buying into speculative asset bubbles that promise easy wealth forever. These types of scams need to be mentioned because they occur again and again throughout history as well. If the promises of profits sound too good, beware. You should also always "pass" on deal offers that require you to decide quickly and skip the normally long process of due diligence. If a great deal is offered to you "and not others," then ask yourself why you are so lucky to deserve this. As another principle, if a deal from far away makes its way to your door, pass. For instance, if an oil deal from Texas is being sold in New York, then you should suspect that it is a bad deal because if it was a good deal then the local Texans would have already bought it. Ditto it goes for buying bank loans rolled up in a package. If they were really good loans, a bank would be anxious to keep them. The *lack of such basic understanding* on the part of buyers who bought bundled mortgages is what has caused much of the financial mess the world is in today.

You must also be especially wary whenever the public starts believing in some type of "easy money get rich" scheme because its preponderance signals that some market is ready to collapse. For instance, once people start treating the stock market like a casino and stocks like lottery tickets, a bull market is usually near its end. There is no such thing as a perpetual motion machine of easy profits in the stock market, or any market. Unfortunately, reality cannot be such that everyone can simply make money by buying stocks or real estate and then walk away. It must come down to good value selection in the end. The super investor becomes an expert appraiser of value, and sucks up great values when he finds them. That's the key to long term success.

In short, you must be wary and forget "buy and hold" to both grow and preserve your wealth! You must know of all these strange possibilities, including the possibility of war, and what to do should they occur if you want to say you are truly prepared to grow your wealth over the long run. We never assume that any of these things will ever happen, but in a lifespan of seventy or more years you are bound to live through one or more of these situations. At the very least you should know about them! It is one of my advisory principles that every generation can expect to live through a war, banking crisis, economic depression, hyperinflation, fiat currency collapse, period of massive unemployment, loss of freedoms, or some type of political takeover that throws out the established status quo. During your lifetime you will certainly live through some sort of major disaster like this which will threaten all your previous efforts at wealth accumulation.

NORMAL TIMES

While holding real assets, gold and silver, or cash and foreign currencies are common remedies for an end game situation, end games only happen once in awhile. You certainly need to know about these scenarios before they occur, but since you will spend most of your life in "normal times" *you must focus the majority of your attention on the investment methods that work during normal times.* Thus we have gone over extraordinarily successful methods, having unprecedented track records, that have been known to work for many, many decades. You don't have to be a genius to use these super investing techniques. You just have to decide which ones you want to use and then put them to work. If we are seeking proven methods that work reasonably well over the long run, the ones I have taught you pass those tests with flying colors.

These investing methods we have covered truly capture fundamental investment relationships as long as you are not in an end game scenario, so let us put the end game scenario aside and return to the expectations of a continuing prosperous future because this is what we are all counting on. To put any Apocalypse fears to rest, we must all remember the words of Warren Buffett who once aptly reminded us, "In the 20th century, the United States endured two world wars and other traumatic and expensive military conflicts; the Depression; a dozen or so recessions and financial panics; oil shocks; a flu epidemic; and the resignation of a disgraced president. Yet the Dow rose from 66 to 11,497." Thus, there is no such thing as an Armageddon you should be expecting, and you certainly should not plan for any end of the world scenario. The world, and humanity, will not end through any economic crisis we can imagine but will continue to march on through thick and thin. Humans always work things out through reforms and restructurings, and you must simply be cognizant of any ways to help preserve your wealth through difficult situations. That's the only purpose of this discussion.

If we put all the end games and economic crisis possibilities aside, which *you must still know about if you want to be able to grow your wealth throughout all types of future environments*, you now have several proven ways to amass a degree of wealth through the singular route of saving and investing … and they have already worked over the long run through thick and thin. If you start upon a program of consistently saving money, investing it wisely, and compounding that amount over the long term, you now have several possible methods for investing success that can be used in combination to diversify your way to financial freedom. With the crisis investing advice to hold foreign bank accounts in another currency or invest in a physical gold fund such as **PHYS** (Sprott Physical Gold Trust) or **PSLV** (Sprott Physical Silver Trust), you have a safe crisis investment methodology as well. You can also use these avenues as a standard part of your long term portfolio just as you can hold your precious metals in foreign vaults through a service like **GoldMoney.com**, too.

Of all the possible methods for becoming rich, the most common way to amass significant wealth has always been to build your own business, which has many benefits. It is usually the most satisfying course of action, and many have noted it was the core of their true life purpose. You create a business that fulfills some market need, and fulfilling that demand produces income and wealth in turn. That wealth can then multiply many times over if your firm is put on the stock market or sold privately, and then you are left with the task of investing your money once again.

Of course most people cannot act like entrepreneurs and build a business, though for those who do I would suggest reading *Think and Grow Rich*, *The eMyth*, and my own book, *How to Create a Million Dollar Unique Selling Proposition*. All these books were written to help people along that special avenue. For most people, their only hope for becoming wealthy, or simply creating a comfortable retirement rather than a "legacy IRA" that can be left to heirs, is to take the investing road to riches. When you know that fact, you must not only ask what you should be doing for yourself but what you should be teaching your children *now* who have forty to fifty years of investing possibilities ahead of them. You cannot depend upon the government for your future and neither can they. Governments do stupid things at times, as do corporations and people. All are blind to the unintended consequences that sometimes thwart a rosy economic future. Your children must learn how to navigate through such waters. It is one of our duties in life to teach them how to do so.

Governments usually forget that the best bank is storing money among the people, especially the middle class, and through errant policies often lead their countries down the road of middle class wealth destruction rather than creation. Even Plutarch said that economies will be healthier when the wealth is distributed among the poor and middle class instead of concentrated in the hands of a rich few. Governments, however, have a tendency to break their social contracts with their own citizens and let wealth imbalances grow between the rich and poor. For instance, if you protect the errant issuers of debt at the expense of the general public, is this not unprincipled madness that favors the rich over the ordinary man? Should you not prevent this from happening rather than enabling it? The public is not blind to such behavior, so it often leads to tremendous social unrest and eventual political upheaval. Therefore, knowing that you cannot depend on your government, what strategies will you teach your children so that they can accumulate enough money through their lives for their own survival, comfortable living or retirement? Even the mega-wealthy turn to investing, so that's what this book is all about. Many principles I wanted to know about when I was younger, and why different investing methods have succeeded because of those principles, are included in this small book made for you *and your children* who will reap any benefits from it.

With this book, you now have more than five of the best investment techniques possible for hyper-compounding your wealth to financial freedom. I've selected some of the simplest methods possible, rather than the most complicated with better returns because you would have a hard time being able to duplicate them. Few can build a Ned Davis type composite multi-factor investment model for the stock market and then keep it updated to use for investment decisions. But all the methods we have gone over can be duplicated on your own to make you into a super investor.

Therefore, what you have is the *exact information and exact techniques* I personally would have liked to have known myself when I was just getting started on my financial career and the road of investing. You have methods, you have the perspective, and you even have case studies of some individuals who have succeeded beyond anyone's wildest dreams in the field of investing. I sincerely encourage you to talk about some of these concepts with your children who have so much future ahead of them. For instance, sit down with them and make them do an Excel spreadsheet so that they can see how investing earlier can produce more money than getting started later. Show them how changing the rate of return on their money changes how much they can expect to have in their bank account. Parents rarely sit down with their children to teach them these lessons.

Few people are ever provided with any education about the possible ways to invest their money unless taught by others, and so most people do not even know that a consistent 20% return per year is extraordinary. A consistent 15% per year return is extraordinary as well. Rarely do we bother to teach investment literacy to our future generation, as done in *Rich Dad, Poor Dad,* and so I've tried to make it possible for you to open a dialogue along these lines using a collection of the best investment styles I have found. At least one of these styles should appeal to someone. In terms of the rules of investing, also remember to pass on the basic general rules that you *win by not losing, practice diversification, think of value, avoid fees and taxes, don't treat investing like gambling, take the long term view, and prepare for emergencies.*

Many books speak about the various principles we should follow in order to more safely grow our wealth through the long road of investing. First and foremost, they tell us not to adopt a gambler's mentality (as in options and futures trading) where it is okay to lose your principal. Never should we become speculators either because in the long run gamblers and speculators nearly always lose money. Speculation is usually the sign of a need for excitement, which is an emotion that never produces good outcomes in matters of money management. One of the rules for investing is that one should always look at things realistically when it comes to money—one must look clinically at the present rather than trust to hopeful forecasts and expectations—and never become swayed by emotions which readily rise and fall in line with market volatility. When it comes to money, if one does not look at things with an objective, unbiased, unemotional mind, investing often turns into pure speculation.

Once you have lost some money, few realize that percentagewise it is actually harder to make it back. Wealth accumulation clearly depends on the principle of compounding and the principles for maximum compounding are to start investing early, consistently add additional funds to the pot, and get as high a rate of return as possible on your money. Time is ticking away, so it's best to get started as early as possible with investing. Over time, even a very small advantage over normal market returns can produce gargantuan differences in final monetary outcomes, so you must always strive to use investment methodologies that consistently beat the market and rarely lose principal. Because taxes reduce the returns you can earn, to minimize taxes you should also use IRAs, 401(K)'s, trusts and other tax friendly vehicles.

You cannot predict the markets, so you should employ investment methodologies that *do not depend on forecasting* but which set out to make money through other fundamental principles. Even so, historical analysis allows you to identify time periods that represent a potential for higher or lower investment returns in the markets. You definitely can construct various models that accurately classify the current stock market environment as bullish or bearish, favorable or unfavorable, and you can use this information to your advantage in increasing your potential rates of return.

The wealthy investor of the future will also most likely be an international investor who is not permanently wed to his home market. International diversification and asset class diversification should be your best friends in growing your investment portfolio over the decades. Along these lines, relative strength momentum investing can identify the big price movers in the world whose momentum moves will tend to persist, especially when the trends are backed by strong fundamentals.

Through relative strength (momentum) investing, it is much easier to pick the top sectors out of a stock index that will continue outperforming than it is to time every 10% up and down move in the markets. Momentum investing can indeed lead to superior investing returns regardless as to how much the naysayers criticize it. This has been proven time and again. With momentum investing the task is to identify the top trends that currently exist and which are likely to last long enough for you to grab a big bite out of those profits. Since most people cannot do this because of emotions or a lack of discipline, if you select this route of investing then it is often best to turn your relevant funds over to managers who will do it for you. You want to employ disciplined managers who will continually scan numerous markets and follow carefully tested rules to capture momentum trends with religious consistency.

When you are in a mega-bull market, almost all sound investment methodologies work, so you must *never confuse brains with a bull market*. In those mega-bull conditions, the momentum investing methods do extremely well. However, through thick and thin, good times and bad, the value investing methods shine brightly with their consistent long run rates of return. Why? Because they work on the principle of buying assets at a discount and waiting for a mean reversion whereupon the true asset values are eventually recognized. Value investing methods can ignore all sorts of market fluctuations (the market is basically random over the short term) that often penalize momentum investing. Their only real weakness, which is the same for nearly all these techniques, is their implicit, inherent assumption that the country doesn't implode through any of the many crisis situations we have mentioned.

Since the tip off to the end of bull market or bubble is the fact that everyone starts talking about how they are making money in the markets and how they will retire rich, you should take the contrarian's approach to the public mood and rely on your proven investment models at euphoric extremes. I rarely worry about individuals who buy assets when prices are low and the situation looks darkest because it seems that people more often lose money by getting into asset bubbles at their peaks. Investment models, as we have gone over, can tell you when the investing risks are highest near such peaks so that you can wisely take some of your chips off the table when prices are peaking. You might forego some returns for awhile by getting out early, but then look like a genius when a market collapses in a nosedive.

One of the common principles behind achieving extraordinary investment growth is to add additional funds to a successful portfolio over time. Also, while dividends represent ready cash from stocks that can be reinvested, for extra returns you can also learn how to scientifically write call options more safely and collect those premiums to increase your returns on many of these techniques when you are holding stocks, especially during periods where models tell you the investment outlook is less than rosy. You also have a new seasonal methodology to help you do this and a "writing options as a business" course that can help you learn how to make more consistent returns every month.

While not covered in this book, there is also a concept called "infinite banking" using life insurance that investors can look to in order to force themselves to save and further compound their wealth through yet another means that is tax protected. The concept of "**infinite (cash flow) banking**" using life insurance policies is another possibility for those who aim to build a "legacy IRA."

In times of crisis, you are once again reminded that people often look to cash, foreign bank accounts/currencies, or gold and silver as ways to preserve their wealth throughout the chaos, too. Precious metals are problematical in that their shine only lasts so long because they, too, can fall in price when crisis periods are over. They typically do best in negative real interest rate environments rather than simply rise due to inflation. The current financial establishment doesn't want anyone to look to gold and silver as alternatives to holding their paper currency when it is being inflated, but it is a proven fact that the precious metals have been used as a store of value throughout history during periods of economic chaos.

These are just a few of the principles I hope you have picked up from this book. Hopefully you could immediately see how some key principles or rules in each super investing technique were often used by others, which explains part of their success. This commonality of certain key principles used over and over again—such as the use of enforced selling rules—is what creates systems that can achieve 20% per year profits over the long run. Understanding that commonality is very important.

In our first two investing methodologies, we used historically tested models that segmented the stock market into clear buy and sell periods, and then used index funds to invest accordingly. As Warren Buffett once explained in his 1996 annual Berkshire Hathaway report, "Most investors, both institutional and individual, will find that the best way to own common stocks is through an index fund that charges minimal fees. Those following this path are sure to beat the net results (after fees and expenses) delivered by the great majority of investment professionals." No load index funds are the way to go when timing the markets with these simple models.

These simple timing models have worked over many decades and are easy to track, so with just these alone you can forgo the simplistic "buy and hold" strategy that subjects you to "fat tail" or "black swan" catastrophic risks that have not yet appeared in a nation's history. The possibility of large, unexpected, and improbable events should dissuade anyone from firmly trusting in financial forecasts of any kind that always project a rosy future, including the stability of the stock market when its fundamental underpinnings deteriorate.

If you are interested in market timing, these two methods are among the simplest but most robust available. They are not guaranteed, but nothing is truly guaranteed in the investment world. Even guaranteed government debt can default. If the idea of seasonal investing scares you, the Triple 40 Timing model satisfies my preferred principle of combining fundamental and technical information together. It has a simple trend following component that is matched with interest rate fundamentals to keep you on the right side of the market, and still does better than buy and hold. It is simple to compute using any free charting software on the web, and works all the way back to 1929 to produce better returns than the market. One could diversify the returns from these models by using them together, and also by selling call options during opportune periods of the market.

The method of matching price trends with interest rate fundamentals was also used by our European relative strength system and incorporated into John Hussman's market climate methodology, too. O'Shaughnessy's newest growth investing methodology, which returned 20+% per year, also added 4% per year to its rate of return because it included relative strength rankings in its formulas.

Relative strength investing introduced the possibility for safer international investing and better portfolio diversification because it uses various uncorrelated asset classes, ETFs and sector funds. Relative strength, or market momentum, is something you can even monitor yourself through a site like ETFscreen.com. The best possible returns for this technique come from evaluating hundreds of potential assets all the time, which is best accomplished through a disciplined relative strength fund that invests in all those multiple asset classes. Individuals tend to stay too long at a party where they are having one helluva a good time, so by putting your money in a fund that rigidly follows disciplined asset allocation and money management rules you can increase your chances at doing well with this type of investing and get out of top tier assets when they stop gaining.

We also encountered our first superior method for picking individual stocks, CANSLIM, for those interested in the details of stock picking. It is easy to make the connection that when our various models identify very bullish time periods, CANSLIM is likely to outperform because momentum investing will be at its best, so investing in "new highs" or "pattern breakouts" will shine during these periods. When you are in a raging bull market and you want to personally pick stocks, CANSLIM is absolutely fantastic, but it takes much time to learn how to properly apply the methodology. You should start now if you want to learn it, and many books for doing so are available.

One of the keys to the success of CANSLIM is its set of money management rules, and you should know that the main reason people complain about the technique, saying it doesn't work, is because they violate these rules! *This is the case with most investment methodologies*—they "don't work" because people fail to follow the rules. If you have problems with dieting, training for sporting events, or even doing regular chores such as cleaning the house, these might be the symptoms of the lack of discipline, control or confidence necessary to be successful at CANSLIM. You should only try to learn it if you have the strongest desire to be a chart reader and stock picker.

In terms of value investing, we also discovered that the granddaddy of value investing (Benjamin Graham) threw all his complicated analysis away near the end of his life, and settled upon just two or three simple variables (wisely chosen criteria) that he used to produce exceptional outperforming portfolios. Walter Schloss and Greenblatt also confirmed the effectiveness of stock screening simplicity as long as the valuation methodology had a fundamental basis behind it. *The basis is that you are buying dollars for pennies, and thus assets at a discount.* Many of the stocks selected by valuation methodologies perform well because you end up investing in takeover candidates, which is a principle few note. Large corporations grow by takeovers, so if you can identify the likely takeover candidates then you have a basic stock selection system. Warren Buffett, for instance, was not a typical fund manager but a businessman looking to grow his assets through just this sort of mentality.

We also gained insight into how Warren Buffett really gained his investing fortune, which was in part due to his flexibility in using different techniques rather than being strictly wed to Graham and Dodd valuation formulas. Buffett became an expert at *buying different positive cash flow situations* rather than sticking to any one single valuation investing methodology. We discovered that while modern stock analysts engage in stock selection as a game of buying and selling, Buffett pursued the principle of buying steady cash flow money machines, whenever possible, whose funds he promptly reinvested. This led to our last technique of how to "generate cash flows for free" through options writing rather than by concentrating solely on dividends, but doing so in a way that follows business principles rather than the excitement of speculation.

Even Warren Buffett wrote options, as illustrated by one of the biggest deals of his life, although he stated that he is opposed to derivatives and options in general. In this case, it just turned out to be what he thought was a good value proposition that generated a lot of free cash that he could use for investment purposes. Time will tell if his judgment was correct. Few people can actually duplicate the time and research effort that Warren Buffett goes through full time, but as he mentioned, all of his colleagues who practiced a value approach to investing did extremely well over the long term in consistently beating the market by many magnitudes. This is why I like value investing the best out of all these techniques.

The idea of value investing (J. Paul Getty's idea to buy productive assets for less than they are worth) therefore becomes one of the most dependable roads for amassing great wealth, and is one of the true secrets to amassing a great investment fortune. This is why I have emphasized Graham's little known, time-tested investment formula that you can use on your own if you desire. If you use this in conjunction with momentum investing to cover a portion of your portfolio, and also use some market timing methods for index funds, you can say that you have three different large investment techniques for growing your wealth. I would not hesitate to teach this set of investment techniques to any group of people including teenagers, college students, and young professionals. Just going through these ideas will certainly help you get started on your investing career.

All through this, I have also provided indications for the type of investment research you might pursue on your own that might lead to other superior investing methods. For instance, I might take the Graham 2-year and 50% selling rules and combine them with just a few of O'Shaughnessy's criteria to determine if a super dividend investing strategy, or alternative value investing methodology, could be developed. Unfortunately, no one has ever published research studies showing how a dividend fund, low P/E fund, high P/E fund, large cap fund, small cap fund, value fund, growth fund, relative strength fund, etc. would perform under different timing signals and market climates, but you could certainly use that information to help guide your investment decisions as well. Knowing which type of fund or investment methodology performs best under what conditions is a way to do far better than simply follow Wall Street's blind dictum of "buy and hold" once again. Adaptive similarity and factor seasonal analysis, which give you a picture of an asset's typical calendar trading pattern during recessions or business expansion periods, shows how useful such information can be.

Which of these five basic strategies should you use? That, of course, is entirely up to you. I prefer a diversification strategy of using several together, but firmly believe you cannot succeed with using a particular strategy if its style goes against your personality, which is why several different investment strategies have been provided. My preference for busy people is that they find a manager specialized in the technique they like, and leave the management of the funds with them. Check with your investment advisor to discuss your various options, but my personal preference is that any long term investing plan for accumulating wealth should include a major component of value investing and relative strength investing. More powerful techniques are available, as I said, but they are too complicated for most people to duplicate.

Lastly, I am a big proponent of selling out of money options whenever possible to increase your returns for all these strategies, and to this extent the similarity/factor seasonal method, market climate, worst six months of the year, and Triple 40 Timing systems all specify periods when the reward/risk trade-offs for doing this are excellent. You also have an excellent options course recommendation that will teach you how to sell options as a business, and I also wish I had seen it years ago so I could have been using this methodology all those years.

A final word, and my personal hopes for your future ... I think a book on getting rich through investing is meaningless without references to culture, human relationships and the meaning of life and values in general. This is why I always urge young people to read Plutarch's *Lives of the Noble Greeks and Romans*, which brings many such life issues up for discussion. As the story of Crassus well illustrates, the desire to accumulate wealth cannot be divorced from life purpose and the deep concepts of character, ethics, morality and even spirituality. While it may sound strange to some who say to me, "Just tell me the investing rules that will make me rich," I firmly believe that investing success and the accumulation of wealth are not divorced from character and merit, and the discussion of making money alone is of absolutely no interest to me. Like Confucius, I cannot be dissuaded from this opinion. When advising many individuals on their financial matters, the ultimate question comes down to how to put your monies to good use after you accumulate it. It is how you use your money in life that is ultimately the important thing, and so I have sometimes raised examples of individuals who never did anything with the monies they gained but who squandered their chances for what would have definitely been a richer life and higher purpose in the process.

There will definitely be future individuals who can build the mega-fortunes of a Rockefeller or Rothschild family through business or investments, and who can build a legacy fortune of generational wealth that can be used to do great good in the world. My business partners and I definitely subscribe to the "great person" view of history. We have concluded that many extremely beneficial things throughout history were accomplished by individuals who chose to act and personally do something with their time, money, power and influence. Great individuals were sometimes more important, and more responsible for good works than governments or anonymous social forces, so we hope to help empower such individuals. We hope that many people might through disciplined, devoted investing become like Bill Gates, Andrew Carnegie, or Li Ka-shing who all amassed incredible wealth through the avenues of business, but who later became role models of how to use it for philanthropic purposes. Everyone eventually realizes they cannot take their money with them beyond the grave, and therefore those with a higher purpose devote much of their wealth to doing great deeds in the world for the public *while they are still alive*. It is better to work on solving social problems for the many while you are still living. Few investing books ever discuss such issues even though their purpose is actually to take you to such heights which enable that possible greatness.

In short, we will all die one day, and your actions and accomplishments will write your own tombstone. It would be a pity if you succeed in accumulating the great riches everyone desires, but your life story mirrors the biography of a Getty, Crassus or Hetty Green whose only life purpose seemed to be the accumulation of more money for no reason other than to see a yet larger number in the bank account. The right super investing methodologies can enable you to hyper-compound your wealth to an incredibly large number if you start early enough, and while my hope goes out that this book helps you achieve that goal, I also hope you use your success to do good in the world having recognized this as a portion of your own life mission.

APPENDIX

One other contribution to stock market analysts who are using screening software is the following formula. It combines both average returns AND their volatility in *one single measurement* to estimate the expected growth of an asset subject to reinvestment. The formula re-estimates the growth rate when there is some variability, volatility, or variance to it.

There is a little known mathematical formula, derived from quadratic estimates, that can incorporate the variance of a growth series into an estimate of its average future growth rate. If you want to determine the long term growth rate, or CAGR, of constantly reinvesting in a portfolio with expected return, E, and having variance of returns var(r), you can do so by using this formula. You might even use it to produce a more accurate estimate of a company's earnings growth rate. The formula is as follows:

Let E = the average return of the portfolio growth rate, earnings growth rate, dividend rate growth or whatever you are trying to predict. If the return of each period is r, let's call E the average return, which is the average of the series $(r_1, r_2, r_3, \ldots)$. Now, let var(r) stand for the variance of those returns $(r_1, r_2, r_3, \ldots)$ as well. To estimate the compound annual growth rate of reinvesting in a growing sum that grows on average at rate E with variance var(r), we can use the following formula:

$$GRTH = \ln(1+E) - \frac{\frac{1}{2}*var(r)}{(1+E)^2}$$

$$CAGR = e^{GRTH} - 1$$

For example, if the average earnings growth rate is 10%, then E = .10, and if the variance of the growth rate is .04, then $\ln(1.1) - .5(.04)/(1.1)^2 = .0953 - .0165 = .0788$.

Therefore, $\text{CAGR} = e^{.0788} - 1 = .082$, so the rate of growth over the long run can be expected to be 8.2% per annum. In other words, the average growth rate is 10%, but when you factor in volatility, the rate you can expect is more on the order of 8.2%.

This little formula can possibly help people with various stock screening systems when they are trying to estimate various future long run growth rates based on historical data. It assumes that you are always reinvesting your money back into the company, which then internally fuels the growth rate of earnings, so you can only use it under the proper circumstances.

BOOKS OF INTEREST

Chapter 1 – Investing Can Be One of Your Roads to Riches

Allen, Robert. *Multiple Streams of Income: How to Generate a Lifetime of Unlimited Wealth!*

DeMarco, MJ. *The Millionaire Fastlane: Crack the Code to Wealth and Live Rich for a Lifetime.*

Fisher, Kenneth. *The Ten Roads to Riches: The Ways the Wealthy Got There.*

Green, Wayne. *The Secret Guide to Wealth.*

Jones, W. Randall. *The Richest Man in Town: The Twelve Commandments of Wealth.*

Kennedy, Dan. *No B.S. Wealth Attraction for Entrepreneurs.*

Kiyosaki, Robert. *Rich Dad, Poor Dad: What the Rich Teach Their Kids About Money That the Poor and Middle Class Do Not!*

Masterson, Michael. *Automatic Wealth: The Six Steps to Financial Independence.*

Masterson, Michael. *Automatic Wealth for Grads ... and Anyone Else Just Starting Out.*

Reinert, Erik. *How Rich Countries Got Rich and Why Poor Countries Stay Poor.*

Stanley, Thomas and William Danko. *The Millionaire Next Door.*

Stanley, Thomas. *The Millionaire Mind.*

Chapter 2 – What Rate of Return Can Your Expect?

Bach, David. *The Automatic Millionaire: A Powerful One-Step Plan to Live and Finish Rich.*

Bogle, John. *Common Sense on Mutual Funds.*

Bogle, John. *The Little Book of Common Sense Investing: The Only Way to Guarantee Your Fair Share of Stock Market Returns.*

Easterling, Ed. *Probable Outcomes.*

Easterling, Ed. *Unexpected Returns: Understanding Secular Stock Market Cycles.*

Gunther, Max. *The Zurich Axioms.*

Heller, Robert. *The Age of the Common Millionaire.*

Shiller, Robert. *Irrational Exuberance.*

Siegel, Jeremy. *Stocks for the Long Run: The Definitive Guide to Financial Market Returns & Long Term Investment Strategies.*

Chapter 3 - Seasonal Market Timing

Bodri, Bill. *The Commonsense of Seasonal Trading.*

Hirsch, Yale. *The Stock Traders Almanac.*
Lo Kuan-Chung. *Romance of the Three Kingdoms.*
Stovall, Sam. *The Seven Rules of Wall Street: Crash Tested Investment Strategies That Beat the Market.*
Williams, Larry. *The Right Stock at the Right Time: Prospering in the Coming Good Years.*

ChartPattern.com – Dan Zanger's website
StockTradersAlmanac.com
ThinkorSwim.com
MarketTimingResearch.com/seasonalsoftware/ ** FREE Software **

Chapter 4 – <u>Analytically Timing Fundamental Information</u>

Davis, Ned. *Being Right or Making Money.*
Hayes, Timothy. *The Research Driven Investor.*
Sperandeo, Victor. *Trader Vic: Methods of a Wall Street Master.*
Zweig, Marty and Morrie Goldfischer. *Martin Zweig's Winning on Wall Street.*

Formula Research – FormulaResearch.com
Hussman Funds (Cincinnati, OH) –
    HussmanFunds.com/weeklyMarketComment.html
Ned Davis Research (Venice, FL) – NDR.com

Chapter 5 - <u>Winning Momentum Investing</u>

Appel, Gerald and Marvin Appel. *Beating the Market, 3 Months at a Time: A Proven Investing Plan Everyone Can Use.*
Boucher, Mark. *The Hedge Fund Edge: Maximum Profit/Minimum Risk Global Trend Trading Strategies.*
Carr, Michael. *Smarter Investing in Any Economy: The Definitive Guide to Relative Strength Investing.*
Coyle, Daniel. *The Talent Code: Greatness Isn't Born. It's Grown. Here's How.*
Darvis, Nicholas. *How I Made $2,000,000 in the Stock Market.*
O'Neil, William. *24 Essential Lessons for Investment Success.*
O'Neil, William. *How to Make Money in Stocks: A Winning System in Good Times or Bad.*
O'Neil, William. *The Model Book of Greatest Stock Market Winners.*
Morales, Gil and Chris Kacher. *Trade Like an O'Neil Disciple: How We Made 18,000% in the Stock Market.*
Schwager, Jack. *Market Wizards: Interviews With Top Traders.*

Stovall, Sam. *The Seven Rules of Wall Street: Crash-Tested Investment Strategies That Beat the Market.*

Vellum Financial (San Luis Obispo, CA) – VellumFinancial.com
Dorsey Wright Money Management (Pasadena, CA) –
     DorseyWrightMM.com
AAII.com
ETFScreen.com
SectorsPDR.com
SPoutlook.com

Chapter 6 – Superior Value Investing

Carnegie, Andrew. *The Gospel of Wealth.*
Graham, Benjamin. *Common Sense Investing: The Papers of Benjamin Graham.*
Graham, Benjamin and Jason Zweig. *The Intelligent Investor: The Definitive Book on Value Investing. A Book of Practical Counsel.*
Graham, Benjamin and David Dodd. *Security Analysis.*
Getty, J. Paul. *How to Be Rich.*
Greenblatt, Joel. *The Little Book that Beats the Market.*
Greenwald, Bruce, Judd Kahn, Paul Sonkin, and Michael van Biema. *Value Investing: From Graham to Buffett and Beyond.*
Mizrahi, Charles. *Getting Started in Value Investing.*
Plutarch. *Lives of the Noble Romans.*
Winans, Christopher. *The King of Cash: The Inside Story of Lawrence Tisch.*

EastmanPublications.com/iwp/ - Inevitable Wealth Portfolio newsletter

Chapter 7 – Dividends or Options

Ansbacher, Max. *The New Options Market.*
Elias, Samir. *Generate Thousands in Cash on Your Stocks Before Buying or Selling.*
Eisen, Dennis. *Using Options to Buy Stocks.*
O'Shaughnessy, James. *What Works on Wall Street: A Guide to the Best-Performing Investment Strategies of All Time.*

O'Shaughnessy Asset Management (Stamford, CT) – OSAM.com
MarketTimingResearch.com/freevideos.html
MarketTimingResearch.com/optionscourse.html

Chapter 8 – <u>End Games and Conclusions</u>

Acampora, Ralph. *The Fourth Mega-Market, Now Through 2011: How Three Earlier Bull Markets Explain the Present and Predict the Future.*

Acemoglu, Daron and James Robinson. *Why Nations Fail: The Origins of Power, Prosperity, and Poverty.*

Alexander, Michael. *Stock Cycles: Why Stocks Wont Beat Money Markets Over the Next Twenty Years.*

Ahamed Liaquat. *Lords of Finance: The Bankers Who Broke the World.*

Alexander, Michael. *The Kondratiev Cycle: A Generational Interpretation.*

Bernholz, Peter. *Monetary Regimes and Inflation: History, Economic and Political Relationships.*

Bodri, Bill. *How to Create a Million Dollar Unique Selling Proposition.*

Carnegie, Andrew. *The Autobiography of Andrew Carnegie and the Gospel of Wealth.*

Dent, Harry. *The Great Boom Ahead: Your Comprehensive Guide to Personal and Business Profit in the New Era of Prosperity.*

Dent, Harry and Rodney Johnson. *The Great Crash Ahead.*

Dreman, David. *Contrarian Investment Strategies: The Psychological Edge.*

Engdahl William. *Full Spectrum Dominance: Totalitarian Democracy in the New World Order.*

Faber, Marc. *Tomorrow's Gold: Asia's Age of Discovery.*

Foot, David, Daniel Stoffman, and Brian Gable. *Boom, Bust and Echo: Profiting from the Demographic Shift in the 21st Century.*

Franklin, Benjamin. *The Way to Wealth.*

Gerber, Michael. *The eMyth: Why Most Businesses Don't Work and What to Do About It.*

Hill, Napoleon. *Think and Grow Rich.*

Jastram, Roy. *The Golden Constant.*

Kiyosaki, Robert. *Rich Dad's CASHFLOW Quadrant: Rich Dads Guide to Financial Freedom.*

Klare, Michael. *Resource Wars: The New Landscape of Global Conflict With a New Introduction by the Author.*

Luttwak. *The Grand Strategy of the Roman Empire: From the First Century A.D. to the Third.*

Lynch, Peter. *One Up on Wall Street: How to Use What You Already Know to Make Money in the Market.*

Mauldin, John. *Bull's Eye Investing: Targeting Real Returns in a Smoke and Mirrors Market.*

Mauldin, John. *Endgame: The End of the Debt Supercycle and How It Changes Everything.*

Modelski, George and William Thompson. *Leading Sectors and World Powers:*

The Coevolution of Global Economics and Politics.

Modelski, George. *Long Cycles in World Politics.*

Pettis, Michael. *The Volatility Machine.*

Prechter, Robert. *Conquer the Crash: You Can Survive and Prosper in a Deflationary Depression.*

Reinert. Erik. *How Rich Countries Got Rich and Why Poor Countries Stay Poor.*

Reinhart, Carmen and Kenneth Rogoff. *This Time is Different: Eight Centuries of Financial Folly.*

Rickards, James. *Currency Wars: The Making of the Next Global Crisis.*

Rogers, Jim. *Investment Biker: Around the World With Jim Rogers.*

Schiff, Peter. *The Real Crash: America's Coming Bankruptcy – How to Save Yourself and Your Country.*

Schiff, Peter and John Downes. *Crash Proof: How to Profit from the Coming Economic Collapse.*

Schroeder, Alice. *The Snowball: Warren Buffett and the Business of Life.*

Sharma, Ruchir. *Breakout Nations: In Pursuit of the Next Economic Miracles.*

Skarica, David. *The Great Super Cycle: Profit from the Coming Inflation Tidal Wave and Dollar Devaluation.*

Strauss, William and Neil Howe. *The Fourth Turning: An American Prophecy – What the Cycles of History Tell Us About America's Next Rendezvous with Destiny.*

Turchin, Peter and Sergey Nefedov. *Secular Cycles.*

Vittachi, Nury and Marc Faber. *Riding the Millennial Storm: Marc Faber's Path to Profit in the Financial Markets.*

Yellen, Pamela. *Bank on Yourself.*

GoldenJackass.com – Jim Willie's *Hat Trick* newsletter

Made in the USA
Charleston, SC
20 February 2017